Latino Immigrant Youth and Interrupted Schooling

BILINGUAL EDUCATION & BILINGUALISM

Series Editors: Nancy H. Hornberger *(University of Pennsylvania, USA)* and Colin Baker *(Bangor University, Wales, UK)*

Bilingual Education and Bilingualism is an international, multidisciplinary series publishing research on the philosophy, politics, policy, provision and practice of language planning, global English, indigenous and minority language education, multilingualism, multiculturalism, biliteracy, bilingualism and bilingual education. The series aims to mirror current debates and discussions.

Full details of all the books in this series and of all our other publications can be found on http://www.multilingual-matters.com, or by writing to Multilingual Matters, St Nicholas House, 31–34 High Street, Bristol BS1 2AW, UK.

BILINGUAL EDUCATION & BILINGUALISM: 100

Latino Immigrant Youth and Interrupted Schooling

Dropouts, Dreamers and Alternative Pathways to College

Marguerite Lukes

MULTILINGUAL MATTERS
Bristol • Buffalo • Toronto

Library of Congress Cataloging in Publication Data
Lukes, Marguerite.
Latino Immigrant Youth and Interrupted Schooling: Dropouts, Dreamers and Alternative Pathways to College/ Marguerite Lukes.
Bilingual Education and Bilingualism: 100
Includes bibliographical references and index.
1. Hispanic American youth – Education – United States. 2. Hispanic American youth – Social conditions. 3. Immigrants – Education – United States. 4. Immigrants – United States – Social conditions. I. Title.
LC2670.L84 2015
371.829'68073–dc23 2014044414

British Library Cataloguing in Publication Data
A catalogue entry for this book is available from the British Library.

ISBN-13: 978-1-78309-343-4 (hbk)
ISBN-13: 978-1-78309-342-7 (pbk)

Multilingual Matters
UK: St Nicholas House, 31–34 High Street, Bristol BS1 2AW, UK.
USA: UTP, 2250 Military Road, Tonawanda, NY 14150, USA.
Canada: UTP, 5201 Dufferin Street, North York, Ontario M3H 5T8, Canada.

Website: www.multilingual-matters.com
Twitter: Multi_Ling_Mat
Facebook: https://www.facebook.com/multilingualmatters
Blog: www.channelviewpublications.wordpress.com

The policy of Multilingual Matters/Channel View Publications is to use papers that are natural, renewable and recyclable products, made from wood grown in sustainable forests. In the manufacturing process of our books, and to further support our policy, preference is given to printers that have FSC and PEFC Chain of Custody certification. The FSC and/or PEFC logos will appear on those books where full certification has been granted to the printer concerned.

Typeset by R. J. Footring Ltd, Derby
Printed and bound in Great Britain by Short Run Press Ltd

Contents

Figures

Tables

Acknowledgments

This book was made possible through years of dedicated collaborative efforts by adult educators, students and community partners with whom I have had the good fortune to work.

There are not sufficient words to thank the more than 200 immigrants who participated in the research that led to this book, generously giving their time and sharing their experiences with me. Their determination in the face of myriad obstacles has been a constant inspiration throughout my research and the writing of this book. The insistence that their perspectives be shared and their stories told was the impetus that propelled this project to completion. It is my sincere hope that my research can shed light on their experiences and positively impact the lives of my readers.

I am extremely grateful to family, friends, colleagues and study participants who have made this volume possible. My friends and mentors Terry Wiley, Pedro Noguera and Carola Suárez-Orozco repeatedly built fires under me and urged me to keep writing. Jon Zimmerman is to thank for his keen insights, expansive knowledge and keen gift for getting to the essence of the questions. I owe a debt to Dr Robert Smith, whose scholarship and work with new immigrant students in New York City has been a beacon for me. Though his cup runneth over, Rob took time out for me, read my work, challenged me and told me from his heart: 'this work is important'. Thanks to Dr Edward Fergus, who served as a guide and critical friend. I would also like to thank Marcelo Suárez-Orozco, who took time out from his busy schedule to read and comment on my work. I am grateful also to Robert Tobias for his feedback, suggestions and insight, and sense of humor.

I am grateful for the help and support of my friend, colleague and sounding board John Lyons, who mentored, cajoled, supported and egged me on in more ways than can ever be listed here. Thank you to *amiga* Mellie Torres, who came to my aid as I was drowning in data and threw me a life ring so I could see the light at the end of the tunnel. I owe a debt of gratitude to Jenny Hunt for ongoing and invaluable suggestions, feedback and patient cajoling of data. Thank you also to Manlio César Correa for reading and raising important critical questions (¡para variar!). Thank you to Michael Tsuk, Saundra Thomas and Bill Liebeskind, who took the time to read my draft and provide me with honest feedback. Thank you to Claire Sylvan and Joe Luft for their support, jocularity, and sharing expertise. Many thanks to Kristin Brown, who sat with me for hours to nurture the initial seedlings of the idea for this project so they could grow. My gratitude goes to Kevin Rocap and J. David Ramirez for constant, loving cheerleading and support. Many thanks to Dr Colin Baker for his stewardship, insights, hand-holding and generous, kind editorial expertise. Enormous thanks to Tommi Grover for his leadership and commitment.

The generosity and trust of the following individuals deserve special mention: Flor de María Eilets, Juan Castillo, Pedro DeLLano, Guadalupe Martínez, Mimi Blaber, Michael Perrone, Julie Quinton, Aranzazu Borrachero, Eva Raison, Lianne Friedman, Teresa Bell and Barbara Diliberti. These and countless other colleagues in the New York City adult literacy community are without equal.

I would like to thank my children, Amalia and Marcelo, who have provided support well beyond their years, taking part in conversations, attending site visits, listening to stories and remaining ever patient when this author has expressed exasperation. Finally, I owe a debt of gratitude and love to my sisters and my parents, Robert Lukes and Mary Fragomeni Lukes, for modeling generosity of spirit, humanism, resilience and instilling in me a deep curiosity.

1 Introduction

Who, What and Where

The line seemed endless. Starting at the top of the narrow stairs, it wound down the dimly lit hallway with its flickering lights, snaked out the door and onto the sidewalk. Every few moments, someone joined and the line kept growing. I paused to watch and heard the sounds of Arabic, Spanish, Chinese, Polish and Russian being spoken. What were all these people waiting for? I paused near two young men in paint-spattered jeans and baseball caps. '*¿Qué se ofrece aquí?*' (What's being offered here?), I asked. '*Clases de inglés. Pero para grandes*' (English classes, but for grown-ups), they replied. Now it all made sense. This was not some retail giveaway or a visit from a world leader, but a quite typical class registration night at a neighborhood community center. Individuals in the growing line stood, crouched, leaned and balanced from foot to foot, waiting to be interviewed and tested, hoping to be among the lucky immigrants who would score a seat in a preparation class in English as a second language (ESL) or general education development (GED).

You may have a mental image of these aspiring immigrants, adults who left school in their youth, you assume, prematurely dropped out, succumbed to the many teenage temptations that can distract and derail a high school education. A closer look, however, reveals something surprising and perplexing. Among the middle-aged adults and grandparent types are young people. Not just a handful of young people, but young people out in force. Were you to ask them how old they are, they would tell you 23, 22, 21, 20, 19 years old; still others would tell you proudly that they have just turned 18 or are 17 and a handful would shuffle their feet, look both ways and sheepishly admit that they are 16, or even 15, too young to enroll in adult education

1

classes but old enough to lie about their age because they are desperate to attend and complete their high school requirements so they can improve their job status and hopefully enroll in college.

Why would young people show up *en masse* to enroll in adult education classes, classes designed for working adult immigrants seeking to learn English or develop their job skills? Why adult education and why not high school? There is Victor, who came to the US from Honduras alone at age 15, traveling north with a neighbor, then alone on trains and walking. Now 19, tall and fashionably dressed, he is hoping to enroll in GED class. Farther down the line, sandwiched between older adults, is Elena. She is 16, she tells me, looking at her feet, not really old enough to enroll in this adult education class. Why is she not in high school? 'High School no era para mi', she says – high school was not for her – and please, don't tell them her age so she can get a chance at a seat. Ramón is 22 and he is waiting to see if he can enroll in a class to learn English, worried that there is a test that will disqualify him. He came to the US as a teen to work and more than 50 hours of his week are spent at a neighborhood restaurant, washing dishes and preparing food, so that he can send money home to his mother and younger siblings in Mexico. He has never attended a school in the US and now, at age 22, the idea of being in a classroom with other students is nerve-wracking. In Mexico he left school after the second grade and never went back. Altagracia is near the front of the line. She is all of 19, poised and dressed like a professional. College is her goal and she is intent on getting there no matter what it takes.

This scene, and the young people involved, plays itself out again and again in adult education programs across the US – at neighborhood social service agencies, at public schools, churches, libraries and community colleges. My experiences over the course of more than two decades with the Latino immigrant students described in this scene – in my role as a teacher, program developer, researcher and evaluator – are what planted the seeds for this book. Again and again I read research on Latinos and education: the high dropout rates, the failure to enroll in or complete college, the lack of educational aspirations. Coming from my graduate classes and still carrying books from the library, I would visit programs and talk to students like Victor, Elena, Ramón and Altagracia, and come away frustrated by the disconnect between what the research said about the glaring gap between dropout rates of US-born and foreign-born Latinos – 11% versus 34%. I was in the library reading about Latino dropouts and low educational aspirations and in the field seeing young adults of high school age out *en masse* filling the seats of adult education classes and striving to move up in the world. Nowhere in any scholarly work or in public policy literature could I find a discussion of immigrants who had dropped out of school and then dropped back in, nor the nuances of their experiences or the implications for public policy.

Significance and Originality

This brief volume seeks to shed light on a growing population of immigrant young adults who are overlooked, fall through the cracks and risk wasting their potential on the path to becoming permanent members of US society. In this book I examine the lives and experiences of Latino dropouts in a sociopolitical context and provide some food for thought regarding future directions for research, policy and practice. The sections that follow discuss the aims of this book, its importance in addressing gaps in existing research and scholarly literature, its originality, and the research methods used to gather the data that are the foundation of this volume. In addition, I provide a brief overview of current statistics on immigrant Latinos in the US, and in New York City in particular, how research has viewed this population to date, and what gaps must be addressed in research and practice to change the fate of this growing group.

First, a few words about immigrants and public policy. In the advent of globalization, every industrialized country in the world is host to growing numbers of immigrants (Callahan & Gándara, 2014). The US, with only 5% of the world's population, receives 20% of the world's immigrants (Nwosu et al., 2014). Without question, the education of immigrants and their children and their integration into the mainstream continue to be central policy concerns not only in the US, but around the world.

This volume focuses on young adult immigrant new arrivals who have not completed high school.[1] Between 1990 and 2000, some 3.1 million individuals (24% of immigrants) who arrived in the US were between the ages of 15 and 24, compared with 1.1 million (14%) of the foreign-born population who entered in the decade between 1980 and 1989 (US Census Bureau, 2010). Immigrants and children of immigrants account for more than 20% of the young adult population in the US, a figure expected to reach more than 30% by the year 2030, with Latinos by far outnumbering other subgroups (Fry, 2010; Mather, 2009; Rumbaut & Komaie, 2010; Suárez-Orozco et al., 2008).

The numbers of immigrants have grown steadily since the mid-1960s and Latinos continue to be the largest share of the overall immigrant population in the US. Between 1990 and 2008, nearly 17 million new immigrants entered the US, and more than half arrived from Latin America (Migration Policy Institute, 2008). Figures from the 2012 American Community Survey (ACS) revealed that nearly half of the 40 million foreign-born residents of the US (46% or 18.9 million individuals) are Latino (Nwosu et al., 2014). Table 1.1 illustrates how two-fifths of all foreign-born come from just seven countries in Latin America (Pew Hispanic Center, 2013).

Historians, sociologists, educators, psychologists, linguistics, economists and a host of scholars in other fields have come to recognize that a monolithic look at 'Latinos' overshadows complexities and differences

Table 1.1 Place of birth of all foreign-born residents of the US

Country	% of all foreign-born residents of the US	Number in the US (in millions)
Mexico	29.0	11.7
El Salvador	3.1	1.2
Dominican Republic	2.2	0.8
Guatemala	2.1	0.8
Colombia	1.6	0.7
Honduras	1.2	0.5
Ecuador	1.1	0.5
Total	40.3	16.2

Source: Pew Hispanic Center (2013)

among Latinos, not the least important of which are between US-born and foreign-born. Among these new immigrants, children and young adults are on the rise. The number of immigrant children and young adults living in the US is larger than ever before: of the total foreign-born population of 41 million, nearly half (18 million) arrived between the ages of 18 and 34, and 40% (16.4 million) arrived as children under age 18 (Rumbaut & Komaie, 2010), some with parents and siblings, some alone to join family in the US, and some as unaccompanied minors.

Today, more than a third (34%) of foreign-born Latinos between the ages of 16 and 24 have dropped out of high school. Latinos born outside the US are three times more likely to have an incomplete high school education than their US-born Latino peers, 11% of whom have not completed high school. They are nearly six times more likely than US-born Whites to have an incomplete high school education, and three times more likely than US-born Blacks (National Center for Education Statistics, 2008). The high rate of incomplete high school among foreign-born Latinos persists decade after decade, despite documented improvements in high school completion among US-born Latinos (Fry & López, 2012). This book seeks to interrogate these numbers and explore their relevance for education and social policy. Generations of permanent residents with incomplete high school have faced dire prospects for work, earnings and upward mobility, through a cycle of incomplete education in one generation being associated with poor educational performance on the part of their children.

Rates of school interruption differ by immigrant generation, age at arrival and ethnic group. Research reveals a glaring gap between the dropout rates of immigrants to the US who arrive as teens (15–17) and of those who arrive during their elementary school years (Fry, 2005). Immigrant young adults who arrive in the US as young children and complete all of their school years in the US have school non-completion rates that are relatively low, about 5% (Fry, 2005). The compounding factors of age at arrival, labor market pressures, English proficiency and skills, which will be discussed in depth in Chapter 5, all represent obstacles to school completion among adolescent and teen immigrants. Pre-migration factors, discussed in Chapter 3, as well as circumstances of arrival and post-migration educational options (explained in Chapter 4), all make for a complex educational landscape for adolescent and young adult immigrants.

Latinos in New York City

More than half of the 19 million first- and second-generation immigrant young adults in the US come from Spanish-speaking countries in Latin America (Rumbaut & Komaie, 2010). In New York City, more than half (56%) of all individuals aged 18–34 are immigrants or children of immigrants, highlighting the importance of the fates of both the immigrant first as well as the immigrant second generation (Rumbaut & Komaie, 2010). Different from Whites and Blacks in the US, the majority of whom have parents born in the US, more than four-fifths of Latinos in the US are foreign-born or have immigrant parents. The same holds true among school-age students in New York City, where more than half of the adult population is foreign-born, with Latinos by far the largest immigrant subgroup (Rosen et al., 2005). According to data compiled by the Migration Policy Institute, about 28% of immigrant New Yorkers entered in the 1990s, and about one-third after 2000. In New York City, a total of 302,168 immigrant Latinos entered between 1990 and 1999 and an additional 389,000 between 2000 and 2010 (Bergad, 2011). The most numerous of the new arrivals are from Colombia, Ecuador, the Dominican Republic and Mexico (Table 1.2), with Puerto Ricans, who are US citizens, making up a still significant but decreasing proportion of the resident population (Bergad, 2011).

Viewed as a whole, Latinos have become an extremely linguistically and culturally diverse subgroup that has changed the fabric of US society and culture. Far from being a monolithic block, Latinos residing in the US represent the broadest spectrum possible in terms of economic status, linguistic background and educational attainment. Certainly Latinos in New York City have both the highest and lowest educational levels (Fiscal Policy Institute, 2010; Rosen et al., 2005). While among the Latino group as a whole there is a broad spectrum of both racial background and nationality (country of origin), the 'ethnic diversity of contemporary immigrants pales in comparison to their social class origins' (Rumbaut & Komaie, 2010: 47).

Table 1.2 Country of origin of all foreign-born Latinos in New York City, 2010

Country of origin	Puerto Rico (born on island)	Dominican Republic	Mexico	Ecuador	Colombia	Other Latin American
City population in 2010	212,457	387,256	197,368	141,870	67,497	235,121

Source: Bergad (2011)

Moreover, their social class origins are closely tied to educational attainment, underscoring the importance of examining not simply a mythically generic 'immigrant experience', but gaining a deeper understanding of specific subgroups. Across the US, those with the lowest levels of educational attainment on average are Mexicans and those who have the highest poverty rate among all immigrant groups are Dominicans (Rumbaut & Komaie, 2010); both groups feature largely in the present study. According to the Center for the Study of Brooklyn (2012) at the City University of New York, 41% of immigrants aged 16–24 in New York City are Latino (a total of 112,415). Of this group, nearly 27% (30,059) are official dropouts and not enrolled in school.

The two largest and fastest-growing immigrant Latino subgroups in New York City – excluding Puerto Ricans, who are US nationals – are Mexicans and Dominicans (Limonic, 2007). Adults in both groups demonstrate above average levels of poverty, with more than a third of each group below the poverty line, and relatively poor educational attainment (Table 1.3). Nearly 65% of adult Mexican and more than 50% of adult Dominican New Yorkers report not having completed high school (Cortina & Gendreau, 2003; Limonic, 2007; New York City Department of City Planning, 2004). Among Mexicans in New York City, older arrivals have non-enrollment rates over 40%, yet Mexicans who arrive at younger ages are enrolled in school at rates nearly comparable to those of US-born youth, revealing a link between age at arrival and educational attainment. Among foreign-born Mexicans residing in New York City, 40% have completed six or fewer years of education, with 25% having completed some or all of high school, and 5% have college degrees (Rosen *et al.*, 2005).

As can be seen from Table 1.3, foreign-born Dominicans and Mexicans have the lowest levels of educational attainment among Latino immigrant subgroups in New York City. For Mexicans, the data are presented graphically in Figure 1.1 and for Dominicans in Figure 1.2. Among Dominicans aged 25 and over in New York City, 29% have completed elementary school or less and another 25% have completed high school or less (Figure 1.2). Only 9% have college degrees (Rosen *et al.*, 2005).

Table 1.3 Educational attainment of major Latino subgroups in New York City, 2010

		% with no high school diploma or GED	% with some college, AA, BA or higher[1]
Mexico	Men, US-born	19.8	60.9
	Men, foreign-born	54.8	14.6
	Women, US-born	11.8	77.8
	Women, foreign-born	59.7	13.1
Puerto Rico[2]	Men, US-born	26.9	40.5
	Men, foreign-born	52.3	21.3
	Women, US-born	24.0	50.8
	Women, foreign-born	49.5	23.6
Dominican Republic	Men, US-born	17.6	57.9
	Men, foreign-born	44.4	30.2
	Women, US-born	9.2	73.6
	Women, foreign-born	43.4	32.6
Ecuador	Men, US-born	10.2	66.4
	Men, foreign-born	42.1	27.3
	Women, US-born	15.7	70.6
	Women, foreign-born	39.7	28.7
Colombia	Men, US-born	10.9	62.1
	Men, foreign-born	19.6	5.9
	Women, US-born	15.3	78.0
	Women, foreign-born	25.9	43.0

1. GED, General Education Development; AA, Associate of Arts degree; BA, Bachelor of Arts degree.
2. Foreign-born means born on the island.
Source: Bergad (2011)

Among first-generation immigrants, young adults are also numerous: immigrants aged 17–24 were nearly 25% of total entrants in the 2000 Census, up from 13% in 1990 (US Census Bureau, 2010). Nearly 20% of New York State's immigrants are between the ages of 17 and 24 years, and constitute nearly 40% of workers among the youngest age group, 16–24 (New York City Department of City Planning, 2004). With employment that ranges from part time to full time (and beyond, with more than one job), school and work compete with each other for these young people's energy and attention.

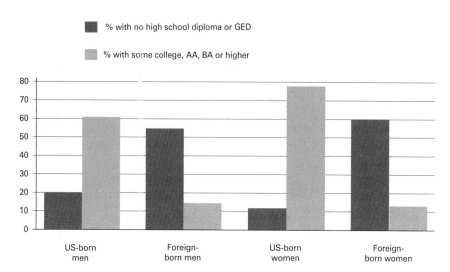

Figure 1.1 Educational attainment of Mexicans in New York City, 2010
Source: Bergad (2011)

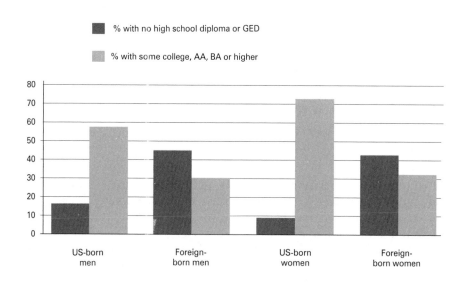

Figure 1.2 Educational attainment of Dominicans in New York City, 2010
Source: Bergad (2011)

Latinos as a Permanent Sector of the US Population

Due to the recent global economic downturn and stagnant wages, many Latino immigrants' dreams of returning home have been put on hold temporarily for financial reasons; this has been compounded by increasingly stringent border control policies, as re-entry is seen as risky enterprise (Massey *et al*, 2002; Smith, 2006, 2013). The result is less circular migration and more permanent residency among this group, which includes especially high numbers of undocumented minors who arrive alone without parents or adult guardians (Smith, 2006), primarily from Mexico and Central America (National Conference of State Legislatures, 2005, 2014; United Nations High Commissioner for Refugees, 2014). In 2013, tens of thousands of unaccompanied young people arrived in the US with no adult, 40,000 alone from Mexico, Honduras, Guatemala and El Salvador and crossing the border from Mexico (United Nations High Commissioner for Refugees, 2014). These young adults, the focus of this volume, are of working age; some are even parents of young children, while some migrated alone. They serve as a significant source of financial support for their families in their country of origin. Despite the differences in the circumstances of their migration, they have striking similarities in high school completion and graduation rates.

The students who have come to be known as 'Generation 1.5' students in the US have much in common with Latino migrant young adults. These young people come from immigrant families and while most came to the US under age 13 but spent their formative schooling years in US schools, some were born in the US but still speak a language other than English at home with immigrant parents. Although they are not newcomers, they share many characteristics with newcomer immigrant learners, as Generation 1.5 students often struggle with academic English, especially writing (Harklau, 2003; Thonus, 2003) and some languish for years in programs for English as a second language and some are classified as 'long-term English language learners' (Menken *et al.*, 2012).

Existing Research on the Latino Population

To date, US educational research on immigrants has focused on school achievement, integration into K-12 contexts (kindergarten to grade 12), and graduation and college enrollment rates, with some studies examining segmented assimilation or the differences between groups.

Research on the graduation rates of Latino students in the US has primarily examined the traditional high school to college pathway. Yet there exists an entire subset of immigrant youth and young adults – those who arrive in the US at high school age (around 14 or 15) up through the Census cut-off for 'young adult' (age 24) – who have to date been rendered 'invisible' – there is little in the way of reliable and detailed data, as research agendas overlook them. The pages that follow focus on these overlooked young adults who arrive in the US without having completed a high school education in their home country and then are counted among the vast and undifferentiated pool of dropouts in the US Census. High schools view these immigrant young adults as hard to serve, and rising standards and accountability requirements for schools serve as a disincentive to serve them. Public school enrollment data reveal a trend to discharge them soon after enrollment and prior to their having completed the requirements for a high school diploma. Increasing numbers turn to adult and alternative education programs, seeking a 'second chance' pathway to college and job training, viewing education as the pathway to attaining a foothold in the economy and the mainstream.

To date, research on this population has focused on their singular status as 'dropouts', while ignoring the growing numbers who seek out adult and second-chance educational programs to continue their education. The aspirations and experiences of the growing population of immigrant youth with interrupted secondary schooling have great significance for national efforts to address post-secondary readiness and success in the US. To date, no study has explored the realities of immigrants who have left high school but who have taken to heart the oft-intoned national mantra that education is the road to success and thus re-enter educational pathways (adult education) seeking a second chance. With a lack of data on this population, the concept that Latinos with incomplete high school are 'dropouts' remains unchallenged, as does the very idea that immigrant dropouts make a measured 'choice' to discontinue their schooling. This volume presents the first research of its kind to incorporate the voices and experiences of Latino immigrant youth 'dropouts' who have self-selected a path of re-entry into an array of US second-chance educational pathways. By no means can they be understood solely as *dropouts*, as they have self-selected a pathway of re-entry into schooling.

Education is the 21st-century mantra. There is a growing understanding of immigrants and migration. With its focus on the education of Latinos as a swelling population group, this book will turn up the volume on the voices of students who to date have been overlooked and ignored, and potentially misunderstood. To borrow from the title of the Urban Institute's compelling study, these young people are 'overlooked and underserved' in schools (Ruiz-de-Velasco *et al.*, 2000), and it is time to shine a bright light to illuminate their experiences. The chapters in this volume draw on new quantitative and qualitative data on immigrant young adults from original mixed methods research. The new quantitative data are interwoven with the voices of the young immigrants in question to provide an engaging and nuanced look at a population that is ubiquitous but invisible. Who are these young Latino dropouts who have chosen to drop back *in* to schooling?

A word or two about dropouts is in order at this point. This volume examines the educational pathways of immigrant Latino young adults who came to the US without completing high school. To date, the roots of their incomplete schooling have not been subjected to inquiry. A central goal of this volume is to fling open that creaky door labeled 'immigrant dropout' and air out its contents. I am not the first to take on this task of examining dropouts, and I follow in the venerable footsteps of Sherman Dorn, Gary Orfield, Michelle Fine, Pedro Noguera and others who have challenged conventional wisdom on this subject. This volume differs markedly from past work in that it focuses solely on immigrant dropouts and that it takes a critical look at the political economy and its impact on experiences both prior to and after migration to the US to explore the causes and consequences of school interruption. In the most objective sense, dropouts are people who have not completed high school, and in this volume I place particular emphasis on young immigrants who come to the US during their formative young adult years (from around 15 to age 24, using the Census categories) with an incomplete high school education. Having crossed the border into the US, their status lands them squarely in the US Census category of 'dropout', a very fuzzy and contested one. For the research world to date, they have been stuck in that vague and shadowy category. My goal in this book is to sharpen the image and look closely at their realities.

Magnifying the Often Overlooked: On Methodology

My interest in the educational pathways and choices of immigrant young adults began years before I started this research, when I was completing my university studies at a public university in Germany prior to its re-unification. I was among a growing cohort of immigrant students from around the world. Among my linguistically and ethnically diverse peers were many students from Latin America and the Caribbean who had made their way to Europe seeking post-secondary education as a pathway out of poverty. Their stories of crossing borders clandestinely, escaping state-sponsored violence, hiding out in the holds of cargo ships bound for European coastal cities led me to develop a nuanced understanding of international migration. These friends and classmates dramatically changed my beliefs and perspectives on access to educational opportunity and cemented my interest in the topic of educational access and equity and the complex interplay of the factors of immigration status and educational attainment.

This book is a product of questions that emerged from more than two decades of my own work with Latino immigrant students in major cities in the US. In schools, universities and community-based organizations, I have designed educational services for Latinos arriving in the first wave of immigrants from their home countries to a new city (Salvadorans and

Guatemalans in Washington, DC; Mexicans in New York City and Los Angeles). During that time, I have heard countless personal accounts and helped many youth and adults document their experiences in writing. Starting with a Title VII grant from the US Department of Education at George Washington University in the early 1990s, much of my professional work has focused on helping immigrants share their immigration stories and experiences, with the goal of helping schools and community-based organizations better meet their needs.

The research presented in this book grew out of work I conducted at New York University at the Metropolitan Center for Urban Education, a research, evaluation and technical assistance provider that serves schools across the US. Immersed in research on immigration, youth and schools, I became increasingly frustrated to discover that existing research studies did not include experiences or statistics on the many youth 'dropouts' I was meeting in adult education classrooms. Not only that, but the research I was reading painted a very different picture from the one I was seeing with my own eyes, out in the field. Many immigrants who arrive in the US between the ages of 15 and 24 with incomplete schooling live outside or on the perimeters of institutional structures, and leave few footprints. Administrative data collected by educational institutions often omit basic information such as years of prior education, age at arrival, or year of entry, making it very difficult to use the kinds of data typically collected by the US Census, school districts or government agencies in order to determine the detailed backgrounds of groups of young adult immigrants. Fortunate to be in a vibrant research community, I set out to fill that gap and to understand what we could learn about Latino immigrant dropouts who found their way back into the educational system via adult education. This volume is the product of that work, and is based on original research conducted over the course of more than a year. It combines new data on immigrant school leavers enrolled in adult education programs in New York City with publicly available statistics on school enrollment, participation, graduation rates and Census figures on educational attainment, poverty rates and college-going.

It is my good fortune to have worked across the divides of adult education, K-12 education and public post-secondary education – what the New York State Education Department refers to as the 'p-16 system' – and thus I am intimately familiar with the many entry points and institutional doors through which young adult immigrants may enter as they seek an educational pathway. A broad and mature professional and personal network provided me with access to programs in ways that would be inconceivable for an outsider.

Because they include individuals who are undocumented as well as those who have never had contact with public institutions in the US, many of the youth in this study could not be identified via formal institutions like public schools. To counter this, I constructed a purposeful sample by recruiting participants from among Latino youth enrolled in one of an array of types of second-chance and adult education programs. Seven sites were selected that provide English as a second language and Spanish GED classes at no cost, have high Latino enrollments, and together provide a broad geographic distribution within New York City. A key consideration in selection of sites was the creation of a sample representing diverse institutions that provide GED and English as a second language services to high numbers of Latino immigrant youth, including community college academic prep programs in English as a second language, community-based social service providers, volunteer-run educational programs and publicly funded adult education programs for immigrants. Within each program, enrollment data were used to select a subset of students who fit the criteria – Latino immigrants who had entered the US as teens and young adults (aged 14–24), native Spanish-speakers, born in Mexico, Central America, South America or the Spanish-speaking Caribbean.

For part of the data collection for this study, I designed and conducted a survey with participants. The design of the survey instrument (see Appendix, pp. 169–185) was based on prior studies of immigrant young people's aspirations and their trajectories conducted by Suárez-Orozco *et al.* (2008) and Portes and Rumbaut (2001). I considered it important to move beyond a purely empirical approach, meaning that I wanted to look past the numbers and statistics on immigrants and schooling and get an up–close, personal sense of who these young people are and what they think and say about the role of education in their lives. Research that I had read kept confounding me, leading me to statistical representations that were thorough, complex and illuminating, but lacked the nuance that qualitative data could provide. To give depth and richness to the study, I chose to conduct focus groups with participants in Spanish, in which participants talked about their school experiences, goals and dreams, and the role that education played in their lives. After conducting these focus groups, I invited a dozen of the participants to speak with me one on one. Ultimately, this mixed methods approach bore fruit: quantitative methods provided a foundation for empirical analysis of detailed demographic and statistical data on young adult immigrant school leavers at the participating study sites; qualitative data in the form of interview and focus group transcripts gave life to the data and told compelling personal stories. Ultimately, the research that is presented here has broken new ground, first by presenting new demographic data on immigrant Latino school leavers, and second by illuminating the voices and experiences of this overlooked subset of immigrant young adults for the first time. (Readers interested in details of the research methodology should refer to the Appendix.)

Researcher Stance

There is no question that every researcher brings a perspective and a bias to the research process. Much of the research on immigrant young adults highlights deficiencies and pathologies; Way (1998) critiques the negative bias of the literature on minority adolescents as being skewed toward a focus on pathologies and challenges, especially when dealing with urban and minority adolescents. The research presented here seeks to move beyond a litany of challenges and to explore deeply what it is that immigrants who have made a choice to pursue education through second-chance options want in their lives. I have sought to be mindful not only of the complexities of their identities and lived experiences, but of avoiding the trap of a deficit view (Spencer & Dornbush, 1990) that would risk eclipsing the strengths, skills and potential of the population in question and could overshadow acknowledgment of their resilience in the face of great geographical and cultural change.

Significant studies of urban youth (Fine, 1991; Olsen, 1997; Way, 1998) have demonstrated the importance of including the voices and perspectives of young people in any study about them, rather than relying exclusively on empirical evidence or administrative data. The research presented here on the educational aspirations and experiences of Latino immigrant youth was designed with the assumption that although empirical data can provide important information about outcomes and student achievement, students' choices and behaviors can be understood only by talking to participants and uncovering their perspectives. I am very fortunate to follow in the path of those who have paved the way in research on young immigrants, and my work has drawn heavily from scholarly work on immigrant assimilation (Kao & Tienda, 1998; Portes & Rumbaut, 2001; Portes & Zhou, 1993; Smith, 2006; Suárez-Orozco et al., 2008). Those researchers cemented our understanding that the choices made by immigrant youth regarding their education and futures are influenced by a complex array of factors that can be understood completely only by examining the components and not simply the outcomes.

Limitations

The research discussed here has a number of inherent limitations. The sample is voluntary, as I had to rely upon a group of young people attending a diverse set of public educational programs in New York City. The participants in this study and the programs in which they are enrolled are a small subset that is significant yet by no means comprehensive. It must be acknowledged that the participants are exceptional individuals in that they have overcome a series of obstacles to migrate to the US and have

Box 1.1 Summary data on US immigrants, 2010

- There were 40 million foreign-born residents of the US, representing 13% of the population.
- 18 million of the total foreign-born population arrived in the US between the ages of 18 and 34 (young adults) and 16.4 million as children (i.e. under age 18).
- 18.8 million of the foreign-born population in the US are Latino.
- Latino foreign-born young adults have dropout rates of nearly 34%, compared with a national average of 8% overall, 6% for other foreign-born, 12% for US-born Latinos, 9% for Blacks, 5% for Whites and 3% for Asian/Pacific Islander youth.

self-selected a path of second-chance education. Every effort had been made in the design of the study to select a sample of diverse programs and students representing different countries, ages and years of schooling completed, and representing both male and female participants. The purpose of this research is not to generalize, but to shed light on a phenomenon that has important implications for policy and practice. Sample selection purposely omitted Latino immigrants who otherwise fitted the criteria but were not enrolled in second-chance educational programs, as the focus of the study was the examination of the aspirations and experiences of those young people who have been flagged as dropouts but who have explicitly chosen an educational pathway as a road to upward mobility. More details on the research methods can be found in the Appendix (pp. 169–185). The next section provides some background information on Latinos in the US (Box 1.1) and the following section briefly reviews the nature of the transition from youth to adulthood from an immigrant perspective.

Research on Immigrants and Immigration

There is no dearth of research on immigration in the US (Cornelius, 2001; Foner, 2013; Gándara & Contreras, 2009; Kasinitz et al., 2008; Klapper, 2007; Massey et al., 2002; Suárez-Orozco, 2000) nor on the educational achievement of immigrants (Hall, 2002; Portes & Rumbaut, 2001, 2006; Ruiz-de-Velasco et al., 2001; Suárez-Orozco et al., 2008). Scholarship on the integration of immigrants into mainstream society, known as 'structural assimilation', has corrected early 20th-century views that all immigrants experience upward mobility (Gordon, 1964; Park & Burgess, 1924; Warner & Srole, 1945; Wirth, 1928). Instead, what has been documented is the segmented nature of immigrant integration for current generations, whereby some immigrants improve their status after coming to the US and others experience downward mobility (Portes & Rumbaut, 1996, 2001; Portes & Zhou, 1993; Suárez-Orozco et al., 2008).

Research and policy reports on the education of Latinos in the US have similarly documented segmented achievement, with some Latinos (both immigrants and their US-born children) doing particularly well, with rising graduation and college-going rates, while others underachieve and drop out in record numbers (Fry, 2002, 2005; Gándara & Contreras, 2009; Ruiz-de-Velasco et al., 2001; Suárez-Orozco et al., 2008). The complex nature of segmented assimilation and resulting divergent achievement patterns in schools give rise to many questions that this volume seeks to address. A key area of exploration for sociologists and educational researchers has been structural and institutional challenges that are unique to ethnic minority and immigrant youth in schools (Gándara et al., 2004; Noguera, 2003; Suárez-Orozco, 2004). Anthropologists, in contrast, have taken a more individual-based view to underscore the important role of culture in achievement (Hall, 2002; Ogbu & Simons, 1998; Togunde, 2008), which has led in some areas to the view that certain groups 'value' education more than others, leading to the persistent conventional wisdom that some immigrant groups are inherently achievers – the model minority myths with which we are all familiar – while other groups are inherently underachievers. Such cultural frameworks are in some ways nuanced, but fail to take into account a complex array of sociopolitical realities, including global economic factors that impact socioeconomic status in immigrants' countries of origin, as well as centuries of geopolitical relations between the US and Latin American that impact migration (Gonzalez, 2000).

Global, institutional or individual frameworks notwithstanding, existing research has examined primarily the educational aspirations and attainments of US-born Hispanics in high school and college (Hanson, 1994; Kao & Tienda, 1998) as well as those of high-achieving immigrant youth through the K-12 to college pathway (Fry, 2002; Immerwahr, 2003). With this nearly exclusive focus on K-12 achievement and the transition from high school to college, there is the need for an examination of 'second chance' learners like those who are the subject of this volume. This is doubly true in this era of public school accountability measures that emphasize so-called 'college-readiness' metrics based on paper-and-pencil test scores. These learners are individuals who either circumvent or leave K-12 schooling and enter alternative and adult education (Ross & Gray, 2005) with the goal of improving their status and work prospects and grasping the brass ring of upward mobility. Research has not explored how participation in second-chance education for immigrants or attainment of a GED or engagement in education outside of these traditional institutions could impact the assimilation process and whether it could break this cycle of social reproduction. In the US, adult education continues to provide an additional opportunity for US-born and immigrant students alike.

The belief that anyone in the US can succeed economically through hard work has long been characterized as the 'American Dream'. The 21st-century twist on the American Dream incorporates education: more education will get you a better job and that will get you a better life. New immigrants in the US have historically embraced the education mantra, known to scholars as the 'achievement ideology' (McClelland, 1990: 225), and generally view both economic and educational opportunities in the US as superior to those in their country of origin (Hochschild, 1995). Formal institutions like schools have been shown to serve a key role in helping immigrants integrate into the mainstream and achieve upward mobility (Alba & Nee, 2003; Hall, 2002). Yet these same institutions have been found to reproduce social inequality from one generation to the next (Macleod, 1995), perpetuating the same social stratification and inequities that exist in the larger society (Bourdieu & Passeron, 1977; MacLeod, 1995). Extensive literature has also explored the societal structures that constrain or facilitate choices and pathways of assimilation (Alba & Nee, 2003; Bourdieu & Passeron, 1977; Portes & Rumbaut, 2006; Rumbaut, 1997), while critics of school reform have examined how the political economy of the US has severely limited choices and opportunities for low-wage workers (Anyon, 2005).

Immigrant youth in the research presented here arrived in the US with interrupted education from low-status/high-poverty backgrounds in their countries of origin. Socioeconomic status has been shown to be a strong predictor of achievement (Blau & Duncan, 1967; Coleman et al., 1966; McClelland, 1990; Orfield & Eaton, 1997; Orfield et al., 2004; Sewell et al., 1969), yet it is often not considered when immigrants are viewed as a monolithic whole, with no attention to family histories and personal migration experiences. This oversight ignores sociopolitical factors that may spur migration north, as well as structural and economic issues of equity of opportunity and access to education in immigrants' countries of origin that impact their educational trajectories both before and after migration. A focus on individual achievement can overlook the important role that social capital and networks can play in facilitating educational access, support and achievement (Fine, 1991; Gaytan, 2010; Nee & Sanders, 2001; Noguera, 2003; Portes, 2000; Suárez-Orozco et al., 2008). For children and young adults, peers have been shown to play a significant role in achievement and integration.

Transitions From Youth to Adulthood

Depending on the discipline, the terms 'youth' and 'young adult' are often used interchangeably. Scholarly work on immigrant education has been built upon a developmental view of childhood and youth based on Erikson's (1968) stages of psychosocial development, with age as the primary marker of each stage. More recent theories of human development view late adolescence as a distinct phase, examining challenges that face emerging adults as they transition on a fairly linear path first from home then on to post-secondary schooling and then into the world of full-time work (Arnett, 2004; Eccles & Zarrett, 2006). Left unaddressed in research on post-secondary pathways for immigrant students are the complex life experiences of teenage labor migrants, whose lives do not follow such linear and step-wise developmental trajectories. Is a four-year high school pathway even still relevant for them? Young adults like Victor, Elena, Ramón and Altagracia are in a stage of development that bridges adolescence and young adulthood, but they and many like them have nonetheless taken on some very adult responsibilities, such as having children and supporting families. Many immigrant youth were thrust into these adult roles at a young age and serve as financial anchors for families in their countries of origin (Martinez, 2009), supporting families with remittances (Somerville et al., 2008), serve as liaisons between parents and US institutions, and make major life decisions in the absence of adults. Arnett's paradigm of 'emerging adult' involves a 'second chance' (Arnett, 2004: 204) 'for people from difficult backgrounds to transform their lives' (Arnett, 2004: 189–190). For older adolescents and young adults who are drawn to the US for economic reasons or because of family ties, challenges to this process of self-realization and transformation include language, displacement, financial instability, lack of knowledge of institutional structures (Gándara & Contreras, 2009; Ruiz-de-Velasco et al., 2001; Smith, 2006) as well as the political economy (Anyon, 2005). Central to the immigration process is a quest for improvement, yet immigrants with low levels of schooling are often assumed to be solely labor migrants or to fall into the category of dropouts (Fry, 2002; Immerwahr, 2003), ignoring what is known about the complexity of the migration processes and the impact of globalization on roles and social expectations (Smith, 2006). The focus on aspirations and pathways of immigrants in a range of educational programs outside traditional high schools, a view of them as emerging adults outside the definition of 'adolescent' as a young person in need of socialization, and beyond the simple definition of dropout will lead to a more complete and complex understanding of a phenomenon that is relevant in a global society beyond the scope of New York City, New York State and the US. The research presented here proposes a new frame of reference to understand this growing group whose educational pathways have great relevance to the future of society, and whose presence in educational programs invites an analysis of existing opportunities and understandings.

Overview of Contents

This volume proceeds by laying a foundation, examining the complex nature of identifying school leavers. Chapter 2 explores the term *dropout*: its roots, history and the complexities of its connotations and how it is calculated. The second chapter also presents a demographic profile of Latinos in New York City – who they are, where they are and what we know about their educational trajectories, including who is counted and who is not among Census categories, exploring the difficulties of identifying and codifying Latino immigrant young adults. Chapter 3 traces Latino immigrants' educational trajectories by exploring the sociopolitical context of migration and school interruption, examining the political economy of the US and many Latin American sender nations and how it impacts school participation. Original data from participants' own perspectives in Chapter 3 illuminates particular circumstances that led to school interruption prior to arrival in the US. The third chapter also explores the paradigm of 'choice' in sociopolitical context as well as the concept of value put on education. Chapter 4 shifts to the post-migration experience, presenting the ways in which immigrant school leavers navigate educational options after they arrive in the US. An array of educational entry points for immigrant young adults is presented in Chapter 4, including high school and the GED for immigrants, as well as existing federal and state policies that impact young people, including those who are disconnected, over-age or undocumented. Participants share their perspectives in Chapter 4 on perceived obstacles to education, their choices and life goals, and we come to understand their contextual knowledge of existing educational opportunities. Chapter 5 provides a nuanced look at school leavers by presenting three distinct subgroups of immigrant dropouts who have made the choice to drop back in to education: pushouts, shutouts and holdouts. These three distinct categories shed light on the political economy and institutional realities. Chapter 6 takes a deeper look at educational experiences by examining the role of language, English proficiency, literacy and academic skills in access to educational options. Research on multilingual approaches to academic English development and existing policies and practices for students with interrupted formal education is also discussed in Chapter 6. Using original data on educational goals, both pre- and post-migration, the chapter challenges perceptions that Latinos, especially labor migrants and persons with emergent literacy, do not value education. The final chapter of this volume, Chapter 7, examines, challenges and critiques existing public policies, opportunities and institutional constraints that impact the young adults discussed here. Promising models, opportunities and directions for future research and persisting questions conclude this volume.

Goals of the Book

This volume is presented with four goals in mind. The first is to begin to bridge the glaring gap in existing research and scholarship on immigrant youth dropouts by presenting original data on a significant but overlooked population. This volume scrutinizes data about immigrant school leavers, but it seeks to enrich the conversation by putting names and faces to the numbers, in an effort to deepen our collective understanding of the lives of these young adults. I hope to expand our knowledge of their demographic characteristics, data on their educational trajectories both before and after migration, their beliefs about education and the goals they articulate for themselves. Second, this volume explores how the political economy of the US impacts the educational trajectories of these immigrant young adults and their educational and labor market options, both those with incomplete high school education and those who have attained the coveted college degree, as well as the factors that impact their integration into the cultural, social and economic mainstream of the US. Third, I seek to expand and challenge existing views on immigrant school leavers by exploring the pre- and post-migration factors that lead to interrupted schooling, as well as the options for their educational integration outside traditional high school. Finally, this volume examines the opportunities and challenges that these immigrant young adults face in pursuing their goals and discusses directions for the future. Ultimately, I hope to share the compelling stories of these young adults, all of whom without exception were eager to share their experiences. Time and again they reminded me that this type of research is important because, as one youth explained, *'de verdad no nos ven'* ('they don't really see us').

The study of this population of second-chance learners is important in multiple ways. First, in order to best serve students seeking a second chance via education, it is vital to understand what happens during their first attempt that may have derailed them. We would not want to make the same mistakes or replicate the same conditions, especially if public dollars and young futures are at stake. Second, if there is more to dropouts than, well, leaving school, then this demands examination as well. Perhaps our paradigm for school leavers needs to shift in such a way as to better impact public policy and thus prevent such rampant school leaving in the first place. Third, if education can be provided effectively via second-chance mechanisms such as adult education or via alternative programs that take into account the unique circumstances of immigrant young adults, then it is worth exploring the conditions needed for success. And finally, as the majority minority, it is important to understand the nuances within this diverse population. Most Latinos are not on a path of circular migration: roots have been laid in the US and the success of subsequent generations, the children of these immigrants, is greatly impacted by the success, educational attainment and subsequent labor force prospects of their parents.

By examining the educational backgrounds and trajectories of a group of immigrant Latinos categorized as 'dropouts' and their experiences in the US as they seek to continue their education, this study provides insights for current discourse on graduation rates, dropouts, immigrants' access to education and policies on access to post-secondary education. Within the national context of increasing emphasis on college-readiness and career preparation, this research seeks to understand immigrant school leavers beyond the simplistic status label of 'dropout' in order to focus not on their exit from formal school pathways but on possible re-entry points that could lead to upward mobility. A constructive focus on their futures should lead to a sense of shared national responsibility for their fates. The research presented in this volume reveals why a unique subset of immigrants invests energy and time in non-traditional educational options and what may facilitate the achievement of their goals.

Note

(1) For the most part in this volume, the age range for 'young immigrant adult' (or youth) is taken from the US Census, as 15–24 years. In the US high school is grades 9–12 (see Table 3.3), typically covering an age range of 13–18. However, it is possible to retake a grade, and older students remain entitled to schooling. The specifics vary across the individual states; in New York State, young people are eligible to remain in high school until age 21. Kindergarten education begins around 4–6 years and the education system from then through to grade 12 is commonly denoted K-12 schooling. Educational pathways are discussed in Chapter 5.

2 Understanding Dropouts: Math and History

Introduction and Overview

Look around. They are everywhere, but you may not have noticed them. Immigrant young adults are preparing your food, washing the dishes and bussing the tables in your favorite restaurant. They are delivering your dry cleaning, picking your lettuce, repaving your street and laying the foundation for that building down the block. They are carrying sheetrock, cleaning the floors and vacuuming your office. They are changing your babies' diapers and doing your laundry. They are stocking the shelves at your supermarket, taking charge of the checkout at the drugstore, rehanging the clothes from the fitting room. They are sewing jeans and blouses, assembling purses, making sandwiches, plucking chickens and delivering bread. They are painting, varnishing, jackhammering and hauling debris. Likely you've noticed them at work in these jobs, but you may not have imagined the other facets of the lives that some of them lead: dusting off after a work-week of 50 hours or more and running to class, thumbing through the dictionary to complete their next assignment, preparing for the next English test.

This book focuses on a very specific subset of the population: Latino young adults who immigrated to the US as adolescents and young adults after interrupting their high school education; they are technically dropouts. Because immigrants like Victor, Elena, Ramón and Altagracia are folded into the overall statistics for Latinos and for dropouts, we know little about them. To understand the situations of Latino immigrant dropouts, this chapter presents data on Latino immigration to the US and to New York City more specifically, and explores the challenges and complexities of locating, identifying, describing and studying this subset of the young adult population. Who are these young people? How and where can they be found and identified?

The chapter begins by dissecting the history of the term *dropout* in the US and examines concepts of high school dropouts to gain a better understanding of this complex and contested construct. Using research, Census data and school enrollment figures, it provides readers with a nuanced image of immigrant school leavers.

Roots of the Dropout Crisis

Without question, the term *dropout* is not a compliment. It is akin to 'illiterate', which in its original Latin means 'not furnished with letters' but has been used as a word that implies ignorance and a general lack of culture. *Dropout*, when used in the vernacular, is not a nice word. More often than not it is used not as a description, but as a quasi-epithet, with the goal of insulting its target. Dropouts have bad reputations. They are viewed as unmotivated underachievers, borderline social deviants with no aspirations. Conventional wisdom would have us believe that dropouts do not see the value of an education or of hard work. The Puritan ideals of the US lead us to look askance at the dropout, for how could someone who has left school of his or her own accord possibly be up to any good? Dropouts are the ostensible ne'er-do-wells in a society that puts its stock in upward mobility and self-improvement, heavy weights dragging down upward strivers.

Yet *dropout* is a surprisingly young term. In his in-depth historical exploration of the concept, scholar Sherman Dorn (1996) reveals that, until the 1960s, neither the concept of a high school dropout nor the term itself even existed. What has changed in the educational landscape of the US that has resulted in such a shift in focus?

The national goal of universal high school education in the US is only about 50 years old. In the 19th century, graduation from high school was neither necessity nor expectation, because child labor laws allowed adolescents to work and many were forced to do so by economic realities (Dorn, 1996). High school education was for reserved for the rich, the upper class and the elite. After laws were passed, child labor still existed, but it became increasingly difficult for young adults to find jobs. More high schools were built, as adolescents became slowly more excluded from the workforce, increasing high school attendance. In the 20th century, schools in the US began to be the place where children spent their adolescence, rather than the workplace. As a result, high school came to be seen as 'the natural place for teenagers' (Dorn, 1996: 18).

At the start of the 20th century, fewer than 20% of all youth of high school age attended high school (Finn & Jackson, 1989). Up until the mid-20th century, less than half of all adolescents enrolled in high school, and the majority of Americans, whether foreign-born or US-born, did not expect to obtain a high school diploma. As fewer teenagers entered the workforce and as child labor laws became stricter and prevented adolescents from working, more began entering high school, one of the many institutions created for 'warehousing' youth. As more demand was created, more schools were built. In fact, there was no such thing as 'truancy' up until that point, and the creation of an image of out-of-school adolescents as delinquents and social deviants is the direct result of a push for universal high school (Dorn, 1996; Fine, 1991).

High schools in the 20th century offered something that other institutions for youth could not: a credential that guaranteed a payoff in the labor market (Dorn, 1996). Time spent away from work and in the classroom meant lost wages, but it was an investment with a good return. This simple equation led high school to gain in popularity. If the high school credential had not promised a payoff, adolescents would not have abandoned a booming labor market to sit in a classroom for four years.

As the high school movement gained in force in the US, the schools became the institutions that were expected to supervise and socialize American youth. Up until that time, there was no great social concern in the US about keeping young people in high school until they graduated. As a result, the choice to leave school – for most immigrants, to work – was not viewed as a mistake or a demonstration of deviance. A dramatic shift had occurred in only one century. By the late 20th century, high schools had become institutions responsible for comprehensive education of *all* adolescents, thus generating the perception that schools are failing, and that students like Victor, Elena, Ramón and Altagracia, who have no diploma, are failures.

Who and What is a High School Education For?

At the start of the 21st century, current stagnant wages and high levels of unemployment have made a high school diploma a necessity, a minimum standard for the lowest-wage employment. Most recently, high school has been redefined as a place to get adolescents in the US 'college and career ready', a phrase coined during the Obama administration. College has become the 21st-century universal goal in the US, and high schools should produce graduates who are 'college ready', although there is no consensus on what exactly that entails. What that looks like and how to measure it are under debate, but there is general agreement that everyone should attend high school and should leave with a diploma. What happens inside the school, whose needs are met and how, are unresolved, even as universal attendance as a goal continues.

For many, including school reformers of all political leanings, schools are institutions that exist to socialize young people (Hammack, 1996; Kronick & Hargis, 1998). Their most rudimentary and uninspiring mission, in the worst case, is to get adolescents off the streets and keep them out of trouble. Others view high schools as the great socializer, preparing youth in the US to be active, thoughtful, law-abiding and productive members of society (Nakkula, 2006). Schooling, mandatory attendance and even school reform reflect two rather conservative visions of schools. The first relates to *socialization* – schools will form young people into law-abiding citizens who can contribute to society (Finn & Jackson, 1989). The second relates to *sorting*: schools should funnel students into an appropriate pathway based on perceived ability, and maintain quality by funneling 'unmotivated' (or in this case hard-to-serve) students into other options, like GED or workforce development.

Politically progressive scholars have vehemently critiqued the credentialing and socialization visions of schooling as highly conservative, aiming to mold youth to best serve the interests of society, recreate the social structure based on income and race, and preserve the status quo by 'sorting' students: smart from dumb, academic from vocational, achievers from underachievers, college-bound from prison-bound (Alexander, 2010; Fine, 1991; Noguera, 2003; Orfield *et al.*, 2004). Some educational reformers have called for more democratic visions of schooling, in which young people are trained to be critical thinkers, engaged in their communities, activists and problem solvers working toward a more equitable society (Fine, 1991; Noguera, 2003; Orfield *et al.*, 2004). Some have critiqued the idea of universal high school graduation, on the grounds that it weakens the quality of high schools (Toby & Armor, 1992). Let the underachievers leave, they say, because if they are not interested in school they ruin the experience for those who are. This view overlooks the stark differences in expectations and quality of schooling, which vary by location, racial group, social class and other factors. Ultimately, high school provides a credential that can lead to post-secondary education and the workforce for both US-born students and immigrants alike. There are some notable and extremely successful high school dropouts, such as journalist Peter Jennings, Kodak's founder George Eastman and film director Quentin Tarantino. Yet these individuals remain the exception, and few students in the first decades of the 21st century can expect professional success, fame or fortune with no high school credential. At this point in US history, it is viewed as the absolute minimum ticket to upward mobility and success in adulthood.

Again, the idea that all teens and adolescents should attend and complete high school is a relatively recent one in the US. Prior to the 1960s, the booming post-war economy produced rising wages and ample employment and, as a result, the large numbers of young people who left high school to enter the workforce were not seen as constituting a 'crisis'. Ironically, concerns about dropouts arose in the 1960s alongside a steady *increase* in high school attendance rates, an increase that was especially marked among African-Americans in the South, who earlier had had the lowest high school attendance. Rates of attendance and the gap between racial groups were narrowing, but high school completion was still far from universal across the country. The current fear of stagnant growth of the economy, alongside federal pressures for universal high achievement and 100% graduation rates, have led to the conclusion that the US has a crisis on its hands.

Whether or not the rates of high school completion and dropout, which have remained fairly stagnant over time for some groups and increased for others, indeed constitute a crisis is arguable (Tyler & Lofstrom, 2009). What cannot be denied is that an incomplete high school education has a momentous impact both on individuals and on society as a whole. For young people like Victor, Elena, Ramón and Altagracia, lack of a high school credential translates directly into lower earnings over the lifespan, as individuals with a high school credential tend to earn more that dropouts (Belfield & Levin, 2007; Tyler & Lofstrom, 2009). Lower wages mean fewer tax contributions to the federal coffers. The cost to society comes in other forms too, as lower levels of education are correlated with poorer health, higher levels of incarceration and crime, greater reliance on federal support programs – such as food stamps, Temporary Assistance to Needy Families (TANF) and Medicaid – and lower levels of educational attainment for children (Belfield & Levin, 2007). The 2006 American Community Survey reveals a notable education-based differential between median earnings of men of all races: those with incomplete high school earned $22,151, compared with $31,715 for men with a high school diploma or GED. Female high school early leavers had median earnings of $13,255 in 2006, whereas those with high school diplomas earned $20,650, those with some college $26,300 and those with a four-year college degree $36,875 (Webster & Bishaw, 2007). The median income men for men who had obtained an associate's degree or completed some college was $40,217, compared with a median income of $55,446 for men with a bachelor's degree (Webster & Bishaw, 2007). Table 2.1 provides an overview of the data.

These differences between earnings of high school dropouts and high school completers are noteworthy. The difference in median earnings between men with no high school diploma and those who have completed high school is 43.2%, and between female high school dropouts and high school completers is 55.8%. Over the lifetime of any one individual, this

Table 2.1 Earnings differential based on high school completion

	Incomplete high school	*High school diploma*	*% difference*
Men	$22,151	$31,715	43.2%
Women	$13,255	$20,650	55.8%

Source: Webster and Bishaw (2007)

reflects a staggering differential in personal income, tax contributions and family resources. Although immigrants in the US comprise individuals in both the highest- and lowest-earning cohorts, on average, Latinos with incomplete high school or a high school diploma alone earn less than all other subgroups in the US (Carnevale *et al.*, 2011).

To date in the US, universal high school completion has never reached 100%. A look at some historical data on high school enrollment and completion will reveal significant trends over time. First, though, it is useful to examine how the figures are calculated.

More Than Simple Math: Calculating Numbers of Dropouts

Simple math

Determining who attends and completes high school should be a relatively simple calculation. Students register and enroll in school, starting in ninth grade (generally at age 13 or 14). Of that pool of adolescents, whom statisticians refer to as the 'entering freshman cohort', some abandon school before finishing their high school diploma in grade 12. Logically speaking, it would make sense to calculate the dropout rate by taking the number of students who dropped out and dividing it by the number of students who entered high school as freshmen, as can be seen in the equation below:

$$\frac{Number\ of\ dropouts}{Number\ of\ students\ who\ started\ school} = Dropout\ rate$$

If, for example, at Central City High School, we have 500 entering freshman and 100 of them dropped out of school, we divide 100 by 500 to give a dropout rate of 20%. Similarly, if we take the number of students who graduate (400) and divide it by the number of students who entered as high school freshmen (500, the total number in that 'entering freshman cohort') we arrive at the equation below, which gives us the overall high school graduation rate:

$$\frac{Number\ of\ graduates}{Number\ in\ the\ freshman\ cohort} = Graduation\ rate$$

At Central City High, the resulting numbers would be 400 graduates divided by 500 entering freshman, and a graduation rate of 80%. This seems straightforward, and a calculation of this type should lead to unambiguous results. Not surprisingly, things are not as simple as they seem. A few factors complicate our equation, and a few perspectives on who is and who is not a dropout complicate the official rates even more. The first complication is created by the data we enter into this simple equation.

What numbers do statisticians and school administrators use to calculate dropouts and graduates? Federal agencies in the US compile an array of datasets that are used for different calculations related to educational achievement. Census data are collected every 10 years to provide an overview of the entire US population and, additionally, each month the US Bureau of Labor Statistics collaborates with the US Census Bureau to compile the Current Population Survey (CPS), which provides a snapshot of demographic and employment data across the country. In addition, the US Department of Education compiles an annual report on the demographics, attendance patterns and other factors of public school students in a large dataset called the Common Core of Data (CCD). CPS data are compiled at the regional level, not at the school district level. In contrast, CCD are yearly snapshots, but they provide a view solely of public school students and not of private or parochial school attendance (New York City's Independent Budget Office has data that count about 240,000 students in private schools and 1,100,000 in public schools), home-schooled children or young adults who may have completed a high school diploma but did not attend school within the US. The CCD data are used to calculate an 'average freshman graduation rate' as follows:

$$\frac{\textit{Number of students who obtain a high school diploma after four years}}{\textit{Number of entering freshman}} = \textit{Average freshman graduation rate}$$

In looking at the above equation it is important to remember that any adult (i.e. anyone aged over 18) who is counted in the US Census or monthly CPS as having 'completed high school' may have followed any one of several quite different paths: completion of a high school diploma in four years; completion of a high school diploma in five or six years; completion of high school at a private, parochial or non-US high school; or, finally, General Education Development diploma, commonly referred to simply as 'GED'. This final pathway of high school completion is the one that complicates calculations the most.

The GED or high school equivalency credential

The GED diploma is a credential that is available to anyone, whether US-born or foreign-born, who is able to pass the written test, which, as of 2013, was available in English, French and Spanish. In New York State, a new test was adopted in 2014 (TASC, Test Assessing Secondary Completion) to adhere more closely to the Common Core State Standards and to provide a credential that better reflects the goals of college and career readiness sought of high schools. To be eligible to take the test, a person must be aged over 17 and not already possess a US high school diploma, though it is possible to take the GED test after having completed high school abroad.

The GED and high school equivalency credential option was developed in the 1940s in the US, originally as a test of basic skills to screen for eligibility for the armed forces, but since then it has become a credential recognized by employers and post-secondary institutions. Some entry-level jobs require only a high school diploma or GED, and most colleges accept GED credentials as entry requirements. More than 18 million people in the US have completed a GED, with the numbers of test takers rising steadily over the years. In 2011 alone, nearly a million adults took the test. Every year in the US, some students leave school to pursue a GED diploma, and although the number of people attempting the test can be calculated easily from test registration records collected by the GED Testing Service, these data cannot reveal much about the pathways taken by GED aspirants. The GED data do not tell us when and if they were enrolled in school prior to the test (and not what school or program they were enrolled in), whether or not they left high school to pursue a GED, whether they attended, circumvented or dropped out of a GED program or, in the case of recent immigrants, what their level of school attainment was prior to taking the test (i.e. whether they had already complete a high school diploma in their country of origin) (Chapman *et al.*, 2011).

Because it is a valid US high school credential, the GED (and now the TASC in New York State) complicates our calculations of the dropout rate. For the purposes of dropout statistics, current calculations at the state and federal level have determined that any high school student who elects to leave high school and go in search of an alternative high school credential will not be counted in the calculation of dropouts. This subgroup of 'GED aspirants' is subtracted from the denominator of our equation, as below:

$$\frac{\textit{Number of students completing a high school diploma}}{\begin{array}{c}\textit{[Number of entering freshman} - \\ \textit{number of students who left school to obtain a GED]}\end{array}} = \textit{Dropout rate}$$

Returning to the example of Central City High School, let us imagine that of those 100 students who left school, 50 dropped out with the intention of pursuing an equivalency diploma or GED. Our equation then becomes:

$$\frac{\textit{400 graduates}}{\textit{[500 entering freshman} - \textit{50 GED seekers]}} = \textit{89\%}$$

Our graduation rate has risen from 80% to 89% using a simple change to the equation. Suddenly Central City's performance looks much better, without having produced any additional graduates! Conversely, it would seem to make sense that the graduation rate could be calculated by taking GED completers into account, as follows, changing our previously quite simple equation:

$$\frac{[Number\ of\ people\ who\ passed\ the\ GED\ test\ +\ Number\ of\ high\ school\ graduates]}{Number\ of\ students\ in\ freshmen\ cohort} = Graduation\ rate$$

However, the above does not make for a viable calculation, as it may include immigrants who have a high school diploma from their country of origin but have pursued a GED because it is a US credential, as well as immigrants with incomplete high school who have never attended US schools but elected to pursue a GED. As we know already from a description of how data on GED test takers are collected, we are not able to trace any GED test taker back to the freshman cohort from which the student may have come, making it impossible to align GEDs with high school leavers. In the case of Central City High School, we cannot determine which of those 50 students who left to take the GED test actually took the test and, if they did take the test, whether or not they passed. Who seeks to get a GED, who actually takes the test, who passes and where they were prior to the test are untraceable in existing data. There may also be high school students who dropped out one year and later had a change of heart and elected to get a GED. Considering these different profiles of GED takers, including them all in the numerator risks double counting. Clearly, the question of the GED complicates our calculation of the graduation rate.

Other math: National metrics

In an effort both to simplify and to differentiate, the National Center for Education Statistics (NCES) has compiled statistics on three important metrics: the *event dropout rate*, the *status dropout rate* and the *status completion rate*. The event dropout rate shows from one year to the next how many students leave high school without receiving a diploma. Students who leave high school to pursue a GED are not included as dropouts in this calculation. So, for example, if I leave school at age 16 and tell my counselor that I am going to get a GED instead of a high school diploma, I am not counted as a dropout, even though (1) I may never take the high school equivalency test; (2) I may take and fail the high school equivalency test; and (3) there is no mechanism in place to follow up on my educational trajectory after I have left high school. Schools in New York State are newly accountable for tracking down students who left school to attempt to pass the GED test. The seemingly straightforward calculation of the event dropout rate is limited by its simplicity. Because it shows us only how many students left public school within any given year – and not how many left and came back, how many went off to pursue a GED, why they left or what may have happened to them – it is a fairly static number. In New York State, schools that cannot confirm with certainty that students passed the GED must count those students in their dropout rates. Confirmed GEDs add no value for accountability purposes in New York State. For the purposes of understanding immigrant dropouts and their educational histories and trajectories, the dropout rate remains a vague metric that does not provide sufficient detail to tell much of a story, other than that a certain proportion of people do not have a diploma.

NCES's *status completion rate* and the *status dropout rate* both refer to the total pool of young adults in the US aged 18–24. Status completion is the number of young adults in this age group who hold a high school credential, which can include a public, private, parochial school diploma, a GED or, in the case of immigrants, a high school diploma from another country. In that sense, GED holders may have dropped out of high school but if they pass the GED test, they are counted as high school graduates and are thus added to the status completion rate. The status completion rate can tell us effectively how many immigrant adults aged 18–24 completed high school, but it cannot tell us whether or not they completed high school specifically in the US, whether they have a GED, nor whether they were passed along from grade to grade and barely graduated or were valedictorian. Status dropouts are young people aged 18–24 who do not have a high school credential of any kind or a GED diploma. This number, along with Census data on the number of immigrants aged 18–24 in the US, can reveal a bit more about the scale of the population of immigrant young adults who are officially dropouts. Overall, though, high school completion simply means completing high school – regardless of how requirements may differ from state to state – and receiving a diploma. To summarize, individuals who have completed a GED are not included in status dropout counts but are included in status completion rates.

Critics have much to say about the calculation of dropout and graduation rates. Scholars have argued that including GED diploma holders in the calculation of total numbers of high school graduates overshadows marked differences between subgroups, while others claim that overall high school completion rates should not include foreign-born school interrupters whose education was terminated before coming to the US (Oropesa & Landale, 2009; Perreira *et al.*, 2006). Some have argued that high school graduation rates should be calculated solely using the numbers of youth who have attended and completed high school in the US and that GED holders should not be included in this equation. Figure 2.1 illustrates differences in high

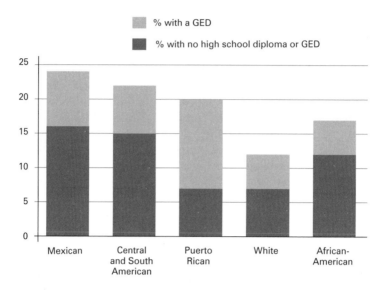

Figure 2.1 Percentage of 18- to 26-year-olds with incomplete high school education
Source: Perreira *et al.* (2006)

school completion rates of different racial and ethnic subgroups, broken down by school leavers with and without a GED.

More complicated calculations: Discharge

Another complication to our simple dropout calculation is what is referred to as 'discharge' in schools. Discharge rates are complex, and include students who have left school for a variety of reasons: returned to their country of origin; moved out of the school district; left public school to attend a private or parochial school; were referred by counselors or administrators to a 'second chance' educational program such as GED preparation or job training; died; or lost interest and decided to drop out. Typically, school districts do not collect detailed information on discharged students, nor do they seek to verify students' reasons for being discharged and, perhaps most importantly, there are really no administrative mechanisms in place to determine what happens to discharged students. The paperwork burden of high school is very high and this may lead to artificially elevated dropout rates where it is deemed to be worth simply recording 'dropped out' rather than detailing a discharge.

In New York State, an increase in discharges over the decade 2000–10 parallels both the increased enrollment of high school age youth in adult education and GED programs, as well as an increase in the graduation rate (US Department of Education, 2010a). Across the US, it has become a documented practice to encourage students older than average for their grade, or those with few credits toward graduation, to abandon high school and instead pursue a GED (Gotbaum & Advocates for Children, 2002; Jennings & Haimson, 2009; Orfield *et al.*, 2004). The discharge process is something that school administrators are not eager to talk about publicly, as it often entails some creative bookkeeping – making students disappear from a school's attendance records when they have stopped attending or accumulating credits. Over the years I have encountered more than a few school employees who were 'encouraged' by higher-ups to suggest to students – or urge, pressure or beg – that they leave school, as their presence without graduating threatened the school's graduation rate.

Some researchers suggest that the current means of calculating of national, state and local dropout statistics are influenced by federal pressures on schools to increase graduation rates, and that the statistics on dropouts reported by the NCES are in fact far lower than the actual dropout rates in high school across the US (Fine, 1991; Noguera, 2003; Orfield *et al.*, 2004).

Regarding our increasingly more complex dropout calculation, discharges make a great deal of difference. Although we cannot really be sure if discharged students end up ever completing high school, the students who are coded in school enrollment records as discharged are subtracted from the entering freshman cohort (the denominator of our equation) and, as a result, graduation rates rise. The equation looks like this:

$$\frac{Number\ of\ high\ school\ graduates}{[Number\ of\ entering\ freshman\ -\ number\ of\ discharged\ students]} = Graduation\ rate$$

Returning to Central City High School, suppose, of the 100 students who left, we know that 50 went in pursuit of the GED, as indicated previously, and we are not sure about the remaining 50. If we indicate that this additional 50 have also been discharged for a variety of the reasons we listed, then we have the following calculation:

$$\frac{400\ graduates}{[500\ entering\ freshman\ -\ 100\ discharges]} = 100\%\ graduation\ rate$$

We now have no dropouts and 100% graduation! Of course, as discussed previously, the US average for high school graduation has increased since the 1960s but has never reached 100%. What our simple calculation reveals is what a significant difference it makes how students are tagged and coded in the data. If we were to recalculate our equation by retaining both the

GED seekers as well as the discharged students in the denominator of our equation – perhaps we assume that most fail to move on and complete high school – our graduation rate would drop back to 80%! With pressure to increase the performance of schools, it is in the best interests of administrators and school record keepers to identify students as discharged or send them off to take the GED rather than risk their dropping out. Critics of the discharge rate have tracked trends over time in large cities like New York, and have determined that discharge rates have gone up or stayed the same while graduation rates have risen (Jennings & Haimson, 2009). From the equations shown, it is clear how this might have happened. Once we begin to move students from the category of *dropout* to the category of *discharged* or GED seeker, our denominator shrinks and our graduation rate rises. Growing concern about the impact of school accountability pressures on low-income, new immigrant, minority and underperforming students raises questions about the processes used to discharge students; critics say there is 'a loosely regulated loophole that can be used to inflate graduation rates by pushing at-risk students out of school' (Jennings & Haimson, 2009: 2).

Ultimately, the accuracy of graduation rates and dropout rates comes down to reporting. Reporting comes down to individuals. The administrative burden to track down students who have stopped attending school is great and staff are often challenged to document precisely what happened to students. Differences in dropout rates studied vary by as much as 50 percentage points (Hammack, 1986; Jennings & Haimson, 2009) and stem from the ways in which schools determine how a student who is no longer attending is to be defined. In New York City, some of the large comprehensive high schools discharged anywhere from a quarter to a half all entering students. An analysis of public data from 2001 for New York City revealed that of about 250 high schools, a total of 31 reported more students as discharged than as graduates, and 48 additional schools had discharge rates that were more than 50% of their graduation rates (Gotbaum & Advocates for Children, 2002). As seen above, recalculation of high school graduation rates to take discharges into account leads to much lower graduation rates for all racial and ethnic subgroups (Jennings & Haimson, 2009). Any discrepancy – or questionable ethics – in how student data are coded can have a significant impact on the dropout and graduation rate (Hammack, 1986).

Data on New York City schools indicate that nearly one-third of English language learners (29%) and slightly more than one-fifth of native English speakers (22%) were discharged soon after entering the ninth grade (Jennings & Haimson, 2009). This is not to say that we should discount all calculations related to dropout rates and graduation metrics. The discussion of the complexities of dropout rate calculations underscores how difficult some groups of non-traditional students are to track. In the US, the data collection mechanisms focus on the majority of students at this point – those who are enrolled in traditional high schools and complete within four years. We cannot ignore statistics on dropout and graduation rates, as these large-scale datasets provide a snapshot of trends in the population. A deeper understanding of the complexities of both the data collection and the calculations of these rates can provide a much more nuanced understanding of issues implicit in any policy discussion of high school completion as well as conventional understandings of the ostensible dropout crisis. Such information underpins an understanding of how these numbers have changed over time and helps us to delve into what we know about school attendance and completion on the part of specific subgroups. This leads us to a discussion of national and local trends.

Dropout and Graduation Trends Over Time

In the US, the percentage of status dropouts has decreased over the years within all population subgroups. Despite increases in high school attendance and completion over time, Latinos aged 16–24 have consistency lagged Blacks and Whites in high school graduation rates, meaning that their rates of dropout were much higher. Trends over the period 1972–2009 are shown in Figure 2.2.

Status dropout rates among Whites and Blacks decreased significantly in the years between 1972 and 2009; the rate for Whites fell from 12.3% to 5.2%, and the rate for Blacks declined from 21.3% to 9.3%. In this same period, Latino status dropout rates showed some peaks and valleys, but they have been decreasing since 2009, falling from 32.4% to 17.6% (Chapman *et al.*, 2011). Notable, however, is that Latinos have led other subgroups in

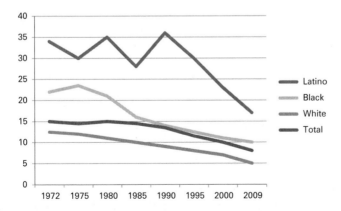

Figure 2.2 US status dropout rates of 16- to 24-year-olds, by racial background
Source: Chapman *et al.* (2011)

dropouts consistently since 1972, when these data were first collected on a large scale. Within that subgroup of Latino dropouts, immigrants have the highest status dropout rates and, at nearly 34%, significantly higher status dropout rates than their US-born peers. In 2009, some 63.0% of foreign-born Latinos aged 18–24 who were not currently enrolled in high school had completed a diploma. Compared with foreign-born Latinos, status completion rates were higher for Latinos born in the US (83.7% for 'first generation' and 86.7% for 'second generation or higher'). Among the immigrant cohort, Latino immigrants accounted for 22.6% of all dropouts, while non-Hispanic immigrants accounted for only 4.0% (Chapman *et al.*, 2011).

Graduates and Dropouts in New York State

A great deal of attention is paid to graduation rates as a measure of school effectiveness across the US. We must be mindful, however, that the decentralized nature of US public schools means that 'high school diploma' can mean something quite different in each of the 50 states. Standards for graduation vary markedly from state to state, and may include different types of diplomas (vocational versus academic versus special needs). High school graduation requirements may also differ between districts, schools and programs within a state.

In an effort to respond to the criticism of dropout rate calculations and mismanagement of reporting systems, New York State has developed its own particular definition of dropout, which begins with failure to re-enroll. If students do not appear on the school's attendance roster from one year to the next, a school is instructed to mark them as dropouts unless the school can document that the student has graduated, transferred to another school or GED program, left the country or died.

Up until the end of the 20th century, New York State had offered an array of high school diplomas that varied in academic rigor. The 'local diploma', which began to be phased out starting in 1996, differed from the academic 'Regents diploma', the latter being a more rigorous qualification that required students to pass a series of exit exams. Currently, in addition to the Regents diploma there is an 'advanced Regents diploma', which students can obtain if they demonstrate a higher level of academic proficiency. New statewide diploma guidelines have phased out the 'local diploma' and now nearly all graduating public high school students must pass a series of academic exams (in a minimum of five subject areas) to obtain a public high school diploma from New York State. This includes students who were born in the US and entered in kindergarten as well as immigrant students who may have started high school in the US knowing little English.[2] When looking across the US, however, at high school graduation rates, the type of diploma matters little and the only significant metric is high school completion.

How does New York State fare in high school completion rates? According to a 2011 report by the New York State Board of Regents, the average four-year graduation rate in New York is 73.4%, meaning that slightly more than a quarter of students who entered high school in 2006 did not graduate within four years (New York State Education Department, 2013b). This rate represents an increase in the graduation rate over the years; only 66% of the cohort of students who entered in 2001 graduated in four years. As said, this rate is calculated by dividing the number of graduates by the total number of entering ninth graders. Graduation rates for New York City included local diplomas, Regents diplomas, IEP (special education) diplomas and the GED. For New York City's entering 2006 class of ninth graders, 61% graduated in four years (up from 59% for the 2005 cohort) (New York State Education Department, 2013b). This rate increases to 69% after six years, as students can stay in school until they are 21 if they wish. Among English language learners who entered in 2006 as ninth graders, 40% graduated after four years, but adding two additional years made a significant difference for this subgroup. Interestingly, although six-year graduation rates are higher for significant subgroups, they are rarely reported in discussions about graduation rates and schools receive only 'partial credit' for graduating students after more than four years. Figure 2.3 reveals differences in graduation rates at four, five and six years for New York City.

Disaggregating the statistics presented above by race and ethnicity presents a very different picture. There is a nearly 30% point gap between White, Black and Hispanic students when it comes to graduation rate, although according to the New York State Board of Regents, this gap is narrowing, but still unacceptable. A total of 57.3% of Hispanic students in New York City graduated in four years, of those entering ninth grade in 2006. Students graduating in five and six years in New York City are predominantly Black and Latino (New York State Education Department, 2013b).

In 2001, New York City collected data indicating that approximately 55,000 students were discharged from New York City public schools, 14,500 dropped out officially and 33,500 graduated from the same group of schools (Gotbaum & Advocates for Children, 2002). No disaggregated numbers are available on students who qualify as 'discharged' but, given national dropout statistics, it can be assumed that the majority are Latino, language minority and from low-income backgrounds (Lopez, 2009). In New York City on average, immigrant students graduated at a slightly higher rate than US-born students, but a breakdown by immigrant subgroup revealed that country of origin is a deciding factor in graduation rates. Black and Latino students in New York City were nearly twice as likely to drop out or to be discharged from school as their Asian peers. Of the class of 2009, 18.9% were discharged, about 25% to attend private or parochial schools (New York State Education Department, 2013b). For the remainder, a total of nearly

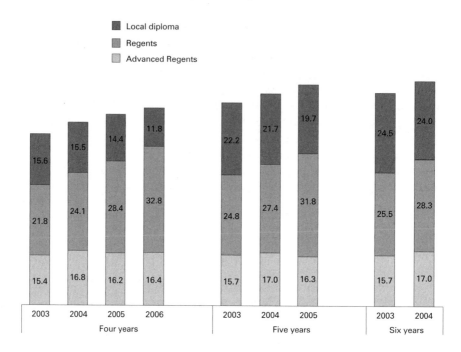

Figure 2.3 Percentage of New York City freshman cohort receiving three diploma types, 2003–06
Source: New York State Education Department (2013b)

14% of the class of 2009, we do not have enough information to form a clear picture of their educational paths before or after discharge from high school. Ultimately, lack of data on certain young adults is the greatest challenge to identifying them, making it very easy to overlook their experiences.

Age at arrival and country of origin of immigrant youth appear to be two of the most significant factors that contribute to the risk of not completing high school. This will be discussed in more depth in the next chapter. A comparison between school non-completion rates of US-born and foreign-born youth is presented in Figure 2.4, based on data from the 2000 US Census:

New York City public schools have placed emphasis in the past decade on students with gaps in formal schooling. Although 16,000 students entering ninth grade in 2009 had been identified as 'students with interrupted formal education' (SIFE), amounting to nearly half the total, procedures to identify and keep track of these students in New York City are new and applied inconsistently, making tracking their progress within the system a challenge. Among immigrant students formally classified as SIFE, Latinos made up the vast majority (New York City Department of Education, 2009).

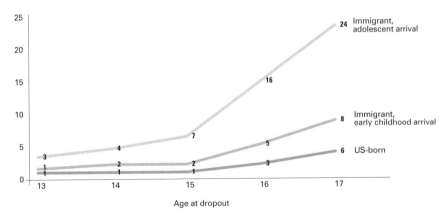

Figure 2.4 Percentage dropout rate, by age at arrival
Source: Fry (2005)

In the Dominican Republic, education is compulsory for primary school and several years of secondary school but, as in Mexico, there are contrasts in attendance between urban areas and rural zones where distances to school are large (UNICEF, 2010). Due to grade retention and economic demands that send children into the workforce, 44% of Dominican elementary school students and 60% of secondary students are older than average for their grade (UNICEF, 2010). The practice of placing teenage immigrants aged over 16 into the ninth grade when they arrive in New York City schools is logical, but has dire consequences, as students' prior education, knowledge and skills are not in line with grade-level requirements.

The Double-Edged Sword of Educational Accountability

'Accountability' has become a key word throughout education. Of all the terms and overarching concepts that have dominated educational discourse in the past 40 years, accountability is near the top of the list.

In the US, the 1990s were marked by a national focus on improving the achievement of all students, with the Improving America's Schools Act 1994 and Goals 2000 setting forth overarching national goals for all students. In their wake, the No Child Left Behind Act (NCLB) of 2001 (US Department of Education, 2002) presented a complex accountability system and a set of quantifiable achievement targets for every student subgroup in every state, to increase yearly (ostensibly until 100% of students would demonstrate proficiency in English and math in every grade). Original proponents of the law, which was an unfunded mandate, applauded its emphasis on providing a more nuanced picture of the achievement of subpopulations, something new in the world of school reporting and considered by many activists for low-income and minority students to be long overdue.

What did the accountability metrics look like in practical terms? Rather than report average performance of all students collectively within a school, each school was for the first time required to disaggregate student data and report achievement based on racial subgroups (White, African-American, Asian and Pacific Islander, Hispanic), Title I (low-income students), English language learners (ELLs) and special education students. Previously, high-performing districts and schools were able to mask poor achievement of certain subgroups by providing averages across all groups. For example, if 90% of students at one school were White and from middle-income families, and their average achievement was high, but 10% of the students at that same school were recently arrived English language learners from low-income backgrounds for whom achievement lagged behind that of the first group, the poor achievement would tend to 'disappear in the average'. Looking at such school-wide averages alone does not provide detail on the complexities of the performance of each subgroup. NCLB required schools to report on each subpopulation and strive to reach targets of 'annual yearly progress' (AYP) for each. Many advocates for minority groups, low-income students, and special populations like ELLs and special education students initially viewed the law as a long-awaited opportunity to illuminate poor achievement of certain groups of students and improve it. It would be a chance to shed light on a long-standing problem and ensure that schools served all students well. Not surprisingly, things did not turn out quite as expected.

Accountability had unintended consequences. Stringent accountability systems that punished schools for not meeting (at times unrealistic) targets for hard-to-serve populations ended up creating the kinds of *institutional constraints* that translate directly into barriers for older youth who are ELLs and who seek to enter high schools. If a school is punished for the less than stellar academic performance of a student like Ramón and not rewarded because he may require additional resources, what incentives exist to admit him? Just as in the case of so many students presented in this volume, if schools perceive them as being a risk for overall achievement targets, why admit them?

Federal and state policies, such as those requiring the four-year graduation rate calculations that are used to measure 'school success' in the US, tend to create disincentives for serving certain subpopulations of students, most notably ELLs and students older than average for their grade, as well as students who may enter school with significant academic gaps, such as some Generation 1.5 students classified as 'long-term ELLs' (Harklau, 2003; Thonus, 2003). The US has failed systemically and nearly without exception to create incentives for schools to serve students of high school age who have gaps in literacy, English proficiency and academic skills. The very system that was created to hold schools accountable for ensuring high achievement of all students has perpetuated a dogged deficit-oriented view of certain students. With so much riding on individual students' achievement, schools take an enormous risk by enrolling those who have enormous potential but face challenges academically. By being compelled by accountability pressures to view such students as 'risks' to school-wide achievement, administrators are often blind to their resilience, strengths and potential. When I see before me an over-age student who may not graduate in four years, I may not recognize the motivation that enables him to travel thousands of miles, often alone, work full time, support family and still try to get a high school diploma.

This is not to shift blame away from staff who bend and break the rules, discharging students *en masse*, lying to students and telling them they are too old or don't have the necessary papers to enroll, testing students and then punting them to another school or into a high school equivalency program rather than granting them a seat. With accountability pressures that subtly – but explicitly – encourage schools to 'cream' the best students off the top to show progress, students who might take longer to graduate or require more resources than others may be perceived as a risk or an investment that pays limited dividends. To frame students as dropouts means they are basically the throwaway students – if they are destined to drop out, why even bother? Let someone else deal with them.

Accountability is a double-edged sword, providing an opportunity to collect potentially valuable data but with inherent weaknesses. This is not to argue against accountability. Educators and advocates who were hopeful at the potential of NCLB were reacting to the long-term neglect of specific services for certain groups. It may be easy to point fingers at schools or administrators who skirt, bend or break the rules in the hope of ensuring the survival of their schools. Members of staff at the school level are merely implementing policies, but at the same time are clearly making personal choices that shut out or undermine particular students. In the course of my research, I spoke with many principals, registration staff, guidance counselors and teachers who refused to be quoted lest they incur the wrath of their superiors. I heard many accounts of high schools receiving students that another school had tested and rejected as too difficult to serve; staff being pressured to 'disappear' students who were older than average and with few accumulated credits; principals pressuring staff to refuse a seat, a test or a referral to students like Victor, Elena, Ramón, Altagracia and others.

Locating School Leavers: The Invisibility Factor

Having explored the challenges inherent in dropout rate calculations and the additional complications added to the equation by discharged students, we are faced with the task of identifying immigrant students with incomplete schooling. At this point in our discussion, let us shift our perspective slightly and think in terms of *school leavers* rather than *dropouts*. Why this change in terminology? Because dropout is such a laden term, here we will focus on students who have interrupted their schooling before completing high school: who are they and where can we find them? In Chapters 3 and 4, we will learn a bit more about the students in question and examine their reasons for leaving school.

Our first difficulty is tracking the students who leave school. In New York City, students who complete ninth grade without having accumulated any credits toward graduation appear to be at greatest risk for interrupting their schooling (Meade *et al.*, 2009). Data from the New York City public school graduation cohort reveal that some students, especially immigrant ELLs, simply disappear from enrollment rosters sometime between ninth and eleventh grade, leaving no clue as to their whereabouts. Existing data do not enable us to keep track of those who left school before graduating. This means that the large datasets that allow for powerful statistical calculations don't do us much good when we want to determine what caused students to leave school. We must look for those students in person, one by one.

Our second difficulty stems from the diversity among the Latino population enrolled in public schools. Students who enter the school system designated as 'limited English proficient' are by no means a homogeneous group. These ELLs – students whose level of academic English proficiency means that they need services in English as a second language – reflect the diversity among immigrants in New York City: they are among the wealthiest students, but also among the poorest students, the least educated and the most educated. Some come from middle- and upper-class families with highly educated parents and have attended rigorous schools before coming to the US, while some come from poor families with parents who have limited formal education and very limited knowledge of the English language and the US school system. All of these factors impact students' needs. Yet when ELLs enter the school system, no data are collected on their backgrounds that would allow us to understand this diversity. The same limitations hold true for Census data: we cannot tease out who came to the US with few years of education and who with many, whose parents were highly educated and whose were not, nor can we investigate the socioeconomic status of a student that would help us to understand his or her background better. In a sense, data forces us to look at Latino students as one big homogenous lump, even though we know from research that the differences between and among groups have a significant impact on their academic outcomes.

Our third difficulty results from divergent paths: not all immigrants who enter the US at high school age end up enrolling in high school, for a variety of reasons that we will explore in Chapters 4 and 5. Often, those immigrants who arrive in the US as young adults with incomplete schooling live their lives outside of the structures of formal institutions. As a result, they leave few footprints. Data collected by educational programs often omit information such as years of prior education or age at arrival, making a random sample impossible in this case. Although large-scale administrative datasets exist, they do not include the entire population of immigrant school leavers who reside in the US, simply because some exist on the margins of society. Some immigrant young adults are undocumented. Others have steady employment but exclusively in the cash economy and are thus not part of any Department of Labor statistics. A reliance solely on the large-scale administrative datasets discussed earlier in this chapter means that a portion of the population goes uncounted. Existing large datasets like High School and Beyond and the American Council on Education's GED testing data do not capture information on age at entry into the country. Thus administrative data on immigrant youth who arrive in the US in their mid-teens are difficult to use to investigate the educational pathways of this population.

The invisibility of this group in research is largely a result of two key challenges: lack of systematic data and access. The lives of teens and young adults who arrive in the US with incomplete schooling – many of them undocumented – unfold primarily outside of mainstream institutions and many cannot be tracked statistically.[3] Those who seek services at schools or social service agencies enter through a myriad of doors, but these agencies generally do not gather demographic data with sufficient detail on pre-migration educational attainment, reasons for leaving school or circumstances of migration, rendering this group of school leavers virtually invisible. Despite their different reasons for leaving school, they have generally been lumped together in research and policy literature simply as *dropouts*. Neither *shutouts* – students eligible to enroll in high school but barred from entering – nor *holdouts* – labor migrants who return to school via adult education after years in low-wage jobs – have been discussed in research. With few educational options and limited knowledge of the US school system, a significant number find their way into adult education. People in this age group (16–24) make up more than one-third of participants in federally funded adult education – 36%, of nearly 2.5 million adult education students served annually – a total of more than 900,000 young adults across the US (World Education, 2010).[4] Their engagement in adult education programs reveals aspirations to continue their education.

As a result, their total numbers must be estimated, from sources such as the Current Population Surveys (CPS), New York City Department of Education high school cohort and discharge data, and adult education enrollment data from New York State (US Department of Education, 2010a). Because data on immigrant youth who arrive in the US in their teens are not disaggregated in enrollment and achievement data from K-12 and adult education, their pathways are neither documented nor scrutinized by research, and thus policy analyses about high school completion and post-secondary access ignore them.

Their economic realities and financial obligations to family (Fuligni, 2007) drive them into the labor force, yet they are neither simply 'labor migrants' nor 'dropouts' who have rejected schooling. Without high school diplomas, they are not part of the K-12 to college pipeline. When they pursue education, it is in options that have been labeled 'second chance' mechanisms, often designed for adults. Their presence in these alternative educational settings bespeaks aspirations that have still to be examined, yet research has not explored what they say they want for their futures and how they expect to reach their goals.

Summary

Key in our analysis of dropouts and their trajectories is the issue of definitions introduced at the start of this chapter. Conventional wisdom would lead us to conclude that 'dropouts' are students who merely lost interest and did not complete high school. Once students are tagged and coded as 'dropouts', the conceptual frame and associated assumptions about abandoning school appear to force a certain type of analysis – 'school failure' – rather than a reframing that questions whether or not these young adults have made a conscious decision to leave school. In the current educational landscape, where rising standards put incredible pressure on schools to demonstrate quantifiable progress in very strict terms, there is little incentive to serve these students or to support the teachers and schools who choose to attempt to meet their needs. This understanding is rooted in the American mythos of individualism in which everyone has an equal chance at success, but extensive exploration of the social order and examination of differential opportunities and contexts has shown that is not the reality. Nonetheless, an analysis of the myriad ways that dropout and graduation rates are calculated, as well as discrepancies in the data about who is included and who disappears from the calculations, reveals the complexity involved in the simple term 'dropout'. Added to that complexity is the difficulty of identifying and locating Latino immigrant students who have interrupted their schooling and who are high school dropouts according to definitions used by the US Census.

It would be tempting to say that Latino immigrant school leavers are 'invisible', yet that is not entirely the case. As workers in the low-wage sector of the economy, they are certainly ubiquitous. Discussions in this chapter have highlighted the size of this group, leading us to conclude that they are overlooked, not invisible. Formal mechanisms for 'seeing', identifying and following the lives of young people like Victor, Elena, Ramón and Altagracia are not designed to make sense of the complexities of their lives, thus leaving large gaps in what we know about them. The overarching assumption – unchallenged in countless research studies – is that immigrant young adults who are primarily working and not attending high school do not value what education has to offer and have no interest in it. This fallacy is undeniably simplistic and founded on the belief that non-participation is a 'choice'. The concept of *dropout* implies that the choice to leave school is an individual one that involves weighing all the options. Now that we have explored the history and the mathematics of dropouts, the next chapter will provide some background on the pre-migration experiences of the type of young adults we met in Chapter 1 to help us understand how and why they came to abandon school in the first place.

Additional resources

American Community Survey, at https://www.census.gov/acs/www.

Common Core of Data, at http://nces.ed.gov/ccd. The Common Core of Data (CCD) is a program of the US Department of Education's National Center for Education Statistics that annually collects fiscal and non-fiscal data about all public schools, public school districts and state education agencies in the US.

Current Population Survey, at http://www.census.gov/cps. The Current Population Survey (CPS), sponsored jointly by the US Census Bureau and the US Bureau of Labor Statistics (BLS), is the primary source of labor force statistics for the population of the US. The CPS is the source of numerous high-profile economic statistics, including the national unemployment rate, and provides data on a wide range of issues relating to employment and earnings. The CPS also collects extensive demographic data that complement and enhance our understanding of labor market conditions in the nation overall, among many different population groups, in the states and in substate areas.

Latino Data Project, Center for Latin American, Caribbean and Latino Studies Graduate Center, City University of New York, at http://clacls.gc.cuny.edu/courses.

Public Advocate for the City of New York, Betsy Gotbaum and Advocates for Children, *Pushing Out At-Risk Students: An Analysis of High School Discharge Figures*, at http://www.advocatesforchildren.org/sites/default/files/library/pushing_out_2002.pdf?pt=1.

To learn more about New York State graduation requirements, visit http://www.p12.nysed.gov/ciai/gradreq/intro.html and http://www.p12.nysed.gov/part100/pages/1005.html

Notes

(1) In many states, including New York, the GED is being phased out, and there is a shift toward different tests to demonstrate high school completion and college readiness. The GED is therefore becoming just one example of a high school equivalency diploma. In the present volume, though, the discussion generally refers to the GED, for the sake of convenience.

(2) There is an exception for students who attend public schools that have received a state waiver to administer portfolio and performance-based assessments.

(3) The number of immigrants who arrive in the US between the ages of 15 and 24 is not disaggregated in K-12 and adult education enrollment and achievement data. As

a result, their total numbers must be estimated, from sources such as the Current Population Surveys (CPS), New York City Department of Education high school cohort and discharge data, and adult education enrollment data from New York State (US Department of Education, 2010a).

(4) This number is likely an underestimate, as only those adult education programs receiving public funding are counted in federal data on adult education participation and outcomes. Nationally, programs include non-profit, for-profit, volunteer-run, church-based and publicly funded programs in English as a second language, literacy classes in Spanish and high school equivalency (GED) classes in Spanish or English, many of them run without public funds. National and state statistics on for-profit, private and volunteer-led programs are not available.

3 Pre-Migration Educational 'Choices': Interrupted Education in Context

Introduction

Were one to look merely at the statistics on dropouts, all of the young people we meet in this book would look more or less the same, as not one has completed high school. Yet Ramón and Altagracia's experiences alone could not be more different. Ramón left Mexico by himself as a young teen, with no papers, initially to work in the back room of a Brooklyn deli, a job that 'was already waiting', he told me, arranged by friends of friends in New York City. Altagracia, who said 'Lloré al llegar acá' ('I cried when they told me I had to come' to the US), was on the brink of finishing high school in the Dominican Republic when she had to leave for New York City, as the visa her family members there had obtained for her would expire after she reached 18 years of age. When Ramón told her how much he misses his family, she asked him why he doesn't go and visit after five years and he was stunned by her question. A temporary visit home is a huge risk that necessitates coming back cross the US–Mexico border undetected. Ramón is an undocumented immigrant working full time and living with friends, while Altagracia is a legal permanent resident living with family. The Dominican and Mexican communities in which they live are both growing rapidly and include individuals with a wide range of educational and social class backgrounds, differences that are exacerbated by immigration status. Other than the fact that they are immigrants with interrupted schooling, what do we know of Ramón and Altagracia's lives before they entered our field of vision?

Though we may be tempted to reduce the lives of the foreign-born to their circumstances after coming to the US, it is informative to take a step back and examine the ways in which who and what they *were before* have led to who and what they *are now*. Prior to migrating, they were family members, workers, students and community members. Where do they come from? What do we know about their experiences before coming to the US? What led them to abandon school? What happened to Ramón, Altagracia, Victor and Elena and others like them *prior to* coming to the US? What were their school experiences? What factors contributed to their abandoning school? Why did they migrate north? What differentiates them from other immigrants?

This chapter explores the circumstances in the Latin American countries of origin of immigrant school leavers, examining factors that impact their incomplete education as well as the historical and sociopolitical forces that led to their migration. Against a sociohistorical backdrop, this chapter weaves connections among four types of evidence and information. The first is a description of the history of US–Latin American relations that sheds light on the broader sociopolitical context of migration northward. The second are statistical data and research based on large-scale empirical studies of large populations, such as global data from the World Bank and United Nations on literacy and education. The third includes statistical evidence from my own original research, based not on a representative segment of the entire population but rather on a purposeful sample of immigrant school leavers in New York City who made their way back into school through adult education. Finally, qualitative data gathered through interviews and focus groups are presented as personal stories of migration.

Without question, large statistical datasets provide powerful evidence across a representative segment of the population in ways that case studies from a small sample such as mine cannot. Due to limitations of such large datasets, it is not possible to create a representative sample of this population with incomplete schooling, as discussed in detail in Chapters 1 and 2. Nonetheless, it is notable what questions emerge by examining data on this small group. My research explores a facet of the immigrant population and, though significant, the resulting data are not meant to be generalized the way large statistically powerful samples are. Finally, individual cases of Latino immigrant dropouts are presented in this chapter, not to 'prove' any theories about education, but to illustrate, exemplify and provide some contours for the reader regarding the characteristics of young immigrants who are often overlooked. These data open the conversation about broader societal and institutional realities that impact immigrants in the US and migrants across the world.

The immigrant voices and experiences presented here can enhance and extend the power of existing data on high school dropouts. In this and the following chapters, immigrant dropouts share their stories and illuminate the circumstances that led them to abandon high school in their countries of origin and later to seek entry into a US educational pipeline. While the young adults in this book are unique, their experiences can reveal how their circumstances have been forged in a complex sociopolitical and economic context. In addition to exploring their personal stories, this chapter adopts a global perspective to examine some of the factors that impact not only school interruption but also the decision to relocate to the US. By exploring historical, economic and sociopolitical factors that impact migration flows and school participation, this chapter sheds light on broader forces that impact personal choices among immigrants. Ultimately, this chapter offers the opportunity to understand factors that impact immigration and school completion and invites the reader to challenge conventional wisdom that would have us believe that the process of leaving home, family and country is an isolated personal *choice*.

Manifest Destiny and US Expansion

Without a doubt, the history and destiny of the US and the countries of Latin America and the Caribbean are inextricably linked. Since the founding of the colonies and the time of the American Revolution, the US has been perpetually involved in the politics and the economy of Latin America, starting with acquisition of North American territories that were colonized by the Spanish. US expansion into the territories of Latin America has been framed by some authors as 'manifest destiny' and by others as colonialism (Gonzalez, 2000; Loewen, 1995; Takaki, 1993). Regardless of what we call it, this expansion considerably weakened economies and governments in Latin America. Weakening and overthrowing governments in Latin America and encroaching on territory (Mexico, Puerto Rico, Panama) helped to expand US power both politically and economically. Throughout the 20th and into the 21st century, 'Latin Americans were made into a steady source of cheap labor for U.S. multinational corporations' (Gonzalez, 2000: 28) and the 21st century has seen Latinos transformed into the 'majority minority' in the US, outnumbering African-Americans for the first time.

In his comprehensive historical account of Latin Americans in the US, Juan Gonzalez (2000) underscores that immigration of Latin Americans to the US has differed drastically from the waves of European immigrants, not primarily due to language or skin color. The central difference has been that Latin American immigration is the result of US expansionist policies in Latin America – both economic and political expansion and, more often, the combination of the two. This has included the US as a recipient of refugees that resulted from US foreign policy in Latin America (e.g. in Cuba, El Salvador, Guatemala and the Dominican Republic), as well as the recruitment of labor migrants to meet expanding US demands for inexpensive workers, Mexico being the prime example, but also Puerto Rico.

The popular debate swirling around immigration from Latin America in the second decade of the 21st century is often reduced to a monochromatic discussion of undocumented immigrants from Mexico. Yet Gonzalez (2000) makes it clear that geographic expansion of the US into Latin American territories and between north and south has a two-century history, starting in the 18th century. Examples of the US annexation of Puerto Rico, conquest of territories that formerly belonged to Mexico and expansion into Panama to build the canal all resulted in further linkages between the US and its neighbors to the south. The interchange of capital and labor is exemplified both in US corporate interests in Latin America and in programs that draw workers north, as well as in the North American Free Trade Agreement (NAFTA).

During the first decade of the 21st century, domestic battles focusing on immigration reform coincided with the largest number of Latin American immigrant entrants in US history. Nonetheless, the US had a higher percentage of immigrants relative to size population in the last decades of the 19th century and at the start of the 20th (Migration Policy Institute, n.d.). Rather than an 'us' and a 'them' that is often evoked in discussions of how to 'fix' the immigration 'problem' – the paradigm being that the flow of Latin American citizens northward is an anomaly to be halted – a thorough look at the historical connections between the US and Latin America reveals that the American continent is one, and the fates of those in the north and south are inextricably linked. Migration north is a policy outcome that results from relationships between the US and Latin America. In Gonzalez's view, 'one would not exist without the other' (Gonzalez, 2000: xviii).

Destiny and Choice in the Context of Migration

Migration has existed since the dawn of civilization. The modern phenomenon of border-crossing comprises both legal and illegal immigration. *Legal* immigration involves international work permits, temporary labor agreements, student or tourist visas, while *illegal* immigration refers to unauthorized entry into a country. With the existence of clearly delineated borders, national policies seek to govern entry. In the US, between 20% and 25% of undocumented immigrants enter from Asia, Europe and Africa combined, with the remainder largely coming from Latin America. Scholars insist that illegal immigration is the direct result of poverty and regional imbalances in the standard of living (St Bernard, 2003) as well as an unavoidable consequence of labor practices that rely upon subsistence-wage workers (Cornelius, 2001; Suárez-Orozco, 2000). In the US, illegal immigration has been the subject of furious debate and political standoffs for decades.

While the extent of illegal migration defies measurement and remains elusive, the persistence of poverty, relative deprivation and the quest for an enhanced quality of life will continue to sustain individual urges to migrate illegally. (St Bernard, 2003: 14)

Whether poverty is a result or a merely a symptom of massive migration, the resulting flows of capital and people go in both directions, north and south. Corporate investments from the US move south, while profits from US corporations move northward, out of their host communities. Laborers move north, while earnings from their work move south in the form of remittances (Somerville *et al.*, 2008). NAFTA, passed into law in 1994 during the Clinton administration, immediately eliminated existing tariffs on more than 50% of imports and exports between Mexico and the US and phased out remaining tariffs. CAFTA, the Central American Free Trade Agreement (in 2004 adapted into CAFTA-DR to include the Dominican Republic), has created a free trade agreement between North America and El Salvador, Honduras, Costa Rica, Nicaragua and the Dominican Republic. Critics say that NAFTA and CAFTA have undermined industry and small farmers and in the US led to depressed wages and the loss of more than half a million jobs (Aguilar, 2012; Scott, 2011). Economists analyzing NAFTA's impact on the Mexican economy also point to resulting adverse working conditions along the US–Mexico border and the loss of more than 1 million agricultural jobs that resulted from subsidized low-cost corn – one of Mexico's staples – flooding in from the north (Bacon, 2004; Scott, 2011).

The labor that flows northward from South America snakes its way on land through Central America and Mexico. Since NAFTA and CAFTA came into effect, the number of Mexican-born people in the US went from 4.5 million to 12.7 million and countries in Central America saw a significant exodus of their residents in large waves of out-migration (Bacon, 2004; Scott, 2011). Table 3.1 gives a breakdown of the numbers for net out-migration by year (not specifically to the US).

Let us return to the young people and learn more about the specifics of their migration experiences. What can we learn about the economic and political contexts in their home countries and how these influenced their out-migration?

Table 3.1 Average annual net out-migration, 1995–2000

Sending country	Number of leavers
Mexico	300,000
Guatemala	30,000
Nicaragua	12,000
El Salvador	8,000

Source: St Bernard (2003)

Migration from Latin America to the US: Some history

US-born residents often hear about immigrants from Latin America in news reports or encounter them in local communities as neighbors, workers and peers. While the immigration debate has focused primarily on immigration from Mexico, the US is home to a broad spectrum of Latinos. New York City is unlike many US cities in that Latino migration includes large numbers of Latin Americans from a variety of countries. For the purposes of my research, the number of young adults with whom I spoke is in direct proportion to their numbers in the New York City population, with Dominicans the most numerous (in fact second to Puerto Ricans, who are US citizens, but because of this fact were not included in my research), then Mexicans, Central Americans and South Americans. Table 3.2 shows the numbers of young people with whom I interacted; again, they were sought out purposefully, as dropouts who had made their way back into the educational system via adult and alternative education pathways.

Dominicans

A group that tends to be overlooked outside of the northeast, Dominicans are a large presence in New York City, being the largest group of immigrants from Latin America, second only to Puerto Ricans, who are US citizens. The national spotlight shone brightly on New York Dominicans in 2008 when Dominican-born Junot Díaz was awarded the Pulitzer Prize for Fiction for his novel *The Brief Wondrous Life of Oscar Wao*. The novel, written in complex Spanish-infused English, weaves the social and political history of the repressive years under the Trujillo dictatorship in the Dominican Republic with a coming-of-age story of a young Dominican boy in New Jersey. In lengthy footnotes, Díaz provides background on the political context that led to a massive flow of Dominicans to the US 'for those of you who missed your obligatory two seconds of Dominican history' (Díaz, 2008: 2). So, what do we need to know?

Dominicans became a presence in New York City only in the second half of the 20th century, beginning primarily after the assassination of the violent and repressive dictator Rafael Trujillo, 'El Chivo', on May 30,

Table 3.2 Country of origin of study participants

	Number	%
Dominican Republic	67	45
Mexico	51	34
Central America	13	9
Ecuador, Colombia, Peru	18	12
Total	149	100

1961. Subsequent promises to establish a democratic government were complicated by the US invasion of the island and the resulting repression of the US-backed Balaguer regime. By 2010 there were 2.2 million Dominican immigrants in the US, nearly half of them residing in New York City. Dominicans, many of them highly educated, came primarily as refugees to New York City and quickly gained a foothold in the economy. Nearly 50 years after the first wave began to come, New York City boasts prominent Dominican elected officials, numerous Dominican businesses and a significant number of Dominican immigrants and their children in positions of power in the city's business and politics.

Altagracia comes from a family with uncles and aunts in the US and a father who is a naturalized citizen. She reunited with him when she came to the US just months shy of her 18th birthday. She moved to upper Manhattan, the core of New York City's Dominican community, where her father had made a home for himself in the 15 years since he had left Santo Domingo. Reuniting with him was hard, she told me, and she was reluctant to leave her friends on the island. Yet she had no choice in coming, she told me, and had hoped to graduate high school, go to college and, in her words, *ser alguien* ('become somebody').

Yet not all Dominicans came as refugees, nor were all highly educated. The mass exodus based initially on political repression later continued as a result of poverty and weak domestic infrastructure. Dominicans with family in New York, especially naturalized citizens, were able to bring family members on visas to the US, but those who had no family ties in the US resorted to immigrating via Puerto Rico, without papers.

Geraldo is among the latter group. He came from the Dominican Republic and is working on completing his GED. His family was poor and when they moved from the countryside to urban Santo Domingo he went to work to support his mother and his younger siblings. Unlike Altagracia, he had no family members in the US, so he left on his own, making the journey via raft to Puerto Rico with no visa. He told me:

> *Mi mama no quería que yo viniera. Lloraba. Mi idea era trabajar unos seis meses, ganar como $5000, y regresar. La cosa se ve diferente cuando estás aquí.* My mother tried to convince me not to go. My idea was to work for six months, earn $5000, and go back. Six months. Things look different once you are here.

Now, after five years, he has friends, a wife and a network of fellow Dominicans. Returning to the island is not on the horizon.

Mexicans

Mexicans have had a presence in the US since its inception. The saying in Mexico persists: 'We didn't cross the border; the border crossed us'. This is no exaggeration. In 1824, before the Alamo and the annexation of the Mexican territories, the country known as *Mexico* was exactly as large in square miles as the US, with 6 million inhabitants to the US's 9 million (Gonzalez, 2000). California is Mexican-dominated for the very reason that it *was* Mexico up until the mid-19th century. New York, by comparison, and other parts of the northeast, are relatively recent destinations for Mexican immigrants. So, why New York City?

New York and much of the northeast were not destinations for large numbers of immigrants from Mexico until the explosion of immigration in the early 1990s, primarily from the Mixteca region of Puebla (Smith, 2006, 2013). Economic changes spurred by NAFTA, the devaluation of the Mexican currency and changes in immigration laws led to a stream of Mexicans to New York. They found ample jobs in service industries, in delis and restaurants, where those with no legal working papers were paid a fraction of the minimum wage (Rivera-Batiz, 2004; Smith, 2006). By the early 2000s, Mexicans were the fastest-growing immigrant group in New York City.

Ramón followed a well-worn path from his native state of Puebla in Mexico, where countless men had migrated north to New York City to find jobs and work. *'Ya tenían trabajo para mi'* ('they already had a job for me'), he told me. His uncles had settled in Brooklyn and one by one his friends began to migrate to *Nueva York*. He works in a restaurant, in the kitchen, washing dishes and occasionally preparing food. Ramón tells me, *'allá la cosa está dura'* ('things are hard over there'). He goes on to say:

> *Gracias a Dios que pueda ayudar a mi familia, trabajar, ayudar a mi mama. Ella vive en mi casa allá. Y puedo ayudar a mi sobrina, la mantengo.*
> Thank God I can help my family, work, help my mom – she lives in my house over there – and I can help my niece who I am supporting.

His first job when he came to New York City was in a deli, stocking shelves, loading and unloading supplies. He earned a weekly wage of $200 for 60 hours each week (six days at 10 hours a day).

Central America

Poverty, US-funded investments, internal social unrest and violent political conflicts in Central America have made El Salvador, Guatemala, Honduras and Nicaragua among the top 20 immigrant sender nations to the US. In total, more than 7 million immigrants from these countries reside in the US. Yet the vast majority of these individuals have arrived in the US since 1980. Economies in El Salvador, Nicaragua, Honduras and Guatemala were weakened from that date, and in the next two decades the gross domestic product per person actually went down, resulting in desperate conditions among the poorest residents (Gonzalez, 2000). Violent internal civil conflicts in Nicaragua, El Salvador and Guatemala resulted in thousands dead and disappeared, and families fled north to the US to escape the violence. Since peace accords were signed, these countries have nevertheless been fraught with persistent poverty and the violence that has resulted from thousands of armed soldiers being released from service with no skills, combined with the rampant availability of guns.

Antonio fled neighborhood violence in his native El Salvador, where local armed gangs had wreaked havoc in his local town. He is one of a new wave of unaccompanied minors (under the age of 18) from Central America who are crossing the southern border of the US in alarming numbers, setting off a humanitarian crisis and renewed debate about border control (United Nations High Commissioner for Refugees, 2014). In El Salvador his uncles were affiliated with the M-18 gang, he told me, while they lived in the territory of the more well-known MS-13 gang, often referred to as 'La Mara' in the US. When retaliation erupted into violence against family members in his neighborhood, Antonio travelled north alone to test his fate. He crossed the border after traveling through Guatemala and Mexico alone as a 16-year-old. Upon attempting to cross into the US, he was detained and sent to a US immigration detention center. After admitting his age, he entered the legal system as an unaccompanied minor and was transferred into the custody of his mother and stepfather, who live in New York City. He is but one among tens of thousands of unaccompanied minors who are intercepted while crossing the border into the US from Mexico every year, most fleeing violence in their homes and communities (United Nations High Commissioner for Refugees, 2014).

Victor is the oldest of five siblings who left school at age 12 to earn money for his family in rural Honduras. A neighbor was leaving for the US and had procured a *coyote*, a human trafficker, who would help them get into the US. At 15, fleeing poverty, hoping to earn enough to send his younger siblings to school and, he admits, seeking adventure and to get out from under the thumb of his authoritarian stepfather, he left for the journey north. He described for me his journey as a 15-year-old hitchhiking and traveling alone by train from Honduras through Guatemala and Mexico, across the border and up through Texas, Louisiana and the southeast to New York City.

South Americans: Ecuadorians, Colombians

Both Colombians and Ecuadorians live in New York City in large numbers, but their reasons for coming and histories differ. Colombians, many of them educated and middle class, came to the US starting in the 1960s, settling primarily in south Florida and New York City. This first wave has been referred to as economic migrants (Gonzalez, 2000), but a conversation with Colombians who have come since the 1980s makes clear the role of political unrest and violence in their decisions to move north. Colombians in the US have among the highest levels of education of Latino immigrants, with large numbers arriving with completed professional degrees.

Ecuadorians came to the US in two waves as primarily economic immigrants, when political instability and a devaluation of currency led many to leave. The first wave, starting in the 1970s, resulted in large numbers of undocumented immigrants, many of whom legalized their status as a result of the 1986 Immigration Reform and Control Act (IRCA). The second wave started in the late 1990s, as a result of the oil crisis that plunged the Ecuadorian economy into instability yet again. Carmen is among this new wave of immigrants. As the oldest of a rural family that lives from handicrafts and farming in the highland regions around Otavalo, she left her home in the mountains of Ecuador at age 17 without a visa and made her way to New York City by land, a distance of more than 4000 miles. Things are not as she had imagined them, she tells me, and opportunities are limited because she is a woman and because she is undocumented. 'Pero quedarse en el Ecuador no era opción' ('but staying in Ecuador was not an option'), she tells me, her eyes filled with tears.

In School, Out of School: Pre-Migration Educational Experiences

Altagracia was close to completing her high school 'pre-baccalaureate' studies in the Dominican Republic before she ended her schooling. Ramón, in contrast, left school in Mexico after second grade, at around age eight, to work and contribute to the family income. Victor left school after elementary school, *primaria*, in his native Honduras, and hopes his younger siblings can break this pattern and complete high school. Elena left school at age 15 to migrate to the US. In the sections that follow, we will learn more about the connections between the US and the countries of origin of the young people in this study in order to better understand how they came to leave school and what led them to migrate north.

Educational attainment in Latin America

Higher levels of educational attainment are linked to increased participation in the labor market, higher wages and generally with upward mobility, and there is a trickle-down effect on children, that is, children of parents with more education tend to reach higher levels of formal education themselves (Blau & Duncan, 1967; Kao & Tienda, 1998; Murnane *et al.*, 2000; Togunde, 2008; Tyler & Lofstrom, 2005; Tyler *et al.*, 1998; UNESCO, 2011). The highest level of schooling a person has completed – often referred to by statisticians as *educational attainment* – has been a significant focus in the area of international development. Among the United Nation's Millennium Development Goals is universal primary schooling by the year 2015 (United Nations, 2000). This should give us pause. The US has heightened concerns about the high school graduation 'crisis' while some segments of the world population are still struggling to attain the first six years of basic education.

To provide a global perspective on educational attainment and participation in school, researchers have constructed large datasets using complex statistical methods. As a result, we know that in the decade 1999–2009 there was a net increase in primary school enrollment worldwide, yet a breakdown of these statistics reveals that this increase took place primarily in Asia and sub-Saharan Africa. Educational attainment in Latin America and the Caribbean varies greatly between and within countries. Illiteracy levels in Latin America were very high in the 1950s and 1960s (Barro & Lee, 2010) and, to address concerns about levels of adult educational attainment, literacy campaigns arose in Cuba, Nicaragua, El Salvador and other countries based on the work of Brazilian educator Paolo Freire (Freire & Macedo, 1987).

An overall picture of school participation and completion rates worldwide is available dating back to the 1950s (Barro & Lee, 2010). Rather than compare grade-by-grade attainment, the data reveal the number and percentage of individuals in countries and regions who have never attended school at all, as well as those who have completed some primary school, some secondary school and some post-secondary or higher education (Figure 3.1).

Since the 1950s, the average number of years of schooling completed by the world population rose from 3.2 years to 7.8 years in 2010 (Barro & Lee, 2010). Even the latter figure, though, is less than junior high or middle school in the US. There have been significant changes in developing

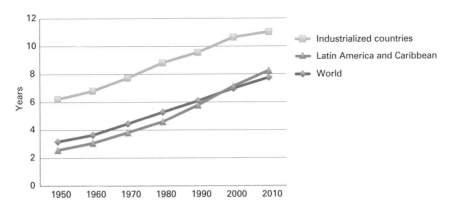

Figure 3.1 Average number of years of schooling in different regions
Source: Barro and Lee (2010)

countries in school participation and educational attainment. The averages reveal that enrollment in secondary education in Latin America and the Caribbean increased from 11 million to 60 million in the 40 years between 1970 and 2009 and that the gap between school-age population and enrollment narrowed (UNESCO, 2011). Primary school enrollment in Latin America and the Caribbean is reported at about 95%, although it decreased by 3% during that same period (UNESCO, 2011). Although averages in the years of schooling attained have increased across the globe, these figures do not tell us much about persistent regional differences in educational enrollment and attainment, nor about disparities in school participation among linguistic and ethnic minorities around the world. In Latin America and the Caribbean, the average number of years of schooling increased from 2.57 in 1950 to 8.26 in 2010. The latter figure represents less than a US high school education. We should take care, though, in differentiating between what constitutes years of compulsory schooling. Table 3.3 provides a point of comparison.

Education in the US begins with elementary school (also referred to as *primary school*), a basic level of schooling that is compulsory in both the US and Latin America. *Lower secondary schooling* is termed *middle school* or *junior high school* in the US and *secundaria* in much of Latin America and the Spanish-speaking Caribbean; it comprises the post-primary years before high school. Confusion is possible because the term *secundaria* used in Spanish-speaking countries is often equated with the US *secondary school* (or *high school*), when in fact the two are not the same. The prerequisite for *post-secondary* (or university level) studies is *high school* (grades 9–12 in the US) and what is referred to as *bachillerato* (upper secondary baccalaureate

Table 3.3 Comparison of compulsory schooling (shaded areas) in Latin America and the Caribbean and the US

	US	Latin America	
Compulsory in the US	Elementary school (grades 1–5)	*Primaria* (grades K–6)	**Compulsory in Latin America**
	Middle school (grades 6–8)	*Secundaria* (grades 7–8) Lower secondary	
	Secondary school or high school (grades 9–12)	*Bachillerato* Upper secondary or 'baccalaureate' studies (grades 9–12)	**Not compulsory in Latin America**
Not compulsory in the US	University (post-secondary or tertiary education)		

studies that are a requirement for admission to university) in Latin America. Much of the confusion is caused by false cognates, as *bachillerato* completion is not equivalent to the US *bachelor's* degree, but to a high school diploma in the US. As is clear, confusion is hardly avoidable when comparing levels of education by name alone, hence the number of years of schooling is often more revealing when examining educational attainment.

Let us now explore the realities of school participation and completion in the main immigrant-sending countries in Latin America. The percentage of the population aged 15 and over in Latin America who completed high school is 25%, while 7% have completed college (Barro & Lee, 1996, 2010). A good starting point for this exploration is a comparison of compulsory schooling requirements between the US and Latin America. Among the top 20 nations that send the most migrants to the US are Mexico, El Salvador, the Dominican Republic, Guatemala, Colombia, Honduras and Ecuador (Pew Hispanic Center, 2013). Table 3.4 presents an overview of compulsory education levels and school participation.

Of course, one of the major challenges in documenting educational attainment and comparing between countries is the lack of consistency in school quality both within and among countries (Barro & Lee, 2010). Quality of schooling is a moving target and includes factors such as time spent in the classroom, quality of materials, instructional design, teacher quality and academic achievement and literacy levels. There are vast differences worldwide between countries in what level of skills and knowledge are attained at any level of schooling. In addition, country-wide averages can be misleading, as significant regional differences in educational participation and attainment can exist within a nation. Not unusual in many

Table 3.4 School participation rates in major Latin American sender nations, 2011

Country	Number of years of compulsory schooling	Enrollment secondary school: % of eligible population	University enrollment: % of eligible population	Literacy rate among 15–24-year-olds
US	12	96%	95%	99%
Colombia	9	97%	43%	98%
Ecuador	9	88% (2010)	40%	99%
El Salvador	9	68%	23%	96%
Dominican Republic	9	76%	no data	97%
Mexico	9	89% (2010)	28%	98%
Honduras	9	74%	21%	95%
Guatemala	11	64%	no data	87%

Source: World Bank (http://data.worldbank.org/indicator/SE.SEC.ENRR)

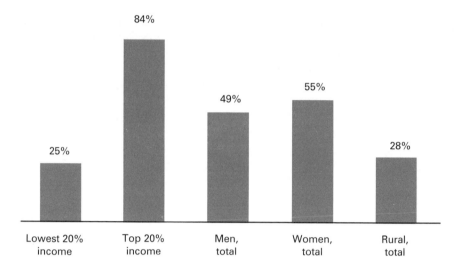

Figure 3.2 Secondary education completion in Latin America, 2011, by persons aged 20–24, by income, sex and rural location

countries in Latin America is a persistent rural–urban divide in education, whereby much higher levels of attendance and access to schools are documented in urban areas than in rural areas and villages. This divide is really a socioeconomic one, for although lower secondary education is compulsory throughout Latin America and the Caribbean, access and participation drop drastically at this level among those on lower incomes (UNESCO, 2011).In some developing countries there is indeed less access to schooling in rural areas (Arnett, 2007; UNICEF, 2010). Worldwide, lower secondary education (i.e. eight or nine years of total schooling) is compulsory in approximately four-fifths of countries (UNESCO, 2011).

Figure 3.2 shows the disparity in secondary school completion by income level, sex and geography. Whereas barely a quarter of all individuals between the ages of 20 and 24 in the bottom fifth of the socioeconomic ladder had completed secondary education in Latin America in 2011, well over four-fifths of those in the highest income bracket had, nearly a four-fold difference. Women outpaced men in school completion in Latin America. Average completion rates in rural areas, which are typically populated by more families in the lowest economic quintiles, were one-third of those for the highest quintile.

Mexico

Because there are such stark differences in educational participation and attainment between countries in Latin America, a closer look at the specifics will be informative. Let us begin with Mexico, the country that sends by far the largest number of immigrants to the US each year, origin of 29% of all foreign-born residents of the US in 2010, or 11.7 million individuals. School dropouts have been a point of policy discussion in Mexico only since the 1990s, when compulsory schooling was raised from six years (elementary school or *primaria*) to nine (lower secondary or *secundaria*) (Arnett, 2007; Instituto Nacional de la Educacion para Adultos, 2009). Mexico's Ministry of Public Education (SEP) has popularized a term unknown in the US, *rezago educativo*, which means literally 'falling behind educationally'. This term refers to persons over the age of 15 who have not completed their compulsory schooling.

Compulsory schooling in Mexico was limited to *primaria* or elementary school (six years) until 1993 (Arnett, 2007; UNICEF, 2010). In Mexico, nearly 17% of those between the ages of 12 and 15 have never attended school, while more than 25% do not finish the six compulsory years of elementary education (Arnett, 2007). Almost 50% of Mexicans leave school after elementary school and another 13% leave without finishing secondary education. Thus, nearly two-thirds of the Mexican population do not complete nine years of education. Not surprisingly, poverty plays a huge role in who attends school in Mexico – 90% of middle-class youth attend school past age 15, as compared with only 18% of poor youth. In Mexico, 'more years of education do not result in greater socioeconomic mobility' (Arnett, 2007: 639).

Moisés is from Mexico, and he is among those who have completed compulsory schooling, although his parents had completed school only up through sixth grade. He completed school through eighth grade, and 'that was it', as he told me. When asked why he abandoned his schooling, he told me:

> *Bueno, necesitaba el dinero. Quería ganar algo. Las cosas sí estaban bien feas. Pues, ya tenía edad, tenías mis 15 años y la familia necesitaba que trabajara.*
> Well, I needed money. I wanted to work for money. The situation was ugly. Anyway, I had already come of age. I had turned 15 and money from me working, well the family needed it.

Mexico, the Dominican Republic and other Latin American and Caribbean countries have invested federal funds over the past decade in programs to provide access to compensatory schooling to anyone aged over 15 wishing to complete primary or secondary school (Instituto Nacional de la Educacion para Adultos, 2010; United Nations, 2011; UNESCO, 2011). Despite these compensatory efforts making an additional three years of education compulsory, nearly half of Mexican students still leave school after six years, and less than half of the population completes upper secondary education (Arnett, 2007; UNESCO, 2011) (see Figure 3.3).

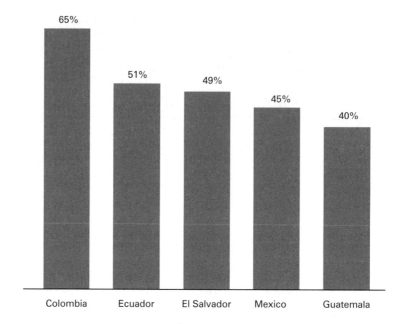

Figure 3.3 Upper secondary completion rates (percentage of population), by country in Latin America, 2011

Central America

In 2013, the US was home to 1.2 million immigrants from El Salvador, a total of more than 3% of all immigrants in the US. Like most countries in Latin America, compulsory education in El Salvador spans nine years and is free. As in most of the rest of Latin America, upper secondary level (*bachillerato*) is not compulsory, but is a requirement for entrance into post-secondary (tertiary) education. A significant drop in participation takes places in El Salvador between primary and lower secondary education, with enrollment rates of nearly 95% of eligible children in primary and 55% in secondary school. Although rates of enrollment and retention have increased in pre-primary, primary and secondary school in El Salvador in the years following the peace accords in 1992, retention across all levels is still less than 70%. Illiteracy rates were extremely high during the first half of the 20th century in El Salvador, with limited access to schooling and poverty being major factors. Current literacy rates are reported at 83%. Persistent issues in Salvadoran education include disparities in attendance and access to schooling between urban and rural areas, participation of women in post-secondary education, student–teacher ratios in rural schools, and high attrition rates in rural areas due to economic hardships and the resultant need for young people to work. These issues are not unique to El Salvador, but are emblematic of how economic inequities impact educational access and attainment across Latin America (United Nations, 2011).

In 2010, more than 2 million Guatemalan immigrants resided in the US. Despite massive reform efforts after the signing of the peace accords in 1996, the country ranks lowest among Spanish-speaking Latin American countries in school enrollment and completion (United Nations, 2011; UNESCO, 2011). Significant disparities can be seen between school enrollment among indigenous and non-indigenous populations, much of it reflecting an urban–rural divide, not unlike other countries in Latin America (UNESCO, 2011).

Individual Dropout Experiences

Judging by statistical representations of them, dropouts from Latin America are all very similar. Yet a closer look reveals stark differences among their experiences. We know from the data presented in Chapter 2 that immigrant students' age at arrival makes a significant difference to their success at completing high school (see page 39). Compared with arrival in the early school years, adolescent arrival of immigrants is more closely correlated with greater levels of incomplete high school. At the same time, other factors impact students' success in school, one being the level of education they completed prior to transitioning into a US school context. A more nuanced view of Latino immigrant populations in the US cautions us not to view this vast subgroup as a monolithic block. As we have seen in an examination of dropout rates (see pages 22–46), there are stark and significant differences between US-born and foreign-born Latinos in high school and college completion rates. Comparing high school graduation rates, we can see that US-born groups often fare better as a whole, although the data also show that more time in the US can lead to poorer educational outcomes for immigrant students (Suárez-Orozco et al., 2008). For foreign-born Latinos, it is instructive to examine educational trajectories prior to arrival in the US to discover trends. But, first, why do we care how much schooling immigrants have before they arrive in the US?

Impact of interrupted schooling

The past matters when it comes to learning. Decades of educational research (August & Shanahan, 2008; Burt & Peyton, 2003; García, 1999; Goldenberg, 2008; Ramirez et al., 1991) have demonstrated the impact that prior education and academic skills in the home language have on immigrants' ability and facility to learn English, especially after the teen years.

Immigrants to the US differ vastly in level of prior education and academic skills, regardless of the age at arrival. They live with family members with a range of educational backgrounds and attend schools with varying levels of support services for English language learners.

Key to understanding the academic progress of immigrant students – the challenges they face and their success – is the research-based finding that among students learning English as a second (or third or fourth) language, those with a more solid academic grounding in their home language have a much easier time both learning English and learning new academic content and skills (Burt & Peyton, 2003). Research on adult immigrants learning English, though limited, indicates that there is a distinct correlation between literacy acquired in the native language and attainment of proficiency in English (Condelli et al., 2009). As a result, among teen, young adult and adult students who seek services in English as a second language, those with high levels of academic skills tend to make regular progress acquiring English, and often even outperform US-born students, while those on the other extreme, with few years of formal schooling and, as a result, limited 'school skills' (how to hold a pencil, how to take notes and study) experience difficulties in reading and writing. As a result, students with gaps in their education in the home language tend to struggle and make limited progress in learning English.

Who completes school and why?

Keeping in mind the vital connection between prior education and later learning, it is informative to explore how much schooling these young adults had completed before arriving in the US. Table 3.5 provides an overview of the educational backgrounds of the young adult Latino immigrants who participated in focus groups that I conducted (see page 181). Each of them, regardless of the number of years of prior education, were attending adult education programs when I met them, making them a decidedly self-selecting yet by no means insignificant group.

Though all the immigrant young adults who participated in this research study had interrupted their schooling prior to immigrating to the US, their prior education varies. About 10% had less than an elementary school

Table 3.5 Number of years of schooling completed by research participants prior to migration

	Number	%
< 6 years	15	10.1
7–8 years	50	33.0
9–11 years	84	56.4

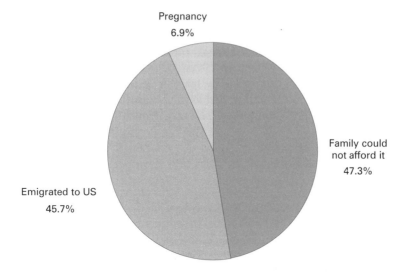

Figure 3.4 Reasons given by study participants for interrupting school in country of origin

education, meaning anywhere from one to six years of total schooling, while a third (33%) had completed primary school and continued on to one or two years of 'lower secondary' schooling for a total of seven to eight years of total education. The remaining 56.4% had begun but not finished their high school college preparatory studies (baccalaureate).

So, why did they not complete their education? The reasons that they gave me for interrupting their schooling fall into three broad categories. The first and most prevalent was a lack of economic resources, given by nearly half of participants (47%). This could be further divided in two: the individual needed to work and contribute to the family income, or could not pursue education because of the lack of free or low-cost schooling. A nearly equal number said they had left school when they had decided to migrate north to the US, a reason given by 46% of the young adults interviewed. Finally, pregnancy (one's own or that of a female partner) was given by 7% of the young people as a reason for interrupting schooling. Figure 3.4 shows the proportions of participants giving the categories of response.

Thus poverty and economic pressures loom large in their explanations for leaving school. Hermenio, from Mexico, shared his experience of combining school with work in the fields with his grandparents, starting at age six. 'Thanks to them I was able to go to school. They paid for everything, the school fees and my personal expenses'. Unfortunately, his grandmother passed away and he was forced to relocate with his mother to another town. As she was too ill to work, he had to go to work to support the family at age 11. Mariano came from a family of eight children: 'There were so many of us. I saw that my family could not afford to send me to school, so I went to work'. These young people came from rural areas and small towns and worked primarily in agricultural settings. For some, being located far from a school meant paying fares for transportation. Despite a persistently popular perception that Latinos in the US place little value on education, the young people with whom I spoke stressed that education became a luxury only when economic needs at home were pressing. Elena, from Ecuador, shared her experience:

> *Bueno, mi mama quería que yo siguiera estudiando, pero yo veía las cosas como estaban, y pues, nosotros somos cuatro, entonces, yo veía que las cosas estaban difíciles. Entonces yo dije que iba a trabajar, para que las cosas sean mejor para ellos que para mi. Entonces les ayudo, poco, no mucho, pero yo les ayudo.*
> Well, my mother wanted me to stay in school but I saw how things were at home, and, well, we are four kids, so, I saw that things were tough. So I said I was going to go out and work so things could at least be better for them than for me. So, I help, a little, not a lot, but I help out.

Their developmental stage is central to this discussion. These young adults, some in their teens, are faced with the unequivocally adult responsibilities of supporting those same individuals to whom they go for advice. They also work long hours, uphold family obligations and face concerns about their future that position them in an adult world. Reasons for leaving school were consistent between men and women, but differed in magnitude (see Figure 3.5). Both young men and young women left school predominantly for economic reasons and to emigrate to the US. Not surprisingly, more young women than men left school because of pregnancy or starting

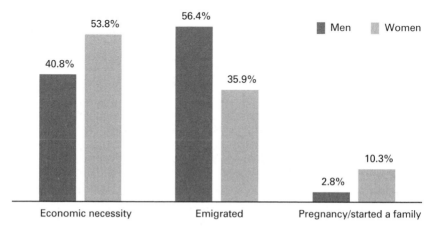

Figure 3.5 Reasons given for interrupting schooling by sex of study participants

a family. More than half of the young women who completed surveys and participated in focus groups cited economic reasons for abandoning school while more than half of the young men cited the decision to migrate as the reason that ended their schooling. In the end, the common denominator is that education was derailed by economic necessity: leaving school to stay at home to care for family, working and then abandoning school, leaving for the US immediately to make money. Victor described it this way:

Pues no, pero yo tenía mis problemas por el dinero que no alcanzaba, pues mis otros hermanos, no sé, entraron al kínder o a la primaria, y tenía que pagar los pasajes y el transporte, entonces, la material y el uniforme, entonces. Primero eché ganas, pero después me di cuenta, no, no, eso no va para más.

Well, it was a problem because there was just not enough money. My younger siblings, they entered kindergarten and elementary school, and you have to pay for transportation, the materials, the uniform. At first, I was still in school and I gave it my best shot, but then I saw, no, no, this is not gonna work.

The reasons for leaving school partly depended upon country of origin in my sample. Among the young men and women from the Dominican Republic who participated in this research, 70.6% told me that they left school to emigrate to the US and reported being enrolled in school up until the time they left home. Altagracia is one of these: she loved school, she told me, and did well in her studies. *'Lloraba por días cuando supe que nos íbamos'* ('I cried for days when I found out I was leaving'). It was not her choice to migrate, she told me, but her family members already in New York had procured a visa, and she had to enter the US on that visa before she turned 18. A year shy of completing her upper secondary high school studies, she left for the US. In contrast, 85% of the young men and women from Mexico reported having interrupted their schooling due to economic necessity before migrating – some as little as a year previously and some as much as 10 years previously. Ramón is among them, having left school as a young teen to work, before migrating at age 15. Among Central Americans who participated in this research, 66.7% reported economic reasons for leaving school, while the remainder reported interrupting schooling upon migrating north. Current reports on the unprecedented level of unaccompanied minors entering the US (United Nations High Commissioner for Refugees, 2014) have documented a four-fold increase in young migrants in the early teen and adolescent years coming to the US across the Mexican border without parents or accompanying adults, fleeing both poverty and violence. Victor, from Honduras, left *'para asegurar que mis hermanitos tengas las oportunidades que no tenía yo'* ('to make sure my younger siblings could have the chances I couldn't'). Why the differences? What can we learn about trends in educational attainment prior to migration?

The Dropout Crisis in Context

How is the reality of being out of school constructed in the social imagination in countries where compulsory schooling includes lower secondary school but not high school completion? As was discussed in Chapter 2, the concept of out-of-school adolescents being 'delinquents' resulted from a push for universal high school and overall increasing high school enrollments in the US. In countries where the scales have not tipped toward majority high school completion, not completing high school is more the norm than the anomaly, at least among lower-income populations. It may be a more accurate reflection of the US dropout rate to omit these young adults from the calculations (Oropesa & Landale, 2009), but to assume that they have consciously weighed the decision to terminate their schooling and thus classify them as 'dropouts' is a logical leap that implies low aspirations while ignoring historical educational policies, limited access, structural constraints and the systemic nature of their limited opportunities. Rising levels of compulsory schooling have resulted in a slow increase in overall years of schooling completed. Nonetheless, the young immigrants with whom I spoke came from families with parents and grandparents whose levels of educational attainment were quite low. Many came from rural areas and low-income families, factors that continue to limit educational access to schooling for people around the world.

Parents' educational levels

Although it is not the only factor impacting participation in school and completion, parents' educational attainment has been shown to be highly correlated with not only the level of schooling completed by children but also their aspirations (Blau & Duncan, 1967; Togunde, 2008). Views of limited opportunity provided by education and intergenerational cycles of poverty have been observed to limit both educational aspirations and attainment. The correlation between poverty and school enrollment makes it clear how a vicious cycle of low educational attainment can be perpetuated across

Table 3.6 Mother's highest level of education completed among study participants

	Percentage of mothers of study participants
0 (never attended school)	4.0
1–6 years	39.5
7–8 years	15.4
High school	12.0
Some college	5.4

generations. A persisting dispute in educational research is the chicken and egg of poverty and schooling: does low educational attainment lead to poverty or does poverty limit educational attainment? In the survey that I used to gather data on educational background, the young adults were asked to indicate the highest level of education that each of their parents, grandparents and siblings had completed. Most were able to say without question how much schooling their mothers had completed (Table 3.6), but knew little about their father's or grandparents' education. Often they had been raised by their mothers and did not have information on their father's level of education or their fathers had never spoken to them about it.

A small number told me that their mothers had never attended school (4%), while nearly 40% reported that their mothers had completed only *primaria*, or 6 years of schooling, in their country of origin. Slightly more than 15% of participants' mothers had completed *secundaria*, lower secondary school. Only 12% of participants' mothers had completed high school education (*bachillerato*), or college-preparation high school education. Only 5.4% indicated that their mothers had attended college, but most were unsure as to whether their mothers had gained a college degree. So, persistently low levels of education can be seen among the families of the individuals with whom I spoke.

Up to this point we have examined trends in educational participation and attainment and experiences of individuals. Yet we have not yet examined the factor that placed them all in a different educational system: the reality of their migration. The next section will consider the political economies in the countries of origin of the immigrants in this sample and how historical relationships between the US and these countries impacted the migration of these young adults.

Re-examining popular discourse: Migration and dropout as *choices*

'But they all chose to come here', I hear repeatedly in discussions about the plight of immigrants, especially when discussion turns to improving conditions or reforming immigration laws. I have presented in this chapter some general background on the educational, political and economic contexts in the countries of origin of the young adults whom we have met. This historical knowledge reveals the importance of reconsidering how we view the concept of 'choice' in their decisions both to migrate and to abandon school. With few exceptions, the young people with whom I spoke rejected the idea that they are *dropouts*. When asked about their interrupted schooling, participants cited issues of access and opportunity, not a lack of interest in school and educational achievement. What of their 'decisions' to leave their countries to go to the US? Was migration a personal choice, or a well-worn pathway resulting from geopolitical and economic forces?

We need not reduce ourselves to semantic haggling, but the examination of social, political and economic forces that impact migration globally should lead us to use the term *choice* cautiously when referring both to school interruption and to immigration. Many of the forces that lead to migration are beyond the control of individual migrants, making the circumstances of their migration less a matter of personal decision than of sociopolitical forces beyond the control of individuals.

Conventional wisdom presents us with an image of young people from Mexico, Central and South America and the Caribbean who one day wake up with the bright idea of migrating north. None of the young people interviewed for this book described their experience in that way. Each came to the US as a teen or young adult, many in their mid-teen years (details are provided in the next chapter, particularly Table 4.1). To listen directly to these young people is to hear an entirely different story than one often characterized in the media.

Most participants reported following in the footsteps of scores of siblings, uncles, parents, cousins and community members into a stream of northward migration that was already a well-worn path. Just as the sons and daughters of Greenwich Village, the Upper West Side and Park Slope have followed a well-worn path to Yale, Harvard, Brown and Stanford, these young people were following in the footsteps of so many others to the deli counters and restaurant kitchens of New York City. 'Choice' is a curious thing – it looks much different to the outsider than it does to the insider purported to be making a selection. For the 'chooser', it may seem less like a fork in the proverbial road and more like the only option.

The discussion of choice raises the question about who values education. Can we, with certainty, say that a family in a country where compulsory schooling lasts nine years and who sends its children to work rather than to complete pre-university studies does not value education? Individuals complete formal schooling – or not – within contexts where access and opportunity are determinants of educational attainment. Although we must look at individuals' personal stories, it is important that we step back to see the broader political and economic factors that drive ostensible 'choices'.

Summary

This chapter has presented background data comparing compulsory schooling requirements in the US and Latin American countries and compared school enrollment and participation rates between countries. For the sample at hand, data were presented on number of years of schooling completed and reasons for abandoning education. A country-by-country analysis has also provided a glimpse into different social and historical factors that led to school interruption and migration. The chapter has also taken a historical look at relations between the US and Latin America to describe factors that can impact migration.

When examining average educational attainment among immigrant groups, statistics can mask the vast differences within groups. Many of the young adults who tell their stories here come from groups with relatively low average levels of educational attainment. Even with data on years of schooling completed, we know that differences in school quality both between countries and within a country mean that we cannot tell a great deal about an individual's skills and knowledge simply by looking at the years of education completed. This truism will be explored in greater depth in Chapter 6.

Finally, this chapter has suggested that the concept of 'choice' when discussing participation in schooling and migration to the US is one worth re-examining. The political economy and international relations between the US and Latin America over many decades have led to generations of immigrants relocating north in search of better opportunities. Whether or not their decision to migrate was determined by economic and political circumstances, the outcome is the same: thousands of young adults each year make the transition northward, many of them of high school age. The next chapter will explore what becomes of their educational paths after arriving in the US.

Additional resources

Novels

Galeano, E. (1997) *The Open Veins of Latin America*. Monthly Review Press, 25th Anniversary Edition.
Gonzalez, J. (2011, rev. edn) *Harvest of Empire: A History of Latinos in America*. Penguin Books.

Data

Migration Information Source, http://www.migrationpolicy.org/programs/migration-information-source
World Bank Open DataSets, http://data.worldbank.org/

Films

El Norte, http://www.criterion.com/films/972-el-norte
Sin Nombre, http://www.focusfeatures.com/sin_nombre
Which Way Home, http://whichwayhome.net/

4 Immigrant Youth Entering the US

Introduction

Victor crossed the border alone, traveling through Mexico from Honduras; Elena came from Ecuador, first on a flight into Mexico and then north. Altagracia came by herself to meet aunts and cousins in Brooklyn whom she had only heard stories about. Nelson rode the trains from El Salvador and was detained while crossing the border, ending up in adult immigration detention because he was afraid to tell officials that he was only 15. Carmen came on a tourist visa from Mexico and stayed on. A look past the numbers and into the personal lives of immigrant young adults reveals a vast diversity of experience. This chapter begins by examining some details of the arrivals of the young immigrant adults in question, then goes on to discuss their views on education, and explores the role they see that education plays in their lives. The chapter also discusses the gap that has been documented between what some articulate as their goals and what they perceive they can actually achieve, and analyzes this gap for the young adults who are the focus of this book.

Arriving in the US

How old were Victor, Elena and their peers when they arrived in the US? A look at US Census data sheds some light on who is entering the US from Latin America and at what age, revealing a trend of youth migrating north to work as young as age 15, with a large subgroup entering the US between the ages of 15 and 24 (National Center for Education Statistics, 2008; United Nations High Commissioner for Refugees, 2014). Young adult migrants from Latin America arrive in the US in a variety of ways, depending on an array of factors, including their age. While some under the age of 18 arrive with

Table 4.1 Age at arrival in the US of the research participants

Age (years)	Number of participants	%
15–16	31	21.3
17	33	22.0
18	27	18.0
19–20	31	20.7
21–24	27	18.0
Total	149	100.0

family, others arrive to join members of their extended family, including cousins, siblings, parents, step-siblings, step-parents, grandparents, or even family friends. The Census data do not provide enough detail to make it possible to know the travel and arrival circumstances of immigrants to the US. Of the young adults with whom I spoke, more than half had traveled alone to the US, and half of those under the age of 18 as unaccompanied minors, a category I will discuss below. Many others arrived with the goal of meeting a family member, in some cases to reunite with a parent who had left some years earlier live in the US. In other cases, the young people had intentions of meeting up with a cousin, an aunt or an uncle in the US, often a relative with whom they had had little prior contact.

In the US, increasing numbers of young people are arriving un-accompanied across the southern border with Mexico (United Nations High Commissioner for Refugees) and the immigrant population in the US is increasingly composed of youth and young adults. The young adults who took part in my research arrived in the US between the ages of 15 and 24. A breakdown of their ages at arrival is given in Table 4.1.

In 2005, more than four-fifths of those entering the US from Latin America (83.4% or 16 million individuals) were of working age, between the ages of 16 and 64. Of the 'recently arrived' (meaning those 19 million foreign-born immigrants who came to the US between 1990 and 2005), a full third (33%) were between the ages of 16 and 29 (Batalova & Terrazas, 2007). While the US population grows older and lives longer, with a growing proportion of senior citizens, the vast majority of those entering the country are of working age (Figure 4.1).

People under the age of 18 are not uncommon among the total popula-tion of migrants to the US, but their numbers are very difficult to track due to the vastly diverse circumstances of their migration (National Center for Education Statistics, 2013a). The United Nations High Commissioner for Refugees reported that in 2013, nearly 40,000 unaccompanied minors arrived at the US border, an increase from some 14,000 in 2012 (US Committee for Refugees and Immigrants, 2013; United Nations High Commissioner

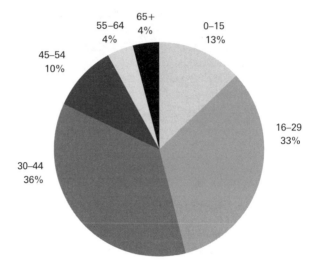

Figure 4.1 Age of recently arrived foreign-born immigrants, 2005
Source: Batalova and Terrazas (2007)

for Refugees, 2014). Young people who enter the country without parents or guardians may interact with a range of federal agencies, including the Department of Health and Human Services (HHS), the Department of Justice (DOJ) and the Department of Homeland Security (DHS) or may 'fly under the radar' and interact with none of the above (Byrne & Miller, 2012). If these immigrant minors enter the US without being apprehended, deported, taken into legal custody, enrolled in school, or interacting with the criminal justice system, they are not 'counted'. Without contact with state or federal public agencies, their existence is not documented within the vast public recordkeeping system.

As a result, it is extremely difficult even to estimate the numbers of unaccompanied minors who stay in the US. It is likely that official records represent a gross under-calculation. In 2014, federal agencies, including the Department of Health and Human Services, began to scramble to respond to an unprecedented surge in the numbers of young people who cross the southern US border alone and without visas (Chishti & Hipsman, 2014; Cowan, 2014; United Nations High Commissioner for Refugees, 2014). Although in the past there had been refugee resettlement programs in place for children (e.g. for Jewish children coming to the US during the Second World War or Cuban children entering the US after the Cuban Revolution), no large-scale programs had been in place for children under 18 who travel without a parent or guardian (Levinson, 2011).

For young adults like many in this study who became full economic contributors to their families at a young age, travel alone across them southern border to the US from Mexico is not unusual. Again, it is important to stress that people who are not apprehended are generally not counted, making it nearly impossible to determine how many unaccompanied minor migrants arrive in the US. Nearly three-quarters of unaccompanied migrants who are apprehended are boys from Mexico, Honduras and El Salvador, many of whom migrate alone or in small groups (Levinson, 2011; United Nations High Commissioner for Refugees, 2014). Many of them enter the workforce upon arrival, often in jobs that have been arranged by acquaintances or family members from their hometowns who are part of an immigrant pipeline. Often they do not interact with the public school system at all.

Who is Working and Where

Census figures reveal that the immigrant labor force has a significantly different composition than the US-born labor force. Nearly half (49%) of all foreign-born workers in the US are Latino, while Latinos make up less than 9% of the US-born labor force (Bureau of Labor Statistics, 2012). While 75% of the immigrant labor force is between the ages of 25 and 54, only 64.5% of US-born workers fall within that age range. Among 16–24-year-olds in 2011, 70% of foreign-born Latinos in this age group were employed, while 64% of US-born Latinos in this age group were employed (Table 4.2). Incomplete high school education differs even more starkly, as 61.6% of foreign-born Latino workers had no high school diploma in 2012 versus 37.1% of US-born Latinos (Bureau of Labor Statistics, 2012).

The figures presented in Table 4.2 are striking when compared with the entire US labor force aged 25 and older. In 2011, a quarter (25.5%) of the foreign-born labor force aged over 25 had not completed high school, compared with 5.3% of the US-born labor force (Bureau of Labor Statistics, 2012). In New York City, immigrants made up more than a third (36.4%) of the total population in 2008 and but nearly half (43%) of the workforce (Napoli & Bleiwas, 2010).

Table 4.2 Comparison of US-born and foreign-born 16- to 24-year-old Latino workers in 2011

	US-born	Foreign-born
Employed	64.0%	70.0%
No high school diploma	37.1%	61.6%

Source, Bureau of Labor Statistics (2012)

Table 4.3 Employment sector of immigrants in this study

Sector where employed	%
Food service	59.6
Health care	10.0
Janitorial	7.0
Retail	10.9
Construction	12.5
Total	100.0

Most of the young people with whom I spoke indicated that they were working in a range of low-wage, low-skill jobs (see Table 4.3). Nearly two-thirds were employed in the category of 'food service' (59.6%), which includes restaurant work, fast food, delis, kitchen staff in food preparation, dishwashing, bussing tables and waiting tables. The remainder worked in health care (10%), janitorial work (7%), retail (including shops, cashiers at supermarkets) (10.9%) and construction (12.5%). These numbers contrast slightly with those for the overall immigrant workforce, as New York City employs immigrants primarily in the service sector, including restaurants and hospitality. Nationally, more than 25.0% of immigrant men work in construction and only 18.6% in service occupations, while 28.2% of immigrant women nationally work in service occupations (Batalova & Terrazas, 2007). In New York City the employment sectors in which immigrants mostly work appear quite different from those nationally. Immigrants make up half or more of all workers in four key labor sectors in New York City: construction, hospitality, manufacturing and retail (Table 4.4).

Participants in this study reported their working hours. Full-time employment in New York City is considered to be 35 hours per week. More than half of the young adults with whom I spoke were working more than full time (including extra hours at one job or working at multiple jobs). A full 25% of those who reported working indicated that they worked

Table 4.4 Immigrants in the New York City workforce, 2008

Sector	Proportion of sector workforce who are immigrants
Construction	56%
Leisure and hospitality (restaurants, hotels, food service)	55%
Manufacturing	53%
Retail and trade	47%

Source: US Census Bureau (2010)

Table 4.5 Hours worked per week by study participants

Number of hours	% of study sample
10–25	31.1
26–35	14.6
36–41	30.1
45–60	23.8

between 45 and 60 hours per week. Not all of this labor is 'on the books' and not all of it is remunerated at minimum wage, which in New York City was raised to $8.00 per hour at the end of 2013 and $8.75 at the end of 2014. Few such jobs in the informal economy offer benefits such as paid sick leave or vacation. Ramón's experience is but one extreme example: his first job, at a small family-owned corner store in Brooklyn, was six days per week, 12 hours per day, for a total of $200 per week. Table 4.5 gives a breakdown of the reported working hours of study participants.

Research examining the life pathways of migrant young adults, especially Mexican labor migrants, posits that a combination of low skills and low aspirations, as well as wages that are higher in comparison with the home country, lead immigrants into the labor force and keep them out of high school (Martinez, 2009; Oropesa & Landale, 2009; Orr, 2009). This idea often morphs into a widespread belief that young adult immigrants who are working full time or more in the labor force are not interested in school. The young adults with whom I spoke were both working but also a self-selected group who had entered adult education programs. What goals did they have for themselves that led them to pursue education? Did they in fact have the 'low aspirations' that is often mentioned in the academic and more general literature?

Aspirations and Goals

When Victor walked into his first pre-GED math class at the community center, he was admittedly nervous. The instructor was from Mexico, like Victor, and the class was conducted in Spanish. Nonetheless, Victor told me: '*Para mi era como si él hablaba en chino, no entendía nada. Quería escaparme, rápidito, y nunca regresar*' ('He might as well have been speaking Chinese, I didn't understand anything. I wanted to run, fast, and not look back'.) His math education in Mexico, he told me, had ended with long division.

Literature on dropouts typically describes school leavers as having low educational and occupational aspirations (Kronick & Hargis, 1998; Rumberger, 1987). Literature specifically focusing on Mexican immigrants – those with among the highest dropout rates in New York City public schools, at 57% – consistently suggests that Mexicans who come to the US to work have no interest in schooling (Martinez, 2009; Treschan & Mehrotra, 2013). Despite available data on working youth of other backgrounds, both foreign-born and US-born, the conventional wisdom that Mexicans are interested only in work and not in schooling is pervasive in both research and policy literature on school participation and attainment. The focus on students' ostensible lack of interest and disengagement with education overshadows the systemic issues that may be linked with low educational attainment. This will be discussed in greater depth in the next chapter (see page 116).

Quite unlike the young people who are disengaged with school, the young adult immigrants who participated in this study spoke very differently about their goals. Nearly three-quarters (73%) expressed a desire to obtain a college degree, ranging from a two-year associate's degree to a doctorate (see Figure 4.2). These aspirations contrast with their collective limited years of formal schooling – nearly half of participants (46.6%) had completed less than eight years of formal schooling in their country of origin when I spoke with them. A statistical analysis of my data shows that their interrupted schooling did not correlate with limited educational or career aspirations among this self-selected group. Data reveal a complexity to these immigrant young adults' educational aspirations and experiences far beyond what the 'dropout' label would suggest.

Figure 4.2 reveals that 24% of those with whom I spoke indicated they aspire to a GED, 31% to a two-year associate's degree, 25% to a bachelor's

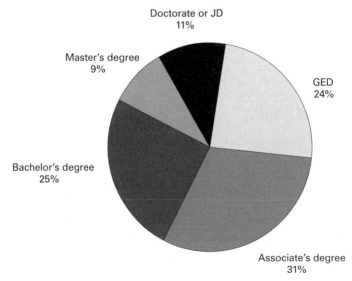

Figure 4.2 Stated educational goals of study participants (JD = juris doctor, a legal qualification)

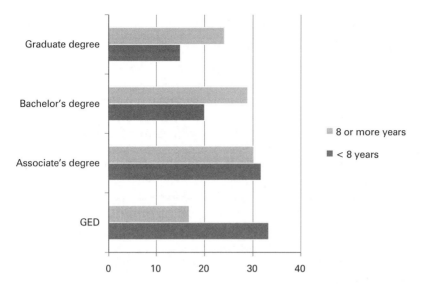

Figure 4.3 Study participants' educational goals, by level of education completed before entering the US

degree, 9% to a master's degree and 11% to a doctorate or law degree. Although, overall, participants' aspirations were high, there is a broad range between completing a high school equivalency and a doctorate. In an attempt to determine whether any factors might explain the different answers, I conducted a series of statistical tests to see if any are significant. In fact, there were no statistical differences between men and women, young adults of different ages, working or not employed, parenting or not, from a rural or urban area. The factors that were statistically significantly correlated with educational goals were level of prior education, parents' level of education and being employed (Figure 4.3). The group who had completed fewer than eight years of schooling had what I would term more 'immediate goals' on the whole: attaining their high school equivalency, entering college, completing an associate's degree. In contrast, those who had already started their high school education in their country of origin aspired to graduate degrees more often. This turned out to be statistically significant (chi-squared test, $p = 0.05$; Mann–Whitney test, $p = 0.05$; $Z = -1.97$; effect size $= 0.026$).

For all of the participants in this study, a high school equivalency diploma is the next milestone toward post-secondary attainment. Those who have already completed eight years of schooling, or lower secondary, as well as those who had started their upper secondary schooling prior to migrating might perceive themselves to be closer to this pre-college goal and thus have higher long-term educational goals than their peers with fewer years of formal education.

Desires Versus Possibilities

Educational researchers and sociologists have long explored the tension between what minority youth say they want for their futures and what they actually expect to achieve. It has become accepted that there is often a gap between such aspirations and expectations (Bohon *et al.*, 2006; Mickelson, 1990). In fact, in the case of the participants in this study, there was little difference between what they hope to achieve and what they actually believe they can achieve, in contrast to much of the literature (Kao & Tienda, 1998; Mickelson, 1990). A phenomenon that has been seen among US-born minority groups is high aspirations – what can be described as a high valuing of education – but then behaviors that undermine achievement as well as real expectations that indicate that these young adults do not believe they can actually attain their goals (Bohon *et al.*, 2006; Kerckhoff, 1976; Mickelson, 1990; Ogbu, 1990).

The latter half of the 20th century saw consistent upward mobility of immigrants, in which subsequent generations moved out of poverty and improved their status, but this is no longer a given in the 21st century. A combination of stagnant wages, job growth primarily in low-wage sectors and mountains of debt from post-secondary schooling mire some young people in situations no better than, or even worse than, the generation before. What is now referred to as 'segmented assimilation' (Portes & Zhou, 1993) means that some immigrant groups improve, while others stagnate and others actually worsen their status the longer they stay in the US.

It may come as a surprise to learn that the 'aspiration–achievement gap' can similarly sometimes widen from one immigrant generation to the next (Suárez-Orozco *et al.*, 2008). This has often been explained away as a difference in 'values', and many of us have heard – or perpetuated – the notion that some groups 'value' education more than others (Ogbu, 1990; Ogbu & Simons, 1998). This has led to myths of model minorities, but also a myth of 'uninterested minorities'. Puerto Ricans, Mexicans and Mexican-Americans are often described as having low aspirations as a result of their values and minority status, and the resulting high dropout rates and achievement gap is attributed to an all-encompassing category of 'culture'.

> One pervasive explanation for low levels of educational attainment among Mexicans and Mexican Americans is that they simply do not hold the same educational values as other adolescents for cultural rather than socioeconomic reasons. We find, however, that some of the differences in expectations and aspirations between Mexicans and non-Hispanic whites and the differences in expectations between Puerto Ricans and non-Hispanic whites can be accounted for by differences in family socioeconomic status. These findings underscore the pervasiveness of Mexican and Puerto Rican education and income disadvantages.

For Mexicans, at least, the high rates of poverty and low levels of parental education are more likely to be factors of historical immigrant streams and modes of incorporation than they are a cultural tendency to undervalue education.... These characteristics have a real impact on aspirations and expectations. (Bohon *et al.*, 2006: 222)

Steele (1997) has developed a compelling theory called 'stereotype threat' to explain the low achievement of women and minorities in certain contexts. His research has focused on women and African-Americans. Using empirical statistical evidence, he shows that in addition to high aspirations, students must be able to overcome persistent negative stereotypes as well as the awareness and fear of other's negative judgments of them in school. His research has shown that stereotype threat can depress the academic performance even of high achievers and leads to disengagement with school.

Overall, participants' educational goals were consistently high, mirroring the commitment to education reflected by their enrollment in non-mandatory second-chance options. Furthermore, labor market participation was correlated statistically with modestly higher educational goals (statistical explanations can be found in the Appendix, pages 182–185). These findings contradict prior research on labor migrants, which views participation in the labor market as a factor that impedes enrollment in high school among new immigrants (Martinez, 2009; Oropesa & Landale, 2009). Most of the young people who spoke to me said that they believed they could attain their goals. Yet for each goal, a portion of those responding indicated that they thought they could achieve an even higher goal, which may be reflective of consistent optimism in the face of myriad obstacles, which I will discuss in Chapter 5.

For the young people in this study, little of the gap between aspirations and expectations that has been described in the literature held true. Why might this be the case? Is their perception of what they can actually achieve a realistic one? Is it possible that they are not entirely aware of the stereotypes that create an image of immigrants who are low achievers? Do they place too much hope in education – especially in the second-chance educational options that provide an opportunity to re-enter the educational pipeline outside of traditional high schools? Are they not aware that a college degree no longer guarantees upward mobility (Anyon, 2005; Ehrenreich, 2001; Rampell, 2013; Stiglitz, 2013)? Is their belief in their ability to attain their goals one born of confidence or naivety?

Specific Career Goals: 'Quiero Ser Profesionista'

During interviews and focus group sessions, young adults talked at length about what they might want to study in college, as well as both general and specific career goals. As mirrored in survey data presented in the previous section, the vast majority (76%) of participants in interviews and focus groups articulated the desire to attend university, and 85% indicated that they thought they would be able to complete at least a two-year college degree. Most (82%) told me that they had enrolled in adult education because they saw it as a stepping stone to a university education, not as an end in itself. One participant summarized succinctly what others had stated: 'Yo estaba tratando de terminar más rápido las cosas para entrar a la universidad' ('I was trying to finish things up quickly so I can go to the university'). University loomed large as a concrete goal to some of them, whereas others viewed it quite idealistically and much more in the abstract.

In focus groups and interviews, there was frequent talk of becoming a professional (*profesionista*) – a lawyer, doctor, forensic scientist, police officer, social worker, day care supervisor, office assistant, civil engineer, architect, computer programmer, graphic designer. All of these professions contrast markedly with the prior work experiences of the group, which were for the most part low wage and low skilled. Something I heard quite frequently was *'quiero tener mi carrera'* ('I want to have a career'), and many explained to me that it was important to finish a university education in order to have a career and support the family. Several interviewees discussed their plan to first complete an associate's degree in a practical area (medical assistant, office worker) in order to procure a good job, and then explore the option of pursuing a four-year degree. Below are some examples.

> *Bueno, yo voy a estudiar eso, como para cuidar bebés ... como, como daycare. Quiero hacer algo que tiene que ver con los niños, porque me encantan los niños. Algo que tiene que ver con eso ... sea pediatra, asistente de pediatra.*
> Well, I want to study that, like taking care of babies ... like, like daycare. I want to do something that has to do with children, because I adore children. Something that is related to that, like pediatrician, pediatrician's assistant.

Some discussed multiple professional and personal goals, as in the case of Victor, who had worked for years in restaurants before concluding that anything less than going to university would mean wasting his time.

> *Quiero tener mi carrera. Computer science. Programación. Voy a hacer esa carrera de dos años. Y también diseñar video juegos. Programar computadoras. Compré una computadora cuando recién ingresé a tomar clases. Quisiera también hacer otra cosa, ayudar a los demás. Como ayudar a gente, pero quiero siempre es como regresar algo que has recibido, alguien te ayudó, y te hace sentir bien, te vas dando cuenta con el tiempo, que es importante.*
> I want to have my career. Computer science. Programming. I am going to do a two- year degree. And also design video games. Program computers.

I bought a computer right after I enrolled in classes. I would also like to do something else, help others. Something like helping people, I want to be able to give back something that I received. Somebody helped you, and it makes you feel good, and in time you realize how important it is.

Some of the professional goals arose from very personal experiences, as in the case of Victor, who, at age 15, had been detained by the US Immigration and Customs Enforcement's border control agents while crossing the US–Mexico border illegally. As an unaccompanied minor, he was assigned to a lawyer and at 20 is now near the process of having his residency legalized. The process had been a long and complex one, as he described it. His goal was to enter university to become a lawyer:

Participant: *Yo quiero ser abogado.*
Marguerite: *Y ¿por qué?*
Participant: *¿Por qué? Por. Poooooor. Por muchas cosas. Defender a los inocentes, ¿me entiendes? Defender a los inocentes, a los inocentes.*
Participant: I want to be a lawyer
Marguerite: Why?
Participant: Why? Because. Because. For many reasons. I want to defend innocent people, you understand? Defend the innocents, the innocents.

In a similar vein, in interviews and focus groups other participants indicated wanting to 'give back' or do jobs that 'help people', like the participant below:

Marguerite: *Si no hubieran obstáculos, ¿qué harías tú, ¿qué tipo de estudio?*
Participant: *Sí, como un estudio, una profesión ¿cómo se llama eso? como ayudar a las personas.*
Marguerite: If there were no obstacles at all, what would you do, what would you study?
Participant: A career, what do you call that, like helping people.

Some participants articulated a clear desire to make choices that contrasted with those of their families, but explicitly stated that their families were not at fault for their priorities because of economic necessity. Some expressed a desire to change their situation, such as Elena, who said she wanted the GED so she could '*ser alguien, como médico o asistente médico*' ('be somebody, like a doctor, or a medical assistant'). Participants did not discuss the salary or earning potential of any specific career, but from their discussions of career goals it was clear that education was a pathway to upward mobility in the workforce, and not an end in itself. Those who spoke of their current labor market situations clearly differentiated between their work in restaurant kitchens, in factories and in construction, and being *una profesionista* ('a professional'). Several expressed the desire to *tener un trabajo limpio* ('have a clean job') or something that they did not view as necessarily easier, but *en una oficina* ('in an office'), a white-collar job versus a blue-collar or manual job. Others discussed the need to *ser útil* ('be useful') and *ser alguien* ('be somebody'). In one focus group, participants discussed the constraining public perception that Mexicans are hard workers:

> *Siempre hablan de la chamba, que bien chambeamos nosotros. Somos mucho más inteligentes de lo que nos pueden aportar. No somos solamente para chambear, por eso vamos a las clases aquí para darle una mejor calidad de vida a las personas que vienen detrás de nosotros, nuestros hijos.*
> They always talk about work, how hard we work. We are much more intelligent than people think. We do not exist just for hard work; that's why we come to school here, to give a better quality of life to people who come after us, our children.

In this case, status in the workplace is closely linked to salary and to upward mobility. When speaking about career and educational goals, participants often mentioned *superación*, which literally translates as 'overcoming' and connotes both self-realization and surmounting obstacles. *Quiero superarme* (I want to overcome) was a common statement, as in this participant's view of his university pathway:

> *Quiero ir a la universidad para superarme. Si puedo graduarme de la universidad puedo tener un trabajo bien. A mí me gusta la arquitectura. Tengo que hacer lo mismo que él, el GED.*
> I want to go to university to overcome. If I can graduate from the university, I can have a good job. I like architecture. I have to do what he is doing, get the GED.

Attitudes Toward Education

Most participants believed that education was the key to their own success and would lead to concrete achievements in the future. An open-ended survey item asked respondents to give advice about education to recently arrived immigrants. This was a means to extend the understanding of abstract educational attitudes and explore variation within the sample. Not a single survey respondent left this question blank. All responses were coded and grouped into four distinct categories, whereby each participant's response fell into one category alone: (1) go to school; (2) make school your priority, not work, (3) learn English and (4) take advantage of all the opportunities in this country. A summary of responses is given in Table 4.6.

Table 4.6 Participants' responses to the survey item 'What advice about education would you give to an immigrant like yourself?'

Advice	%
The key to success in this country is education: go to school	27.0%
Make school your priority, not work	32.0%
Learn English	26.3%
Take advantage of all the opportunities in this country	14.7%

Attitudes were reflected in the specific advice they indicated that they would give to immigrants like themselves, such as the responses below:

- Educate yourself because education is what will help you get ahead in life.
- The best advice is to believe in yourself that anything is possible when you want to improve yourself.
- That you get an education above all else, as education is the most important for any person, the pathway to the best things in life, the top economic and intellectual level. Don't get swept away by what you see and hear, have goals for the future.
- Education is important to triumph.
- Look for help to continue your education because a person with a good education has more opportunities for having a good future.
- The more academic preparation you have, the more opportunities you will have in this country and it is never too late to get good academic preparation.
- Education is important to be somebody.
- The first thing to do is to look for a school here to help you because people who don't go to school are nobody.
- Education is a weapon to get ahead.

The above comments underscore the value participants place on education as a means to success. Many drew a direct link between acquiring formal education and self-realization ('being somebody'). They also equated increased opportunity with higher levels of formal education. Perhaps reflecting some of their late starts in second-chance schooling, some respondents underscored that it is never too late to pursue an education. Education was equated with opportunity and self-realization. Specific comments revealed how they viewed the role of education in helping them achieve their life goals. Nelson explained that he had re-entered education only after realizing that his original plans after migrating were unrealistic:

Mi plan era venir, trabajar, ahorrar y hacerle una casa para mi mama. Y después te das cuenta, todo era un sueño y lo difícil que es.

My plan was to come, work, save, and build a house for my mother. And then you realize, that is just a dream, how hard it really is.

Many participants discussed the concept of the American Dream (*el sueño americano*). The belief in upward mobility through hard work and improved opportunities is a backdrop to migration north as part of the immigrant labor market pipeline. Migration north is a product of the global economy and for many immigrants from Latino America does not represent a personal choice as much as a pre-determined global pathway (Massey *et al.*, 2002; Suárez-Orozco, 2000).

What seems to have shifted for many of the participants was not the meaning of the American Dream, but the pathway to achieve it. They now viewed upward mobility as something that could be attained only through education and self-improvement. Viviana, who comes from a large family in central Mexico, discussed the struggle she faced when she embarked upon an educational pathway different from that of her family members:

Quiero estudiar y me dicen, ¿pero por qué? ¿Estudiar qué? Bueno, les digo, quiero agarrar una carrera. Pero dicen, mejor trabajar, mejor regreses para acá. Es como que … bueno, lo importante para ellos es que trabaje, que ahorre y que regrese. Que me case y esté con ellos. Eso es lo normal, es lo normal. La gran parte de la familia lejana que tenemos, es lo típico, que vienen a Estados Unidos, que van y regresan otra vez, que trabajan tres años, y regresan otra vez y regresan otra vez.

I want to go to school, and they ask 'But why? Study what?' Well, I tell them, I want to have a career. But they say, it's better to work, then come back here. It's like … well, the important thing for them is that you work, save money and go back. Get married and go back to the family. It's normal; that's what is normal. Most of my extended family, that's what they do, come to the United States, work for three years go back, come back here, and go back again.

Family's differing priorities were not prescriptive of the goals articulated by the participants in this study. Qualitative data revealed that not only did some participants come from families with low levels of formal education, but that their family members had not embraced the achievement ideology as they had. This suggests that the belief in 'the education gospel' (Grubb & Lazerson, 2004) happened in the course of adapting to their lives in the US. These participants contrasted their own high aspirations and choices to pursue education with those of their parents and family members. Rosa told me:

Quiero cambiar la historia de mi familia. Nadie quiere estudiar. Pero hacerles entender que sí pueden. Cuando hablo con ellos, les digo, ¿por qué no estudias? Cambiar la mentalidad.
I want to change my family's story. Nobody wants to go to school. But I want to make them understand that they can. When I talk to them I say, 'why don't you go to school?' Change their mentality.

Participants' attitudes to education stand in contrast to those of many of their family members who had experienced economic barriers to accessing education, over generations, which had prevented education from being an option, let alone a pathway to upward mobility. Elena put it this way:

No es que no les importa la educación. Pero allá uno tiene que trabajar y es así simplemente. Nadie en mi familia ha terminado la prepa.
It's not that they don't think education is important. But over there you have to work and it's just like that. Nobody in my family has finished high school.

Ramón clearly explained the importance of study over work in his personal experience, and how he came to see that education is important for him personally and is the top priority:

Allí donde estaba trabajando me salí – porque me di cuenta que prefiero tener más tiempo y trabajar en lo que sea, para dedicarlo a la escuela. Y de allí salía mejor. Nada me garantiza que yo pueda estudiar. Pero no va a ser lo mismo. Si yo logro tener un título o algo, si es que regreso a mi país o algo, no va a ser lo mismo que cuando yo salí. Puede ser vengo aquí a trabajar, pues el dinero va y viene, pero si regreso aunque con las manos vacías pero con el conocimiento, lo tengo, un título lo tengo, y no voy a estancarme y estar en lo mismo.
I left the job I was at – I realized that I want to have more time and work doing whatever so I can focus on school. And it was better. There is no guarantee that I can go to school. But things won't be the same. If I am able to get a degree or something, and if I go back home to my country, it's not going to be like when I left. It's possible that I come here to work, but, well, money comes and goes, and even if I go back empty-handed I will have knowledge, I have it, I have a degree, and I won't stagnate and be stuck the way I was before.

Ramón's choice to make school his overarching goal represents a shift in thinking along three dimensions: (1) a different set of priorities from those of family members, who may see the accumulation of wealth and returning home as the priority, (2) an emphasis on the acquisition of knowledge as opposed to the acquisition of wealth, and (3) an emphasis on making work the aspect of life that must adapt to schooling and not vice versa. This is a shift from both contemporary and historical explorations of immigrant trajectories (Fass, 1991; Hochschild, 1995; Kasinitz *et al.*, 2008, 2013) in which the immigrant first generation focuses exclusively on hard work to benefit the immigrant second generation. Victor discusses how he made a similar shift, deciding that school should be his priority, regardless of his legal situation:

> *Un tiempo pensé que no valía la pena estudiar, por mi situación legal, pero ahora no. Ahora lo que quiero es estudiar. Avanzar, por lo menos. Tener conocimiento de dos, tres cosas. Cosas del destino, si me llegan a sacar, o si tengo que irme bueno, voy a aplicar a una escuela, y bueno, el conocimiento tengo, he aprendido bien.*
> I used to think that it was not worth it to go to school because of my legal situation, but not anymore. Now what I want is to go to school. Get ahead, at least. Have some knowledge of two or three things. If destiny has it that they deport me, or if I have to go back, I'm going to apply to school, and what I learned, I learned it well.

Research has shown that many recent immigrants, especially those who are undocumented, focus on work and remittances with the goal of returning home (Rivera-Batiz, 2004). It appears that for those who have made the shift into second-chance education, these short-term goals were no longer the priority and returning home was no longer the primary goal. Participants indicated that they had sought out school to 'improve themselves' (*quiero superarme)* and 'to be someone' (*quiero ser alguien)*, and that education is the means to that end.

Summary

This chapter has explored some of the diverse circumstances of arrival of immigrant young adults who enter the US with an incomplete high school education. In addition, the chapter has presented and discussed the educational goals articulated by a specific subset of these young adults – Latino immigrants who return to education in 'second chance' pathways after interrupting their high school education.

The chapter has illuminated what scholars have referred to as 'abstract educational attitudes' (Mickelson, 1990) – the beliefs that these young people have about education, their personal views on the value and importance of education. The majority of the young adults with whom I spoke in the course of this study indicated that they wanted to continue their education, not only to finish high school or acquire an equivalency diploma, but to pursue graduate degrees as well as two- and four-year college degrees. A small proportion sought to complete a high school equivalency credential, but also indicated that they hoped they could attend university and study for a professional career. These high aspirations and goals were consistent across years in the US and age of participant. Age, sex, area of the country where the participant had gone to school had no significant effect on stated educational goals. Participants included working adults, those currently not in the labor force, as well as those who were working as part of the cash economy without the benefit of legal immigration status. Those who were employed were exclusively low-wage unskilled laborers with minimal job security. A significant, albeit small, difference was revealed in the educational goals of this latter group. It is possible that they have learned through experience that there is a link between educational preparation and upward mobility in the job market and that their shift into second-chance education reflects this belief.

Their views on schooling and its place in their future reflect what has been demonstrated in the literature on education and labor market outcomes – that post-secondary schooling is, in today's society, a prerequisite for upward mobility (Louie, 2007; Orr, 2009). These views also reflect the beliefs underlying current school reform efforts – education is what improves one's lot, regardless of poverty, geography, family history, race or linguistic background (Anyon, 2005; Cuban, 2004).

In general, young people with whom I spoke expressed a wish to be a professional of some sort, primarily white or pink collar as contrasted with the blue-collar jobs at which they worked. They expressed high expectations, with goals they expected to achieve closely aligned with those they stated for themselves. Although a self-assessment, it reflects a positive and hopeful attitude toward the future that will be explored more in depth in Chapter 5. Overall, educational aspirations were linked to desires to obtain higher levels of education for economic gain. Yet their purposes in gaining an education did not stop at economic and career advancement. Multidimensional reasons for obtaining post-secondary schooling included both labor market advancement and personal improvements. In a sense, education was in participants' eyes something that would give them the essence of being a better person. It would make them 'be somebody' and 'be useful', and was a pathway to overall betterment of themselves as individuals.

The repeated emphasis on education was nearly a mantra among these young people: 'education is the most important thing there is'. They have a solid belief in education's central role for their upward mobility. These views present a direct contradiction to research and scholarship that suggests that immigrants – especially young labor migrants from Latin America – are single-mindedly focused on work, and have little interest in investing in their own educational advancement (Hirshman, 2001; Martinez, 2009; Oropesa & Landale, 2009; Rivera-Batiz, 2004).

Despite homesickness, few had any intention of returning to their country of origin. They had embraced the American value that education is what solves social problems (Anyon, 2005; Apple, 2006; Cuban, 2004).

In contrast to prior generations of immigrants, who generally focused on work to ensure success for the second generation (Fass, 1991; Hochschild, 1995; Kasinitz *et al.*, 2009), education appears to be not only an ideal for this group, but a priority that at least the young people like Ramón, Altagracia, Elena, Victor, Nelson, Rosa and others have acted upon by seeking out and enrolling in educational options. The 'college for all' philosophy in the US leads to the conclusion that the more educated workforce will be one that is also more economically secure, even in the face of persistently high unemployment rates that leave many well-educated young adults with college degrees working part time or not at all.

Now that we have explored these young adults' attitudes to education and where they see themselves going, the next chapter will illuminate what happens to some of them as they see the doors that will lead them toward these goals.

Additional resources

Books

Forty-Cent Tip: Stories of New York City Immigrant Workers (2006). Photo essays by students at three international high schools in New York City about the life, dreams, and disappointments of immigrant workers, published by Next Generation Press. See http://www.nextgenerationpress.org/titles/fortycenttip.html

United Nations High Commissioner for Refugees (2014), *Children on the Run: Unaccompanied Children Leaving Central America and Mexico and the Need for International Protection*. See http://www.unhcrwashington.org/children

Films

Man Push Cart, http://www.raminbahrani.com/films/mpc.html
The Harvest: The Story of the Children Who Feed America, http://theharvestfilm.com/

5 Pushouts, Shutouts and Holdouts: Entering, Exiting and Evading High School in the US

Introduction

The educational pathway through elementary, middle and high school has become a well-worn one for millions of immigrants and their children. This school trajectory is fairly straightforward for a young child of immigrants born in the US or one who arrives to the US as a young child during the primary school years. Students enroll in elementary school, middle school, high school, and then continue on to college (or a community college, in particular if saving money is a key issue or if a student needs to brush up on basic skills).

This is the common schooling trajectory, but not all students, whether US-born or foreign-born, are successful on it, for a variety of reasons. Adolescent and young adult immigrant arrivals to the US encounter few educational programs designed specifically to meet the unique needs of students who may have interrupted schooling and limited English proficiency (García *et al.*, 2008; Ruiz-de-Velasco *et al.*, 2001). In New York City, some immigrant youth who arrive as older adolescents manage to enroll in traditional high schools successfully. Yet significant numbers circumvent high school altogether, or are turned away when they attempt to register, or are discharged before they earn a diploma (Gotbaum & Advocates for Children, 2002; Jennings & Haimson, 2009; Martinez, 2009). This chapter explores the various school options that exist for immigrants aged 15–24 to continue their education once they arrive in the US without a high school diploma.

Take two examples. Altagracia attended two years of high school in New York City before exiting school without a diploma. Ramón, in contrast, had spent about five years working in New York City before taking steps to enter school by approaching a local Mexican community center to take some math classes in preparation for the GED. What accounts for the differences in their school participation? What kinds of educational experiences did Altagracia, Ramón and others like them have after entering the US? This chapter explores how they came to enroll in adult education programs as a means to further their education.

By looking at specific cases of students seeking to enter high schools in New York City, this chapter also sheds light on what can happen to students who seek viable educational pathways once they enter the US. The chapter explores the complex landscape of educational options for immigrant young adults and invites us to share the experiences of individuals who sought to enter the typical US educational pipeline at somewhat atypical ages. To start at the beginning, we'll explore the places where young immigrants can enter the educational pipeline.

Paths and Options

For immigrants who arrive in the US between the ages of 16 and 24, the educational pathways and the entry points open to them are not at all straightforward, and the array of options may differ from their earlier schooling experiences, which can range from an urban setting to a rural environment with solely one school. Young people like Victor, Elena, Altagracia and Ramón suddenly face in the US multiple schooling options – and there are advertisements on billboards, streets and subways for special schools at which to learn English, different colleges, trade schools, classes, and training programs that promise a high school certification and a college degree in one fell swoop. Such young people may well wonder 'what is the right school for me?' and 'where am I even allowed to enter?'

In the US, immigrant children and young adults are granted free access to public elementary, middle and high schools as long as they meet the age requirements and register through the traditional channels. Immigrant status does not limit their legal right to participate in public schools K-12 – or should not, from a legal standpoint. *Plyler v. Doe*, the landmark 1982 Supreme Court decision, granted illegal immigrant students the right to attend public schools K-12 free of charge. The decision altered the landscape of pre-university public schooling for immigrants (Legal Information Institute, n.d.), framing public education as right for all children residing in the US, including all immigrant youth of school age, regardless of their immigration status or the circumstances of their entry into the US. A little more than a decade after the *Plyler v. Doe* decision, access to public education and services for immigrants came under fire in California in the guise of Proposition 187, a bill designed to deny public education and public health services to illegal immigrant children and families. The bill was passed in 1994, but soon after it faced legal challenges and was ultimately deemed unconstitutional because it was a state's attempt to legislate immigration enforcement, which in the US lies solely within the federal domain (Alvarez & Butterfield, 1997; Carter, 1997).

Despite the controversy surrounding universal access to public education for immigrants, enrolling an immigrant child in school is straightforward, in theory. A child is brought to school by parents or relatives and completes the enrollment process, submitting a birth certificate and proof of residence. For older youth and young adults, things are not so easy. A young man like, Felipe, for instance, found the process not as he had anticipated. He arrived from El Salvador at age 18, on his own, to stay with family in New York City and aspired to attend high school. *'Eres demasiado grande'* ('You're too old'), his aunt told him. *'Necesitas papeles'* ('You need papers'), his cousin told him. *'Sin los documentos de la escuela en tu país'* ('Without your school records from your country') said his co-worker at the deli, *'no vas a poder ir a la escuela aquí'* ('you can't go to school here'). Colorful multilingual posters on the subway advertise 'Learn English' and 'Get an international student ID', but at a cost. For some immigrants like Felipe, the assumption is that the cost of schooling and its value are directly proportional, thus they conclude that fee-based or for-profit schools that cater for immigrant students must be of higher quality than free, publicly funded and state-supported institutions. Post-secondary education in the US is not impacted by the landmark *Plyler v. Doe* decision, and not all immigrant students have access to public universities, depending on their state of residence. The question remains: with so many ostensible options, where are the various entry points and which ones are best?

Where are doors 1, 2 and 3? The complex landscape of programs for young adults

A complete understanding of the educational trajectories of immigrants in the United States requires some background on the options that are available, specifically because people aged 16–24 straddle two educational worlds. They are simultaneously well within the age limits of high school attendance (students in the State of New York age out of public high schools at age 21, not at age 18) but students within this age span are also old enough to drop out (at age 16 in New York). In simple terms, there are two pipelines that represent options that are both accessible and affordable: (1) regular public high school and (2) adult education.

Because individual states in the US have the ultimate authority in setting education policy, compulsory schooling requirements vary across the country. In some states, students are mandated to attend school until they graduate or until they turn 18 (e.g. in California, Connecticut, District of Columbia and Hawaii), while in some states this age is 17 (e.g. Arkansas and Mississippi) or 16 (New York, Georgia, Idaho, Indiana), unless they have parental consent (Empire State Coalition for Youth and Family Services,

2013). In New York State, compulsory schooling spans ages 6–16, inclusive. Students may leave school without parental consent at the end of the school year during which they turn 16 (17 in New York City). In contrast, the maximum age at which a student is allowed to attend a public high school in New York is 21. As a result, students have a legal right to attend public high schools in the State of New York until they turn 21 (Bush, 2010).

For immigrant students who arrive in New York City and seek to enter a public high school, the options are vast and complex. New York City has over than 400 high schools, which collectively offer more than 600 academic programs, including accelerated early college courses, and programs in fine arts and music, engineering, and career and technical education. Some of the programs are by application only or are limited to certain students based on test scores and academic level, requiring that interested students submit transcripts or take a written test or be interviewed. There are 'screened' programs in which applicants must meet certain criteria, as well as 'zoned' schools that serve only students in certain neighborhoods. Elite academic high schools admit students on the basis on test scores. Catholic high schools exist alongside private high schools (the latter have annual fees upwards of $40,000 per year and generally do not accept English language learners or students with special needs). New York City also offers some public high schools created specifically for new immigrant students, such as Newcomers High Schools, as well as a network of 15 schools in the Internationals Network for Public Schools, all of which are non-charter public high schools that serve immigrant English language learners who have been in the US four years or less, regardless of the gaps in their formal schooling. Older immigrant youth are viewed by schools as 'hard to serve' due to the age at which they start school, as well as their often low levels of English proficiency. Due to federal and state accountability pressures to graduate students within four years or else be sanctioned (see Chapter 2), high schools are often understandably reluctant to enroll newly arrived teens with limited English proficiency because they will 'bring down the numbers'. As a result, new immigrant English language learners may end up being referred directly to these schools designed for newcomers by district enrollment centers or from high schools reluctant to serve them.

If a student like Victor arrives at a local high school seeking to enroll, he or she must provide identification and proof of residence. Because New York City has a complex application process for high school selection, middle school students seeking a seat in a high school submit an application ranking their school preferences in the fall of their eighth grade year and by the spring semester of their eighth grade year typically know what school or program they will attend the following year. Although there are enrollment centers for public schools around New York City, immigrant teens new to New York City often go directly to a local high school asking to be admitted 'over the counter' (i.e. they were not referred through a middle school application process). Notably, these students do not arrive only at the start of the school year, but arrive at high schools seeking admission from the very first through the very last day of the school year. Enrollment numbers of new immigrant students in local schools in neighborhoods with many immigrants therefore tend to increase over the course of the school year because so many students arrive in the US after the school year begins and ask to enroll. Students who meet the age and residency requirements are legally entitled to a seat in a public high school.

If all goes well, a new immigrant student arrives and enrolls in high school. For a variety of reasons, discussed later in the chapter, things do not always unfold as planned. There are additional options within the public school system for students of regular high school age (and over), managed and funded by the New York City Department of Education. These 'alternative pathways to graduation' include a complex array of programs for people aged 15–24 (New York City Department of Education, 2013a). Many of these have been designed to address the needs and challenges of the growing population of 'disconnected youth' in large urban school systems, young adults who have dropped out of school and may be seeking work but who are unable to find it – hence they are 'disconnected' from both school and work. However, many of the alternative high school options designed for disconnected or at-risk youth are beyond the reach of new immigrant students simply because among their requirements is a year or more of prior attendance at high school or a minimum number of completed credits, criteria which no newly arrived immigrant youth can meet. As a result, new immigrant students may be referred to an alternative program to complete a high school equivalency diploma and learn English. Many such programs fall within the public K-12 system and are free of charge, while others are run by community colleges or community-based organizations.

Outside of the K-12 public education system, all states in the US offer multiple options for young adults seeking to learn English or to complete their high school and basic education. New York is no exception; the variety of programs designed to help immigrant adults learn English is staggering, with classes housed in community centers, libraries, community colleges, churches and religious institutions, union offices, health centers, pre-schools, social service agencies, for-profit and proprietary schools, and community ethnic organizations, among others. Those enrolled in non-high-school educational programs attend a diverse array of second-chance options, including programs in English as a second language designed for adults, high school equivalency (GED) classes and Spanish-language literacy and high school equivalency classes.

Earning a Credential Outside of the K-12 Pipeline: High School Equivalency

For immigrants who enter the US without having completed high school in their country of origin, there are alternative pathways through which they can attain a high school equivalency credential. Entry into post-secondary education or training in the US generally requires a high school credential or its equivalent. The main pathway toward post-secondary education for foreign-born students with incomplete high school is 'high school equivalency', which can be obtained through a series of tests given across the US known popularly as the 'General Education Development' (GED) exams. These were introduced in the 1940s as a means to certify the skills of members of the US armed forces and enable them to transition into jobs in the civilian sector. Since that time, millions of young people and adults across the US have taken the tests, which are also available in French and Spanish, and in versions for the visually and hearing impaired. Until 2013, the GED tests were nationally the single means of earning a high school credential outside of a traditional high school pathway in the US, but starting in 2014 with changes to the test, some states, including New York State, began to adopt a range of tests very similar to the GED but aligned to national Common Core Standards to fulfill this need and to better reflect national shifts in high school curricula. In 2014, the GED Testing Service released a new exam aligned to the new Common Core State Standards and said to better measure 'career and college readiness', the most popular buzzwords in world of US education in the past decade.

> The score report for the new test provides detailed feedback on more than 100 knowledge and skill points, which GED Testing Service says is essential for educators, employers and colleges to better understand a person's strengths and weaknesses. (GED Testing Service, 2014)

Since its launch in 1942, the GED test has dramatically changed the stratification of education in the US (Maralani, 2003). The GED pathway channels 700,000 individuals a year into test centers and awards nearly 450,000 credentials annually (American Council on Education, 2008). Because it is designed as an alternative high school credential, the GED functions as a safety net for students not on a traditional high school pathway but who have post-secondary and workforce aspirations. For those without a high school diploma, a GED certificate is a prerequisite for entry into post-secondary education and training, and it is also required by some employees for consideration for low-skilled or entry-level positions.

In New York State, the GED tests – and, in the future, their equivalent – are free of charge; the credential is known by employers; a passing score allows entry into community college, though holders of the GED certificate often need remediation in much higher proportions than students with a traditional high school diploma (Patterson *et al.*, 2010). Although in New York State people are eligible to remain in high school until age 21, New York City and State administrative data reveal an increase in the number of school-age Latinos taking the GED, although only 39% of these 17–21-year-old Latino GED test takers actually passed the test in 2007–08 (Jennings & Haimson, 2009).

States receive some public funds in the form of block grants to support adult basic education and workforce development, but not all programs for adults receive these – and few programs are funded exclusively with public monies. Programs may be free or fee based, and fees vary. Teaching staff may be trained or untrained volunteers and a combination of full-time and part-time staff. The variety of the programs, their diverse institutional hosts and the vast array of funding sources mean that it is not possible to say how many programs exist, nor how many individuals are served, nor their ages and backgrounds.

Adult education is not mandatory for immigrant young adults and generally functions on a first-come, first-served basis. There is no central-ized hub to refer immigrants to adult education programs, although the US Department of Labor funds Workforce One Centers designed to help un-employed adults gain basic education and training if they can demonstrate their legal right to work in the US. Analysis of existing program data has demonstrated that only a fraction of the need for adult English language services is being met in New York State by publicly funded programs (Colton, 2006). Many other programs exist in settings as diverse as church basements, local community organizations and private businesses, but they are not regulated by public agencies and there is no way to estimate the numbers of students served, nor their ages. Accountability requirements that dictate public funding constraints can result in instability in program options, with new programs being funded and others at risk of losing funding from one year to the next (Barron, 2013). Unlike some state programs, in New York adult education programs do not require potential students to document their immigrant status or residency, unless those programs receive funding from the US Department of Labor.

With existing data, what we do know is that, across the US, adult education programs funded through the Adult Education and Family Literacy Act serve significant numbers of young adults, including those who could legally attend high school. Of the total of slightly more than 2 million individuals who enrolled in these publicly funded programs in 2010–11 (Table 5.1), about one-third (35%, or approximately 700,000) were under the age of 25 (US Department of Education, 2013a, 2013b). Students of high school age are represented in publicly funded adult education programs as well, with more than 200,000 enrollees (11% of the total) being students who are still of high school age.

Table 5.1 National enrollment in adult education, program year 2010–11

Program	Ages of students enrolled											
	16–18		19–24		25–44		45–59		60+		Totals	
	n	%	n	%	n	%	n	%	n	%	n	%
English as a second language	15,011	2	118,010	14	468,143	56	183,814	22	54,421	6	839,399	42
High school equivalency	59,205	24	81,093	33	84,485	34	19,323	8	2,493	1	246,599	12
Adult basic education	137,716	15	281,183	30	370,651	40	118,311	13	18,304	2	926,165	46
Totals	211,932	11	480,286	24	923,279	46	321,448	16	75,218	4	2,012,163	100

Source: US Department of Education (2013a)

In the State of New York, in program year 2010–11, nearly half (43%) of the 123,000 students in publicly funded adult education programs were Latino. Of the total, 5% were aged 16–18 and 21% were aged 19–24 (US Department of Education, 2013a, 2013b). This likely represents an under-count of students of high school age in adult education, as these numbers do not include private or volunteer programs that do not receive public funding. The latter numbers are not compiled.

This examination of the numbers of youth in programs designed for adults leads us to an obvious question: why are they not in high school? The next section explores their pathways into, out of and around high school.

Pushouts, Shutouts, Holdouts

When this research was conducted, the participants in this study were enrolled in adult education second-chance options. More than four-fifths (85%) of the young adults who took part in this study, or a total of 126, were between the ages of 14 and 20 upon arrival in the US (see Table 4.1, page 73), within the age at which they could legally attend high school in New York State.

Although they were eligible to attend high school in the US upon arrival, only slightly more than one-fifth of the sample (22%) had actually attended. Their time in high school was distributed across a wide range, with some attending as little as two months and some as long as three years. The remaining 78% had never attended US high school. Does this confirm the conventional wisdom that they had no interest in high school? The accounts below provide a more nuanced view of their non-participation.

An analysis of their enrollment in high school and their personal accounts presented in the following pages reveal three distinct patterns: (1) students who enrolled in high school and were later 'counseled out' by teachers and counselors – such students have been referred to in educational research as 'pushouts'; (2) immigrant young adults who arrived in the US with the intention of entering traditional high school but were unsuccess-ful – 'shutouts'; and (3) labor migrants who emigrated with no intentions of pursuing education, but re-entered school via adult education after years working in low-wage jobs – 'holdouts'. Each of these three groups is discussed in more detail below.

The first group, *pushouts*, are a familiar focus of analysis and discussion in educational research, starting as early as the 1970s during desegregation efforts in southern school districts (Arnez, 1978; Gotbaum & Advocates for Children, 2002; Orfield *et al.*, 2004). *Pushouts* are students who attended high school but were encouraged to leave to pursue an alternative path to high school certification or to abandon school due to reasons that include age, be-havioral issues, lack of credits and pregnancy. Controversy has surrounded the reasons for this phenomenon, and some scholars have suggested that increasing federal and state accountability standards can undermine those students who are most at risk and create incentives for schools to push out students such as English language learners, teen parents and students who work while attending school (Pallas *et al.*, 1987).

The second group, *shutouts*, are immigrant young adults of high school age who not only intended to enroll in high school upon arriving in the US, but made an effort to do so. Shutouts are unsuccessful in enrolling for a variety of reasons, discussed below. This phenomenon has apparently not yet been discussed in the educational research literature but is relevant to and understanding of immigrant school leavers, and I coined the term *shutout* to differentiate this group from students who have been forced out of school and those who have dropped out. As described below, students in this group never made a conscious choice to abandon their schooling permanently, but were simply unsuccessful at 'dropping in'.

The final group, *holdouts*, has possibly never been examined in educational research and policy literature that explores the realities of labor migrants and immigrant youth with incomplete high school. *Holdout* is a term that I coined to refer to labor migrants who immigrated with no intention of pursuing education, but re-entered education via adult education after years of working in low-wage jobs. With interrupted formal education, these young adults made a conscious effort to drop back into some sort of schooling, but rather than enrolling in high school they entered directly into adult and second-chance educational programs.

Neither *shutouts* nor *holdouts* have been discussed in educational research to date. In the pages that follow, young adults from each group discuss their experiences and reveal their views on their educational paths.

Pushouts

The phenomenon of *pushouts* is not a new one in relation to minority and low-income students (Arnez, 1978; Gotbaum & Advocates for Children, 2002; Orfield *et al.*, 2004). In New York City, students who complete ninth grade without having accumulated any credits toward graduation appear to be at greatest risk of dropping out (Meade *et al.*, 2009). Data from the City's 2007 graduation cohort indicate that some students, especially immigrant English language learners, simply disappear sometime between ninth and eleventh grade, leaving no clue as to their whereabouts. Of the 149 participants in my research sample, 22% indicated that upon immigrating to the US, they had enrolled in high school in New York City. Attendance ranged from one month to four years; each participant was officially discharged by school staff. Among those, eight had attended high school for less than one year and 20 had attended for between one and two years. Four had attended between two and four years of high school and two reported attending for more than four years. Several reported having passed one or more New York State Regents exams before being discharged. While most entered as ninth graders, some received course credit for academic work based on their foreign transcripts and were placed in tenth or eleventh grade upon arrival.

For students, the act of signing discharge papers creates an official record stating that the student left school by personal choice to pursue other options and was thus 'discharged'. The discharge pool is difficult to disaggregate, being a catchall for students who leave the district, those who move to parochial schools, those who leave due to pregnancy or family issues, as well as those counseled out to get a GED or attend a job training program. When students stop attending high school or are counseled out to attend a different program, it is nearly impossible to track them down to determine where they went and why, according to some high school principals with whom I spoke in this research. The practice has been documented at length in New York City and was the centerpiece of a major civil suit against the public school system (in the US District Court in 2003 (see Advocates for Children of New York, n.d.). Data gathered in New York City reveals that some schools have discharged more than half the number of students they graduated (Gotbaum & Advocates for Children, 2002).

Altagracia is a pushout. She approached me one evening when I was speaking with students at her GED program and told me the story of her exit from a New York City public high school. She arrived just shy of her 18th birthday from the Dominican Republic on a visa to reunite with family in New York City. In Santo Domingo, she had been one year away from completing her upper secondary diploma (baccalaureate). Once she arrived in New York City, relatives helped her enroll in a large public high school, where each day she had multiple periods of instruction in English as a second language, mostly focusing on grammar and pronunciation. In her regular classes – biology, American history, geometry – she sat in the back and watched the teacher lecture, struggling to grasp any words. She told me about her interaction with the school's counselor after her sophomore year:

> *Ella me llamó y me dijo que me faltaba tantos grados ... y que si yo no me iba del high school que ellos me iban a botar. Y ella me explicó que 'usted está muy grandecita para estar en high school'. Entonces, yo dije, tengo 19 años, yo firmo, y hago mi GED. Y firmé. Pero en ningún momento me dio la oportunidad de ... digo yo, de buscar un programa, o de que ellos mismos me buscaran un programa.*

> She [the counselor] called and said that I was missing so many credits ... and that if I didn't leave high school they would throw me out. And she explained 'you are a little too grown up to be in high school'. So I said, I am 19, I will sign, and I'll get my GED. And I signed. But she never gave me the chance, I mean, to find a program, or for them to find a program for me.

By signing discharge papers, Altagracia is documented in official records as having made a personal choice to leave school, though her account of what occurred suggests otherwise. She was not referred to a GED program or an alternative pathway to graduation. Nonetheless, many students' own accounts suggest that leaving school was by no means self-motivated. Rising enrollments of young adults in adult education programs suggest that the pushout phenomenon may be growing due to increased pressures on high schools to increase their four-year graduation rates. Across the US, it has become a documented practice for traditional high schools to encourage students to leave if they are older than average for their grade, have gained few credits toward graduation or will need more than four years to graduate; they are generally urged instead to pursue a high school equivalency diploma (GED) (Gotbaum & Advocates for Children, 2002; Jennings & Haimson, 2009; Orfield et al., 2004). In response to accountability pressures to raise test scores and graduation rates or risk closure, schools rid their rolls of under-performing students and English language learners who may lower overall test scores and four-year graduation rates because of skill gaps, low credit accumulation or limited English proficiency (Orfield et al., 2004).

Age and development play a role in the decision to leave. At 18, as legal adults, they are thrust into the position of making serious life choices on their own, often with limited information and an incomplete understanding of the consequences of their decision. At one adult education program that I visited, nearly half of the participants in a Spanish GED class approached me to ask questions about why they had been discharged from high school. Altagracia spoke about her decision to leave school:

> Hablé con mi papa y le dije, mira, la escuela me quiere botar, y el dice, 'bueno, tu eres mayor de edad, sabrás lo que es bueno'. Pero era que si yo no firmaba, de que yo iba de me propia cuenta, que me iban a botar. Es como dicen, el consentimiento de que me yo de mi propia voluntad. Como sin problemas. Pero en ningún momento me explicó los razones o me dijo ... bueno, como me explicaron los razones pero en ningún momento me dijeron, 'mira, hay otras opciones como night school o tal o tal lugar', nadie me dijo, 'bueno tu puedes ir a tal y tal lugar y pasar un año o más y graduar de high school'.
>
> I spoke to my father and told him 'look, they want to kick me out of school'. He says, 'Well, you are an adult, you know what is best'. But the thing was, if I didn't sign they were going to kick me out. I had to sign that I was leaving by choice. With no problems. But nobody ever explained why or said 'Look, there are options like night school or such and such a place and you go for a year or so and graduate high school'.

Literature on disconnected youth (O'Connor, 2008; Ouellette, 2006) cites widespread disengagement on the part of the over-age and under-credited. In contrast, participants in this study had actively sought out educational options and expressed concern about leaving school, worrying that incomplete education might compromise their futures. One said:

> *Bueno, me sentí como media incómoda, diciéndome, guau, como tú puedes dejar la escuela? Yo no puedo, ¿por qué hacen eso? Después, bueno, me sentí mal. ¿Qué va a decir la gente? Después, no [sucks teeth], me sentí mal, como que yo voy a ser una de esas analfabetas ... me voy a quedar analfabeta. ¿Qué va a ser de mi, entonces, después y todo?*
>
> Well, I felt sort of uncomfortable, and said to myself, wow, how can you drop out of school? I can't ... well, I felt bad, what are people going to say? Then, well, [sucks teeth], I felt bad, like I am going to be one of those illiterates... I am going to be illiterate. What will happen to me, afterwards and all?

When asked about their official status as dropouts, the pushouts disagreed:

> *No es que uno quiere dejar la escuela, es como que el sistema obliga a uno dejarla ... el sistema mismo me dijo, o te vas o te botamos.*
>
> It's not that you want to drop out of school; it's like the system forces you to drop out ... the system told me: leave or we will kick you out.

The experiences of the students who were forced out of traditional high school pathways raise serious questions about how federal accountability demands pressure schools to jettison students who may take longer than usual to graduate or who may cause the school graduation statistics to be less than optimal. With so much at stake, schools may be making the conscious choice to leave some of the most vulnerable students behind. For students who are enrolled and making less than optimal progress by standard accountability measures, this means being forced out of the system. For other students, this may mean not being allowed to enroll at all, as discussed in the next section.

Shutouts

The same accountability pressures that may lead schools to push out enrolled immigrant students could in turn serve as incentives for some schools to refuse admission to over-age and under-credited students, especially those who enter in the teenage years with limited English proficiency. New immigrant students, with limited knowledge of their rights within the public education system, are subject to the idiosyncrasies of the institutional process and, in many ways, the subjective decision of the intake and enrollment specialists who process their paperwork and answer their questions at the time of enrollment. Not every school has multilingual staff in its front office to answer the questions of immigrant students and their families, and nor is every individual who makes decisions about enrollment fluent in Spanish or other common immigrant languages.

Shutouts arrive in the US and consider the option of high school, but do not enroll, despite their original intentions. Young adults like Felipe and Rosa reported being told by relatives or friends that at 18 (or 17 or 19) they were too old for high school or did not have the documents required to enroll. Because they had limited information on the school system, they did not realize they had a right to a public education. Felipe never attempted to enroll in school, so vehement were the reports that it would not be possible. Neither Felipe nor his relatives had enough knowledge of the workings of the school system to question the misinformation provided by friends and neighbors.

> Y a mí y a mi hermano me dijeron que igual a que escuela van ustedes los rechazan porque les falta un papel.
> They told me and my brother that it doesn't matter what school you go to, they will turn you away because you don't have all the papers.

Rosa, who arrived from Ecuador on her own after a long journey, made it as far as the enrollment counter of the local high school, where she was told there were no seats for her and sent away. Not sure that she had a right to a seat in a high school class in the US, she was reluctant to question this information or to push for an alternative placement. She and other shutouts reported being told that they were over age for high school; not having school transcripts from the country of origin; and/or schools had no space (no había cupo). More than 10% of the young adults with whom I spoke in the study reported that although they were still under the age of 21 at the time, they were sent directly to a high school equivalency or adult education program from the district enrollment office when they attempted to enroll in high school. Others who were turned away from high school found their way into community-based GED programs and programs in English as a second language, generally through family members or friends. With family, friends and co-workers serving as de facto experts and liaisons to educational pathways, potential students are often misinformed by people who themselves have had little experience navigating public schools in the US. Although friends and family tell them that 'they won't take you without papers', this practice is not legal. Institutional barriers to high school access by immigrant students have been documented by the New York Civil Liberties Union; these include students being asked for immigration papers or social security numbers when arriving to register for school and being turned away when they are not able to present them (American Civil Liberties Union, 2010; Bernstein, 2010). The New York Civil Liberties

Union pressured the New York State Education Department to stop such enrollment practices, which, regardless of their intention, are illegal and discriminatory.

Some students reported me that when they went to enroll in a high school, they were told that there was no space in any program or 'there were no seats'. None of the students had been assessed for academic proficiency or English language proficiency before being referred out. Rosa, who at age 24 was just completing her GED in Spanish, wrote on her survey form for the present study:

> Yo me quejo porque cuando llegue no me aceptaron en la escuela y tenía 17 años y me dijeron que me fuera difícil porque hiba a cumplir los 18 en un pal de días más [sic].
> I would like to complain because when I came they did not accept me in school and I was 17 and they told me that it would be hard for me because I was going to turn 18 in a few days.

Such accounts raise serious questions about institutional practices that limit access to high school by immigrant students, who by state law are allowed to enroll up to age 21. As one participant reported:

> Mi idea era estudiar inglés para después ir al colegio, pero ya que era mayor de edad, no me cogieron para el colegio.
> My idea was to study English so I could go to college, but since I was over age [18] they did not accept me at high school.

As the institutional act of shutting out an applicant is rarely documented – here there are only the anecdotal accounts of the participants – this phenomenon is difficult to investigate. Although New York State regulations indicate that the public school system is to find a space for students under age 21, policy and practice do not always converge. Administrators who confirmed these reports would do so only off the record, as they feared repercussions for reporting these practices. At one site, a conversation during the research orientation with potential participants revealed that 12 participants of 25 had attempted to enroll in high school at age 17 or 18 and were told that there were no seats. Some participants were turned away, while others were referred directly to GED programs, not given the opportunity to choose a public high school from among their options. Contrary to what some research on disconnected youth suggests, failure to enroll in high school thus does not necessarily imply lack of interest (Golstein & Noguera, 2006; Way, 1998).

Holdouts

The third set of participants comprises labor migrants who arrived in the US with work as their primary goal and but who later shifted their priorities to include educational advancement as a priority. Many arrived as young as age 14 and entered the labor market, primarily in low-wage jobs like food service or construction (Rivera-Batiz, 2004; Smith, 2006). They differ from the two previous groups in that their original goals did not include gaining an education. In that sense, their choices confirm the conventional wisdom that labor migrants have little interest in education. One participant put it succinctly: '*Yo quería venir acá por como seis meses y regresar con mil dólares para ayudar allá*' ('I wanted to come here for six months and work and go home with $1,000 to help my family'). Holdouts also shed light on the reasons why they pursued work instead of schooling in the first place: Ramón is one of these holdouts. At 22, he had been in the US for nearly eight years, having arrived in his mid-teens from Mexico. After years of working in the food industry, he made a conscious choice to enter school, and was now on a path to college. Ramón put it this way:

> *Yo tenía mis problemas por el dinero que no alcanzaba, pues mis otros hermanos entraron a la primaria, y tenía que pagar los pasajes y el transporte, entonces, la material y el uniforme. Primero eché ganas, pero después me di cuenta, no, no, eso no va para más. Yo vi que hay jóvenes que estudian y trabajan, pero yo me dije, no, a lo mejor, yo me dedico a trabajar, y tal vez allí más adelante, tal vez voy a estudiar, pero eso era algo así, como muy remoto. Todavía no había cumplido los 15 años.*
>
> I had problems because there was not enough money. My other siblings entered primary school and you have to pay for uniforms and transportation and materials. At first I applied myself, but then I realized, no, no, this just isn't going to work. I saw young people who worked and went to school, but I said to myself, no, maybe I should work and then maybe later I can go back to school, but it was like something not very likely. I hadn't even turned 15.

Despite these intentions, many reported a shift in priorities after working in low-wage jobs, when they realized that the only pathway out of poverty was education. Several participants expressed dismay that their older co-workers who had been in the US for years were still working at menial, low-paying jobs, and they did not want to emulate them:

> *Yo no quiero tener 40 años y andar ambulante buscando un trabajo de construc-ción. No quiero hacer eso. Entonces en este país le dan a uno la oportunidad de estudiar y se tiene que hacerlo.*

I don't want to be 40 years old and walk around looking for a construction job. I don't want to do that. So, in this country you get the opportunity to study and you have to take it.

Fewer than 10% of the young people with whom I spoke could point to any family member, friend or co-worker who had been to college. One shared his watershed moment in talking to a co-worker at a restaurant when he arrived at work exhausted after a late-night party:

Le digo, ah, entonces, también estabas de fiesta, pues, y me dice, no lo que pasa es que estaba yo estudiando toda la noche. ¿Cómo así?, digo, ¿tú estudias arquitectura, no? Dice, pués, sí, está bien difícil ahora … tengo que trabajar para cubrir los gastos. Y me dice, y tú, que pasa, siempre de fiesta, ¿por qué no estudias? Entonces me puse a pensar, bueno, ella está estudiando y yo, no estoy haciendo nada, perdiendo el tiempo … y me di cuenta que sin la escuela, no se puede hacer nada.

And I told her, so, you were out partying last night too, and she tells me, no, I was up all night studying. How so, I ask her, aren't you studying architecture? And she said, yes, it's really hard right now … I have to work to cover my costs. And she asked me, and you? How come you are always partying, why not study? And I started thinking, well, she is studying and I am not doing anything, wasting my time … and I realized later, without school you can't do anything.

Research on immigrant youth reveals the potential of peers in helping recent immigrants navigate their new educational environment (Gaytan, 2010; Suárez-Orozco *et al.*, 2008). Despite working anywhere from 35 to 60 hours, mostly in food service and construction, these young adults juggle family, work and school to enter post-secondary schooling via the GED. All reported economic necessity and the work pipeline leading them to migrate north. Holdouts, despite interrupting their schooling as early as age 10, balked at the notion that they are dropouts, citing economic and institutional factors for their interrupted education: 'I never had the opportunity to realize my intellectual potential', said one.

Similar to both pushouts and shutouts, labor migrant re-entrants present a particular challenge for data collection. As laborers who return to school after years in low-wage jobs (and who often continue working), they are not to be found in the K-12 enrollment data. Those who re-enter education often take classes in community-based, church-run or informal volunteer-led programs that have limited systems to collect enrollment and achievement data. As a result, the unique scale, scope and attributes of this important subgroup are rendered invisible to researchers and policy-makers. What we do know about them is that, up until the point of re-entering the educational pipeline, they conform to a well-documented pattern: they leave school at a young age due to economic pressures to work and support family in their country of origin, and they then travel north to the US to work in low-skilled jobs, often without legal immigration status. At some point, however, holdouts shift their focus to see education as a key goal and an opportunity for advancement. By the time their focus shifts, many in this group have aged out of high school eligibility. For holdouts, as well as for pushouts and shutouts, adult and second-chance educational programs become an entry point for college and job training, as post-secondary education and training programs in the US require a high school credential for entry. Below is a discussion of high school equivalency and the role it plays for immigrant adults and young adults.

Support and Criticism of the GED

In reviews of the usefulness and effectiveness of the GED tests, some scholars and policy-makers laud the GED as an opportunity, a 'low-cost way to integrate hundreds of thousands of off-track individuals back into the mainstream of society, while at the same time providing an efficient means to meet its goals of equality of educational opportunity' (Smith, 2003: 414). For those with an incomplete high school education, the opportunity to gain access to post-secondary education, employment and training via an alternative path means that an incomplete high school career need not represent an educational endpoint. The GED and other alternative high school equivalency credentials provide concrete opportunities to re-enter education and training that are both accessible and affordable.

As much as it represents a viable opportunity, the GED is not without its detractors among scholars and policy-makers. Much of the critique addresses three central issues: (1) the impact of the GED on high school attendance and completion; (2) its effectiveness as an alternative to a four-year high school pathway; and (3) its usefulness in the labor market.

Does the existence of a GED credential lure students to drop out of high school? A visit to any GED preparation program will reveal young adults who left high school because they were bored and frustrated with the teachers, instruction, course content and their peers. Many of these impatient young adults perceive that seeking a GED diploma may be a faster and more efficient way of completing their high school education. As an accessible, low-cost option that is not particularly time-consuming, this deceptively 'easy' alternative to high school completion may in fact entice some students out of high school and into second-chance educational pathways. In contrast, students like Ramón, Altagracia, Felipe and their immigrant peers were not lured away from high school. In fact, many would have preferred to remain in a US high school – or in the case of the shutouts, to enroll in the first place – had they been given the choice or had they developed a more nuanced understanding of the system. The GED as a loophole that draws students out of high school may hold true for students in US high schools, but for the young adults in question here, this is decidedly not the issue. In the scholarly debate around the impact of the GED on earnings, some researchers suggest that if in fact the GED lures students out of high school and into a lower-earning pathway, then any positive impact of the GED is erased (Tyler, 2004; Tyler & Lofstrom, 2005). This claim stands in stark contrast to the reality that the earnings of immigrants with foreign (non-US) high school completion certificates are on average less than those of foreign-born US GED credential holders (Clark & Jaeger, 2006).

Perhaps more controversial in the case of immigrant young adults is the question: does the existence of an alternative to a four-year (or longer) high school pathway provide schools with a seemingly ethical alternative that justifies throwing ostensibly underperforming students overboard? Increasing pressure to adhere to and surpass federal accountability standards means that schools must attend to test scores and four-year graduation rates, two metrics that English language learners who enter as teens put at risk. If the GED is seen as a viable option for these students, why would traditional high schools accept them, rather than send them off to get a GED credential? Dorn presents a scathing critique of the GED:

> GED programs provide an excuse for schools and social critics to ignore the real disparities in educational opportunities between poor and wealthy. By suggesting that drop outs can easily replace four years of high school education with a test, proponents of the GED reduce the mission of secondary education, for poor children at least, to provide a piece of paper and little else. (Dorn, 1996: 141)

For schools that discharge their immigrant students (see Chapter 2, page 32), the GED is viewed as a completely acceptable alternative. Discharging a student with a referral to a GED preparation class is not only common but is viewed as an adequate service for students who may not be faring well in a traditional high school setting. Although reporting standards regarding discharged students grow increasingly more onerous for schools, a student with a GED is often counted as a high school graduate. In continued criticism of the GED as a 'solution' to the dropout problem, 'scholars point to the irony that the most "effective" dropout solution has, in fact, been largely worthless' (Dorn, 1996: 121).

Is the GED really 'largely worthless', as Dorn claims, and does it distract from any real adult second-chance education with substance? To what extent is it an adequate replacement for a four-year high school education, and to what extent is it equivalent? Some social scientists claim that the GED does not help older immigrant youth to gain the skills they need to function, but serves as a mere 'loophole' (García, 1999: 78) for both schools and students. Similarly, critics claim that rather than educating students to become full participants and engaged members of a democratic society, the GED frames a high school education as a way to certify discrete bits of knowledge (Fine, 1991). For both young adults and older adults seeking to continue their education, second-chance education that looks toward high school, an educational pathway designed for adolescents and teens, may in fact be a step backward. New GED tests and their counterparts like New York State's TASC test are aligned to new educational standards that aim to prepare students more adequately for college and the workforce. Nonetheless, there are still criticisms of the direction that public education has taken, becoming increasingly driven by test results and teacher evaluation, a focus that has undermined many public programs and weakened many schools (Karp, 2013).

What do students actually know once they have obtained such an alternative credential? Is it in fact a reflection of a lower level of knowledge and skills than is indicated by a high school diploma? Much of the ongoing scholarly debate revolves around the impact and effects of GED completion, as well as the effectiveness of the GED certificate on the route to post-secondary access and completion (Murnane et al., 2000; Tyler & Lofstrom, 2005, 2009). The largest study of GED recipients to date concluded that '[th]e effectiveness of GED acquisition as a route into post-secondary education is a woefully understudied area' (Tyler & Lofstrom, 2009: 2). What is known from existing data on the skill levels and developmental needs of entering college freshmen in the US is that, regardless of whether students begin post-secondary education having completed a GED credential or a regular high school pathway, a large portion of high school graduates need extensive remediation in the first years of college, especially in community college settings, where the bulk of low-income immigrant students and first-generation college-goers end up (Adelman, 1998; City University of New York, 2008a, 2008b). Yet, the simple fact of having completed a GED credential does not doom a college student to failure. For example, at the City University of New York, GED holders who stay on past the first two semesters academically outperform high school graduates (City University of New York, 2008a). An ongoing longitudinal study of post-secondary outcomes of GED credential holders (Patterson et al., 2010) reveals that more than 70% of GED recipients who had the goal of attending college actually enrolled, and more than two-thirds of those who enrolled in post-secondary pathways attended for at least two semesters, but very few (slightly less than 12%) graduated within six years.

Given the importance that post-secondary education plays in increasing earning potential and the fact that so many GED holders go on to pursue at least some post-secondary education, how do GED holders fare in life as compared with high school graduates and high school dropouts? Studies of earning potential of GED holders leave a significant gap, as they do not include foreign-born or non-English-language test takers (Tyler & Lofstrom, 2005, 2009). What is known, however, is that GED completers earn more in both actual and relative terms than high school dropouts and are much more employable (Tyler *et al.*, 2000). However, this increase in earnings comes slowly over time and, as GED scholar As Tyler explains:

> These earnings figures underscore two important facts. The first is that individuals lacking a regular high school diploma generally have very low average earnings, in part because of low employment rates. The second fact is that even if the high economic returns estimated in this paper represent the causal impact of the GED, acquisition of this creden- tial can only partially ameliorate the harsh economic realities associated with being a dropout in this country. (Tyler, 2004: 596)

Economic mobility is perhaps why so many immigrant dropouts seek entry into GED programs. For immigrants, having the recognized credential of the GED 'seems to lead to substantially higher wages than a traditional high school diploma earned outside the US, and for men and women these results are statistically significant' (Clark & Jaeger, 2006: 4).

How do new immigrant young adults learn about the existence of the GED? The GED has no equivalent in Mexico, Central or South America, so it is not clear how immigrants who were not referred to GED preparation programs from their high schools end up learning about the GED option and even less clear what value they place upon it. What is known, however, is that for immigrant young adults who are not *able* to attend high school in the US – whether institutional barriers prevent them from enrolling or completing or because they are too old to attend – the GED and alternative high school diploma routes open up possibilities that would otherwise not exist for them.

If the GED is a viable pathway, where does it lead for immigrants who have no high school credential from their country of origin and no oppor- tunity to complete high school in the US? Economic pressures on immigrant young adults are great when family members depend upon remittances sent from abroad (Somerville *et al.*, 2008). Most students report that needing to work while attending college posed the greatest challenge to completing a degree (City University of New York, 2008a; Fry, 2002; Johnson *et al.*, 2009). The option to stay in traditional high school and complete a diploma is perhaps ideal, but it is not always a viable one for immigrant students who face the need to earn money together with the challenges of acculturation demands and schools' often low expectations and quality. Immigrant youth may often be led to interrupt their schooling by a combination of the in- stitutional barriers discussed here and family economic pressures (Fuligni, 2007; Martinez, 2009; Oropesa & Landale, 2009).

Discussion and Implications

Despite their differences, the three groups discussed in this chapter – *pushouts*, *holdouts* and *shutouts* – have been generally categorized in research and policy literature within the monolithic category of *dropouts*. Neither *shutouts* – students eligible to enroll in high school but barred from entering – nor *holdouts* – labor migrants who return to school via adult education after years in low wage jobs – have received any attention in research. Evidence presented here suggests that assigning these diverse young people with interrupted schooling to the vague and overly simplistic single category of *dropout* not only serves to limit an understanding of their realities and educational pathways, but also obscures their engagement with schooling and their long-term goals, obfuscating an array of institutional factors that force them out of school prior to migration as well as after they arrive in the US.

The evidence and arguments presented in this chapter contribute to policy discourse on immigrant students and highlight issues (including access to schooling) and policies that impact graduation rates. The results presented here provide perspectives on the educational experiences of immigrant students identified as 'status dropouts' (see Chapter 2, pages 30–32), reveal their reasons for interrupting their schooling and provide a nuanced understanding of their experiences in the US educational system.

The experiences of the young adults whose stories are presented in this chapter serve to underscore the importance of examining how institutional barriers pose particular challenges for students who know little about their rights within the public educational system. In addition, their experiences highlight the ways in which rising educational accountability standards, with the goal of improving student learning, incentivize the abandonment of a whole sector of students, rather than creating an urgency to serve them better. The experiences of the immigrant young adults shared in this chapter underscore the need to re-examine current federal educational policy that focuses on rewards and penalties based exclusively on school performance, with little real incentive to serve those students most in need of academic and social support. Finally, a broader understanding of the constraints that push students out of school suggests a need to re-examine the blanket definition of *dropout* for students who leave high school before completion, to more fully understand the factors that lead them to interrupt their schooling.

Three key findings emerge from data presented in this chapter. First, the term 'dropout' masks issues of equity and access that lead to school interruption for immigrants not only before arriving in the US, but also once they arrive and seek entry into high school. Second, the failure of immigrant young adults to enroll in high school must be understood in the context of economic and institutional barriers and not viewed as individual whims or choices. Third, the education and career development of immigrants with incomplete secondary education is an issue of human capital development, and their success or failure has far-reaching implications for their participation in their communities and in the labor force.

Data presented here suggest that the category of 'dropout' obscures a complete understanding of immigrant learners, overshadowing their engagement with schooling, their aspirations and, perhaps most importantly, structural and institutional barriers that may hinder the opportunity for a high school diploma, as well as access to the pipeline toward college and career. Despite federal and state budget cuts, recent national initiatives emphasize universal high school completion and post-secondary access:

> There is widespread agreement among policymakers, the business community, and educational leaders that the US must raise the educational achievement of its young population. Simply stated, in a 21st century labor market, all high school students must graduate with the knowledge and skills needed to succeed in some form of postsecondary education. (Kirst & Venezia, 2006)

Despite the sweeping emphasis in this and similar reports on universal access and success, the bulk of public policy initiatives aimed at improving post-secondary readiness focus only on the transition from high school to college. This ignores the growing and significant population of students who, as described in this chapter, are jettisoned from high school pathways and are left to catch up via second-chance alternative credentials such as the GED.

Continuing to overlook this growing immigrant subgroup would be to dismiss the unrealized potential of a rising generation who have visibly embraced the US ideal that education is the road to success. It is critical that public policy address the trajectories of immigrant status dropouts such as those in this study, not only to examine institutional constraints that shut or push them out of high schools in the US, but also to examine viable opportunities for educational advancement and success. A focus exclusively on their exit from schooling must be a means to identify possible re-entry points that could lead to their educational success.

The literature on Latino education, dropouts and disconnected youth is undergirded with a subtle cultural deficit theory that perpetuates the idea that Latinos lack educational aspirations. The failure to look more closely at the population of status dropouts to examine barriers to participation in education further perpetuates this deficit model. Further research on this topic must attend to available educational pathways for this group and barriers such as academic skill and knowledge gaps, lack of social capital and knowledge of educational systems, remediation, post-secondary transition planning, and availability of professional and peer support. Research on adult populations reveals that 'stopping out' is a decision that learners make based on life circumstances and often represents a temporary interruption in schooling, rather than a permanent one (Belzer, 1998; Quigley & Uhland, 2000).

The failure to look more closely at the population of dropouts to examine barriers to participation in education perpetuates the idea that Latinos lack educational aspirations. In remedying these concerns, school officials will need to address the barriers noted above. In addition, schools will need to receive the necessary resources to support the success of students who arrive as teens with multiple educational needs.

Saddled with the lowest high school graduation and college completion rates, this growing population of young adult immigrants often relies on adult education providers and policy-makers to understand the complexities of their situations and provide viable solutions. Existing scholarly work indicates that these realities of immigrant youth are not unique to New York City, to large urban areas or to the US itself. In this time of globalization, an understanding of the aspirations and experiences of immigrants who increasingly seek alternative pathways to improve their situation that can inform future adult education research, policy and practice for all immigrant students, in whatever country. Attention to the pathways and needs of this growing population is relevant not only for the youth themselves, but for the host society as well, and will provide insight into these issues and is relevant for immigrant education in other contexts. It is also of the utmost important for adult education providers and policy-makers to fully explore the complexities of the populations they serve, with the goal of designing programs and interventions to best meet their needs. A discussion of such policies and interventions follows in the next two chapters.

Summary

In this chapter, we met three groups of students who took very different paths related to high school once they arrived in the US. The chapter also sheds light on what can happen to students who seek to enter the educational pipeline in the US and discusses how a federal focus on school accountability impacts the willingness of schools to serve immigrant students. With more understanding of why certain immigrant young adults are not enrolled in high school in the US, and understanding the adult education pathways that are available to them as an alternative to high school, the next chapter explores their skills and contextual knowledge as they navigate the realms of adult basic education and post-secondary schooling.

The chapter also examined whether the GED is a viable alternative pathway for immigrant young adults who have been left behind by traditional high schools. In addition to the question of its inherent value in terms of knowledge and certifiable skills, young adult immigrants face the additional dilemma of knowing where, how and what to do with the GED credential once they have obtained it, as their familiarity with the US educational system is shaky at best, riddled with misperceptions, misinformation and lacking information at worst.

The US Department of Education's 2010 *Blueprint for Reform* lists as its top priority 'Every student should graduate from high school ready for college and a career, regardless of income, race, ethnic or language background' (US Department of Education, 2010b). Though the focus of current educational efforts in the US is high standards and proficiency in English and math for 100% of students, many students find themselves shut out or pushed out of schools because their very existence in the institution threatens the unrealistic goals set for schools (Fine, 1991; Noguera, 2003). The White House's 'Education for America' initiative seeks to generate 5 million new college graduates by 2020. Remediation is a key concern in this agenda, and although the *percentage* of remedial students among new college entrants has decreased, the *number* of remedial students has increased (Forderaro, 2010). Among those entering college in need of remediation because of shaky academic skills are students like Victor and Altagracia. Chapter 6 will explore precisely how prepared these young adults are for their continued education, examining their skills, choices and opportunities as they seek to meet their educational goals.

Additional resources

2014 GED Test, http://www.gedtestingservice.com/educators/2014test
New York State Test Assessing Secondary Completion (TASC): http://www.acces.nysed.gov/ged/

Films

I Learn America, http://ilearnamerica.com/i-learn-america/
Living Undocumented, http://www.livingundocumented.com/
Unsockumented, https://www.youtube.com/watch?v=uk9awjmYa7s

6 Hard and Soft Skills: Academic Skills, English and Social Capital Among Migrant Youth

Introduction

Now that he is enrolled in an adult education class, learning English, Victor wants to be a lawyer or 'to do something where I help people'. His experience with the US Immigration and Customs Enforcement (ICE) while being detained crossing the border exposed him to legal aid lawyers, whom he admired and to whom he is grateful. Elena has settled on a two-year degree to begin, but would like to be a teacher or social worker. Once he was settled in New York City, Ramón bought his first computer and would like to study software design or computer programming.

Their perceptions, visions and dreams of what they will do professionally are complicated by a number of factors. First, despite years of working and surviving in nearly adult roles, facing difficult economic decisions and struggling in the labor market, navigating and acclimatizing to a new country, they are still emergent English learners. In the US, with few exceptions, professional training and academic studies require a good command of English. Second, they come to their 'second chance' learning context with a wide range of skills and academic background knowledge, as some have attended only a few years of formal schooling and some have nearly completed high school. Finally, their knowledge of the US educational system – in particular secondary education and workforce development – is shaky at best. As we learned in Chapter 5, their peers and family are not always the best sources of information. How do these three factors impact their opportunities and what can we learn about their unique needs?

In addition to content knowledge and language proficiency, there is recent recognition among researchers that student success is also influenced greatly by strong networks of peers, as well as strong connections to institutional networks of resources and support (Gaytan, 2010; Stanton-Salazar, 1997, 2001). In addition, 'contextual knowledge' of institutional structures and how educational systems function, of where to find academic support, and of how to interact with instructors is also key to ensuring that students are not only academically prepared, but can navigate the school system and make sound decisions along their educational pathways (Conley, 2007; García, 1999).

This chapter explores the complex factors that may make or break a student's educational progress. These include language and academic skills, contextual knowledge, and social networks and relationships. The chapter examines how these factors impact immigrant students who enter US educational settings as young adults with interrupted education from their countries of origin and discusses some key considerations for the design of educational programs for this population. Central to this chapter is the fact that the young people in this study have not completed high school. However, they have made conscious decisions to sign up to educational programs with the goal of attaining upward mobility, although these programs may not be designed to meet their needs. This chapter seeks to unravel the complex interplay of hard and soft skills and knowledge that must be attended to in order to ensure that programs are effective. How do those skills manifest themselves in the lives of our young immigrant adults?

Language and Academic Skills in Context

While completing her survey for this research study, Altagracia asked me to help her calculate how many hours per week she worked. I suggested that she try to multiply the number of days she worked each week by the number of hours she worked per day. She grappled with this calculation (9 hours a day for 6 days a week: 9×6) and finally double-checked on her phone, saying that math was not her strong suit. I was struck by how she seemed to struggle to formulate handwritten answers even in Spanish and how many of her responses were rife with misspellings. Although she had come to the US barely one year shy of completing high school, I wondered how her skills might represent the quality of her prior schooling and how both might impact her ability to attain her goals in the US.

Altagracia is but one among many young adult immigrants who come to the US and seek entry into an educational pipeline. This snapshot from her experience underscores an important consideration when designing programs and interventions for immigrant young adults: number of years of prior schooling matter, but alone they do not provide significant insights into an individual's skills and the potential challenges that lie ahead in seeking to re-enter and continue schooling in the US. Number of years of schooling completed prior to migration cannot provide a flawless indication of skills and need for academic support; nor do they reveal the quality of schooling completed, an individual's literacy level in the native language

(Spanish), English proficiency, nor the academic content knowledge that has been mastered. A group of students who have completed the eighth grade in the US will have a broad range of reading, writing and academic skills, from barely proficient to far beyond grade level.

The majority of immigrant population growth between 2000 and 2020 is projected to be accounted for by individuals with the lowest levels of education (Aud *et al.*, 2011; Migration Policy Institute, 2008). In the US, policy discussions focusing on academic readiness and success focus on education solely in English as the route to academic proficiency. Latino immigrants seeking to transition to college face the double challenge of basic skills and academic content: they must develop both conversational and academic English and acquire academic skills and content knowledge. For immigrants who have re-entered high school or who are now attending adult education programs after having interrupted their schooling, developing academic literacy can be complicated by limited literacy skills in their native language alongside often shaky – and sometimes non-existent – 'classroom skills' (Advocates for Children, 2010; García, 1999; Menken, 2008). These students face challenges not unlike those of Generation 1.5 students, who often are not well versed in the complexities of academic writing and often struggle for years as long-term English language learners (Harklau, 2003; Menken *et al.*, 2012; Oudenhoven, 2006; Thonus, 2003).

For immigrant students who enter US schools as newcomers, there is a two-fold challenge on the educational road ahead. At the same time that English-proficient students are grappling with new and complex academic content in language, arts, math, history and science, immigrant English language learners are additionally struggling to learn sufficient English quickly enough for them to access these academic subjects and pass exams to graduate. This is precisely why transitional bilingual programs were designed to help newcomer students with limited English proficiency keep up with academic subjects while they are in the process of learning academic English. New immigrant English language learners are tackling new academic content that is conceptually challenging even for native speakers of English (history, algebra, chemistry, biology, physics, literature). In addition, they are pushed to become proficient enough in English to be able to write complex essays and analyze text at a very high academic level in order to pass state assessments and be able to graduate from high school in four years. What do we know about what they need to know and are able to do in each of these areas?

English Language Proficiency

Although we can point to a few examples of immigrant entrepreneurs who achieved financial success in the US without speaking English, proficiency in English is undeniably a marketable skill that promotes success in US society. English language ability has been correlated with academic success, higher wages and increased opportunities for advancement in the workforce (Hakimzadeh & Cohn, 2007). Lack of English proficiency has been linked to social isolation, depressed wages and limited opportunities for advancement.

Traditional high school models for new immigrant youth separate discipline-specific classes (e.g. math, science, social studies) from classes designed to teach English. This presents a challenge for students and teachers alike: complex subject area content that even native speakers of English find difficult is made doubly inaccessible for English language learners (ELLs) due to the material itself combined with the complexity of the academic language needed to master the subject. It is one thing to explain to a stranger how to get from Elmhurst Queens to Coney Island on the subway but another altogether to explain the complex processes of cell mitosis, homeostasis or how to find the roots of a quadratic equation.

The impact of these double-duty academic and linguistic challenges for new immigrants at the high school level is reflected clearly in the high school graduation rates for ELLs. While in 2013 the graduation rate for non-ELLs in New York State was about 75%, for ELLs it was nearly half that, at 40% (New York State Education Department, 2013a, 2013b). Nearly two-thirds of students who entered ninth grade as ELLs never made it to graduation in four years (Figure 6.1).

One of the major barriers to the acquisition of English skills that are needed to graduate from high school has been a phenomenon known as

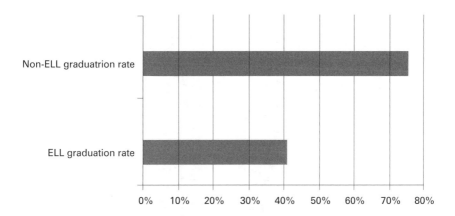

Figure 6.1 Graduation rates of English language learners compared with those of non-English language learners, New York, 2013
Source: New York State Education Department (2013a, 2013b)

'linguistic isolation'. This challenge is one faced by Latino immigrants in numbers higher than the national average for all immigrant groups. A household is 'linguistically isolated' if none of the individuals aged 14 and over are proficient in English. In New York State, 28% of all Spanish-speaking households were linguistically isolated in 2011, more than three times more than the national average of 8.1%. (Migration Policy Institute, n.d.). The proportion of individuals over the age of five in New York State who speak English 'less than very well' is nearly 50% on average across all groups, but more than 70% among individuals for whom Spanish is the first language.

Language skills among new immigrants have been studied at length. The number of individuals in the US who report that they do not speak English well or at all grew from almost 14 million in the 1990 Census to over 21 million in the 2000 Census. Of adults with limited English proficiency (LEP), 50% report having nine or fewer years of education and 64% have less than a high school degree; only 18% have any post-secondary education (Pandya *et al.*, 2011).

Among the young adults with whom I spoke in my research, the majority (58.0%) reported that they knew only 'a little' English, and nearly one-third (31.5%) self-assessed their knowledge of English as merely conversational (Figure 6.2). For young people like Ramón in his dishwashing job and Alta-gracia, helping out at the deli in her predominantly Latino neighborhood, this may suffice, but it does not open doors to employment or academic success. Very few of the young people were on the extremes – few (only 4.3%) said their English skills were 'very good', while only 4.0% reported knowing no English at all. Figure 6.2 is a graphical representation of their

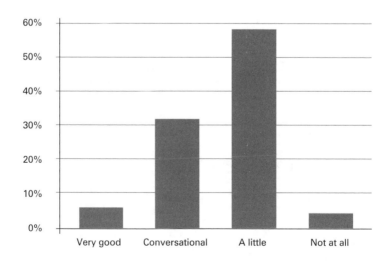

Figure 6.2 Participants' self-reported English proficiency

self-assessed English skills. These data are similar to data collected about the general foreign-born population of Latinos in the US, of whom 23% say that they speak English 'very well' and 12% 'pretty well' (Hakimzadeh & Cohn, 2007).

Success in college demands a high level of academic English, which represents a challenge even for some native speakers of English who have completed 12 years of schooling in the US. Nationally, 40% of students who enter college need remedial or developmental courses to help them gain academic skills, study habits, reading, writing and math skills at a level required of a college freshman (Conley, 2007). What is the impact of remediation? Research on college retention and completion rates has revealed that students entering college in need of developmental coursework to help them become 'college ready' are at higher risk of leaving school or not completing a degree, and that remediation lengthens the time needed to obtain the degree, increases costs on already financially strapped students and hastens dropout (Adelman, 2006; Conley, 2007).

The struggle to develop proficiency in English also takes an emotional toll. Altagracia, Ramón, Elena, Victor and their peers discussed many instances of humiliation when they learned that co-workers were talking about them in English or when clients at restaurants insulted them in English but they did not fully understand and felt unable to respond adequately. Several report feeling motivated to learn English 'para que no me humillen más' ('so they never humiliate me like that again'). Latinos in the US overwhelmingly indicate that they believe English proficiency is one of the most important factors in their success and, correspondingly, that failure to be proficient in English is a major source of discrimination against them (Hakimzadeh & Cohn, 2007).

There is no question that English proficiency – and particularly academic English development – is key to students' success and ability to make headway through schooling to reach their goals. Yet English proficiency is only one part of a complex web of skills. The next section will provide some insight into other skill areas that make a difference for immigrant young adults.

Foundational Knowledge and Skills in the First Language

Conventional wisdom (not based on research in language acquisition) would have us believe (erroneously) that languages are separate – a person learns languages best sequentially and this information is stored in different chambers in the brain. Research has, though, demonstrated the cognitive advantages of multilingualism and the synergistic relationship between the languages spoken by people who are multilingual (García, 1999, 2012;

Thomas & Collier, 2003); it has also demonstrated that one key to the effective acquisition of a second language is a strong academic foundation in the primary language (Cummins, 2009; Slavin & Cheung, 2005).

What does this relationship look like in reality? It means that immigrants who arrive in the US with high levels of formal education, whether as adolescents or as adults, have an advantage in learning English. For immigrant students whose first language is other than English, prior education and formal academic skills in the native language correlate strongly with the development of the academic English proficiency necessary for college success (Burt & Peyton, 2003; Cummins, 2009; Ramirez *et al.*, 1991; Thomas & Collier, 2003). After entering a class to learn English, the process of second language acquisition depends very much on an individual's background.

Students placed on courses in English as a second language (ESL) are a diverse group. Those with academic skills from their home countries tend to progress consistently through ESL and gain academic credits. However, a significant cohort of students, most notably those with interrupted schooling and emergent literacy, are prone to linger in ESL classes while demonstrating slow progress, often as a result of ineffective program designs that fail to address their academic and literacy needs nor leverage opportunities to use their home language.

Research in K-12 contexts has provided solid evidence of the important link between literacy skills and academic proficiency in the native language and English language acquisition (Cummins, 1991; Ramirez *et al.*, 1991; Thomas & Collier, 2003). This phenomenon can been seen among the graduates of New York City public high schools, where valedictorians of many city schools are students who entered high school or middle school as new immigrants with high levels of academic proficiency in their first language. These students not only acquired English rapidly but even outperformed their native English-speaking peers academically in English (Alvarez, 2009). Similar evidence has been provided by two key longitudinal studies contrasting approaches to English language development (Ramirez *et al.*, 1991; Thomas & Collier, 2003).

For young adults who have completed only a few years of school, re-entering a classroom setting presents them with the challenge of learning how to be in a classroom as well as developing literacy skills (and overcoming the tremendous social stigma of being illiterate). Below are some examples that lend clues to the way in which literacy skills may present a basic challenge for young adults as they seek to re-enter an educational pipeline.

Like Altagracia, some participants in my research reported having completed more than eight years of formal schooling before entering the US, but it is difficult to draw any conclusions about their academic strengths without conducting a formal assessment of skills. Conversations with their teachers and the staff in the programs they attended revealed that some students may have reported more years of education than they actually had

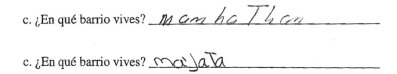

c. ¿En qué barrio vives? _M am ha T h an_____

c. ¿En qué barrio vives? _maJaa_____

Figure 6.3 Two writing samples from different study participants responding to the question (in Spanish, left) 'What neighborhood do you live in?'

completed simply due to embarrassment or for fear of not qualifying for a program. Some, like Altagracia, struggle with math. Some, like Ramón, read slowly, vocalizing the words while holding a pen under each word to keep their place. Despite having lived in New York City for five years or more, some, like Victor, struggled to write the name of the borough or neighborhood in which they lived, as illustrated in Figure 6.3.

The question asks 'What neighborhood do you live in?' In both cases the answer should read 'Manhattan'. The Spanish approximations of the word in Figure 6.2 suggest that students struggle with letter–sound correspondence in English, which is not surprising for Spanish speakers new to the English language (Kalmar, 2001). In addition, the writing in the samples strays from orthographic conventions in multiple ways. In addition to using no upper-case letters at the beginning of the proper name, the both samples have an upper-case letter ('T') in the middle of the word, a characteristic common of beginning writers (Colombi, 2002; Weaver, 1998). In addition, both the size and shape of letter formation suggests a very beginning writer (mis-formed 'J', inconsistent shapes among letters on the line, different spacing between letters, writing both above and below the line). The sample in Figure 6.4 demonstrates somewhat more control of letters, but also reflects inconsistencies characteristic of beginning writers.

The sample above, in response to the question 'How has attending school here helped you?', reads literally 'Very good Ilikeit', with no punctuation. The last two words in the Spanish sentence are connected rather than separated as is the convention in the Spanish phrase 'me gusta'. The sentence begins with a lowercase letter, omits the period and reveals a common Spanish orthographic error of switching the letter 'v' for 'b', as they are the same phoneme in Spanish but two different letters (Colombi, 2002).

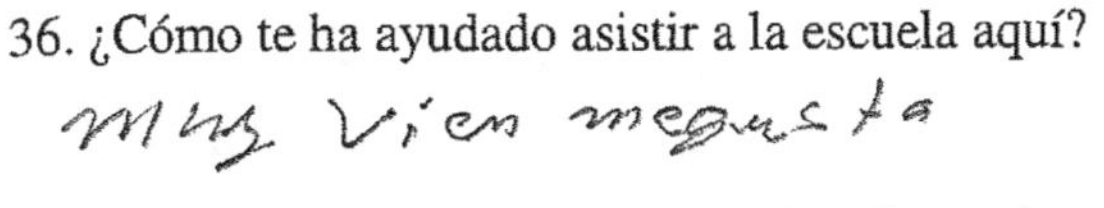

36. ¿Cómo te ha ayudado asistir a la escuela aquí?

M uy Vien megusta

Figure 6.4 A writing sample from a study participant responding to the question (in Spanish, above) 'How has attending school here helped you?'

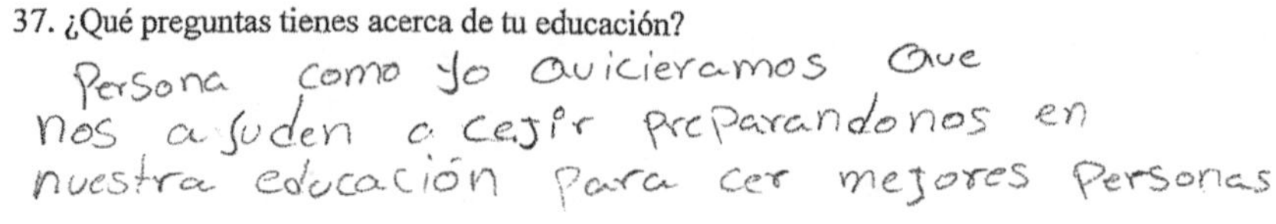

37. ¿Qué preguntas tienes acerca de tu educación?

Persona como Yo Quicieramos Que nos ajuden a cejir preparandonos en nuestra educación para cer mejores personas

Figure 6.5 A writing sample from a study participant responding to the survey prompt 'Other comments'

The sample presented in Figure 6.5 is a participant's comment in response to the survey prompt 'Other comments'. It translates as 'Person like me would like to get help to continue studying in our education to be better people'. An upper-case 'P' starts the sentence, as is the convention but, as in Figure 6.3, there is a mix of upper- and lower-case letters throughout the excerpt, along with several misspellings, and no period at the end of the sentence. The formation of the letters 'y' and 'q' suggest a beginning writer (Colombi, 2002).

While these few writing samples provide some hints regarding possible gaps in skills, the related comments illuminate feelings about the challenge of returning to school after a long interruption. Despite their extensive life experience and obvious survival skills as immigrants navigating a new culture and context, entering a classroom with very few years of schooling is fraught with feelings of fear, embarrassment and sometimes shame. Rosa put it succinctly when she said: 'Me daba pena que no sabía nada, que no había ido a la escuela' ('I didn't know anything, since I had never been to school'). Below, Ramón shares his feelings of surprise and frustration when faced in a high school equivalency preparation class with what he perceived as his own limited skills:

> *El maestro me dice, ven acá, dime las tablas, dime las tablas de multiplicación y yo digo, baaah, no, no puedo eso. Y nos pusimos a estudiar las tablas, y veo este chavo ya bien avanzado y digo, ¿cómo así? ¿Cómo es que él puede y yo no puedo?*
> The teacher says, come here, recite your multiplication tables for me, recite the multiplication tables and I say, baaaah, no, I can't do that. And we got to studying the multiplication tables and I see this guy who was already way ahead and I say to myself, how is that? How come he can do it and I can't?

These are but brief glimpses into feelings about returning to school for young adults who have been pushed out or shut out of a linear educational trajectory. Extensive scholarship in adult education illuminates the tangible affective challenges faced by young adults with emergent literacy skills who make the choice to return to the classroom (Comings et al., 2000; Fingeret, 1994; Lukes, 2009; Mezirow; 1974). This is compounded by the low status that is given to the first languages of English language learners, who are often treated as deficient in programs designed to teach them English, rather than building upon their existing linguistic knowledge (Gándara & Contreras, 2014; García et al., 2008; Lukes, 2009; Reyes, 2011; Wiley & Lukes, 1996).

Research on immigrant education could benefit greatly from formal assessments of literacy, numeracy and content knowledge. The evidence presented here is preliminary, yet it provides important clues as to participants' specific academic challenges, which in turn impact their progress toward their goals. It also underscores the important role of native language assessment for programs serving older youth and young adults, as the number of years of schooling is not itself a valid measure of knowledge and skills, and assessments given in English to students with varying degrees of English language proficiency do not accurately assess background knowledge. These young adults have traveled alone and negotiated various institutions to make a living and find housing and so on. Yet some, like Ramón, cannot explain the orbit of the planets or name the four cardinal directions. The academic issues illustrated here have serious implications for educational program design for this population.

Social Capital and Contextual Knowledge

Many of us have heard of – or know personally – brilliant students with great potential who never made it to college. Some did not view themselves as 'college material', while others were reluctant to apply, or came from families in which no one had ever attended college. Academic skills and English proficiency are not all that it takes to make the leap from high school to college. Scholarship on transitions to post-secondary education divides the field of 'college readiness' skills into multiple dimensions (Conley, 2007) that go beyond academic skills, behaviors and content knowledge to include cognitive abilities (metacognition, analysis, reasoning) and *contextual knowledge* (how, where and when to apply to college, get financial aid, etc.). Colleges and universities now pay a great deal of attention to 'first-generation college students' – those who are the first person in their family to go to college. Plenty of students with great potential miss the opportunity to attend college not due to poor grades, but because they have limited knowledge of the application and admissions process, financial landscape, and the culture and expectations of post-secondary education in the US. Not unlike first-generation college students, young adult immigrants with interrupted high school may have limited or erroneous knowledge and understanding of schooling options, opportunities and pathways that might lead them in the direction in which they hope to go.

As presented in Chapter 4, participants in this study articulated a range of educational goals, from completing their high school equivalency diplomas to finishing graduate or professional degrees. The attainment of any of these goals requires a minimum of academic literacy and content knowledge, but also vast amounts of contextual knowledge of the educational pathways. What exactly does a person need to know to navigate the new terrain of college?

Paths to Post-Secondary Education

In his work on understanding the complexities of college readiness, Conley (2007) uses the term *contextual knowledge* to mean the understanding of the complex landscape of post-secondary education (credits and their value, financial aid, guidance, etc.) and ability to navigate it successfully. The young people with whom I spoke in this study had little prior exposure to conversations about college in general, and few conversations with individuals who had successfully navigated the college transition process. As a result, their perceptions about the details of both the transition to college and the path through college toward a career were often fraught with inaccuracies and riddled with gaps.

Participants' discussions about goals were often linear. When asked about the paths to reach their goals, they typically articulated a sequence of steps: first take the high school equivalency diploma test (in Spanish), then learn English, then enroll in university,[1] then find a job related to the chosen career. Subsequent milestones included buying a house for a parent, getting married and having a family. In focus groups, they worked in teams to create images that reflected their educational and career goals, milestones on their educational paths, and obstacles to reach those goals (see Appendix, pages 182–185). Although goals were very similar across groups, they all reflected a very general sense of 'next steps' in broad strokes, and participants provided scant detail, suggesting that they knew little about the specifics of post-secondary education and career preparation.

Despite relatively low levels of self-reported English proficiency, when asked to name challenges in reaching educational goals, barely one-fifth of the young people with whom I spoke identified English proficiency as a primary obstacle. For the most part, English was something you develop as one step in the path to realizing your goals, not a process lasting many years. They may well have had a somewhat unrealistic assessment of the time it is likely to take to develop the academic proficiency in English required to be successful in a post-secondary environment.

When given the opportunity to pose questions about their educational paths, Altagracia, Victor, Rosa and others demonstrated significant gaps in knowledge about eligibility for college, cost, scholarships, different types of degrees, length of time and requirements to complete a degree, as well as the location of post-secondary institutions ('Where is CUNY?' was a common question). Their peers had general concerns such as '*¿Cómo qué tiempo voy a tomar para hacer la universidad?*' ('About how much time will I take to do the university?'). Other questions illuminated the fact that they had a pathway in mind, but not a clear idea of it, as in the question '*¿Cómo qué tiempo necesito para ser abogado profesional?*' ('About how much time will it take to be a professional lawyer?'). For a student who attends a high school equivalency program in Spanish and has developed some initial proficiency in English, the question reflects a very long-term goal that necessitates both English language proficiency and a high level of academic ability.

Others had questions about paths, including, '*¿Cuánto tiempo dura una carrera de sipcología?*' (How much time is a sychology [*sic*] course of study?') and '*¿A quién debo acercarme para obtener información acerca de una universidad, de acuerdo a nuestros recursos económicos?*' ('Who can I ask to get information about a university based on my economic resources?'). A number of the young adults indicated that among their obstacles was limited knowledge about college. Financial constraints have been shown to be among the greatest barriers to degree completion for students in the US (Johnson *et al.*, 2009). Lack of money was indeed often cited by participants as being an obstacle to reaching educational goals. Nelson put it succinctly by asking '*¿Cómo puedo obtene un Doctorado sin deverle Mucho dinero al gobierno?*' ('How can I get a doctorate without ohwing [*sic*] the goberment [*sic*] a lot of money?'), reflecting not only a concern about financial constraints but also suggesting emergent academic skills in the native language that may reflect shaky academic preparation.

When asked to explain specific steps to enroll in college and earn a degree, few were able to articulate a response beyond '*aprender inglés*' ('learn English') – including some young people who were but months away from sitting for their high school equivalency exam. Altagracia said that she had told the educational counselor: '*No me hables de college hasta que tenga mi diploma de GED en la mano*' ('Don't talk to me about college until I have the GED diploma in my hand'). Counselors at participating sites confirmed students' reluctance to plan ahead, indicating that many focus instead on the immediate goal of passing the GED rather than preparing for the long-term path of post-secondary education and career.

Notable is the extent to which these young adults exhibited determination, on the one hand, but were unaware of, or unwilling to recognize, potential obstacles. '*Estoy decida*' ('I am determined'), wrote one, and '*no hay obstáculos. Tengo fe que voy a lograr mis metas*' ('there are no obstacles. I have faith that I will reach my goals') wrote another, as if willing herself to succeed through sheer determination. Participants' comments reveal a tenacious optimism and belief that goals are within reach, though not without effort, and a conviction that success requires hard work. They appeared to view obstacles as bumps in the road, not as insurmountable barriers:

Yo siempre pienso, uno está donde uno quiere y uno llega a donde uno quiere. Creo que cada barrera que uno pase te hace más fuerte, y tú creces más y más.
I always think, a person is in the place that he wants to be and anyone can achieve what they want. I believe that every barrier that you overcome makes you stronger, you grow more and more.

The overall sentiment among the young people with whom I spoke is that the US has opportunities for anyone who wants to take advantage of them. Victor and others employed relativism when discussing obstacles, saying things like '*Siempre hay alguien quien tiene una situación más difícil. No nos falta nada*' ('There is always someone in a worse situation. We don't lack anything really'). José discussed his aspirations in the context of obstacles and reflected the hopefulness of much of the group that their situations could be improved through education:

La vida no es para siempre para estar trabajando ... la limpieza es buena, porque uno tiene que dar vida a lo que uno hace. Pero yo aspiro a mucho más. Toda en la vida se puede.
Life is not only for working ... being a janitor is good; you have to breathe life into the work you do. But I aspire to much more. Everything in life is attainable.

In their optimistic view, opportunities in the US are much greater than in their countries of origin, and, in their comparative frame of reference, they are currently better off, despite hardships that they recognize (Ogbu & Simons, 1998). Yet there is no guaranteed reward from hard work (MacLeod, 1995) and participants may have failed to recognize that societal inequities and institutional constraints can counter attempts at upward mobility through hard work (Bourdieu & Passeron, 1977). They have embraced the American Dream (in fact the American Myth) that hard work is rewarded and all opportunities are there for those who take advantage of them. Yet their social networks are key in providing information. How do their social networks play into the question of access and success?

Who You Know and What They Know: Social Capital and Peer Networks

While US culture frequently tells us that hard work is duly rewarded, we are increasingly aware of the power of privilege: some people are born into not only more resources, but also more 'access' and more of that difficult to define *something* that makes the difference between getting the job or not. Beginning as early as the 19th century, with Marx, economists and sociologists have been examining, exploring and debating the forms that capital takes – beyond simply money and finances – and what determines an individual's ability to influence the world and achieve his or her goals. These include social connections, cultural knowledge and experience, as well as economic resources. Bourdieu (1986), Coleman (1988), Durkheim (1893) and others have written extensively on forms of capital and their role in both individual choices and preparation for success and upward mobility.

In other words, how do your friends, family, community and peers enhance – or potentially limit – your ability to position yourself to improve your lot in life and reach your goals? Social capital and social networks play a key role for the young adult immigrants who are the subject of this volume. How do the individuals and groups to whom you are connected help you? For immigrant young adults new to the US and all of its institutions, this question has particular relevance because they are entering networks that can influence their futures.

This is perhaps best illustrated by two examples from our group. Fernando came to the US from the Dominican Republic for what he assumed would be only several months, to earn money to help his struggling mother. Soon, a job teaching Tae Kwon Do to children put him in contact with middle-class parents preparing their children for selective high schools and private colleges. Because he is charismatic and outgoing, Fernando developed a rapport with many families, who admired his skill at teaching their children and viewed him as a role model. Many conversations with the parents of his students and questions that he posed about educational opportunities and life in the US gave him ready access to information on career paths and options provided by informed, formally educated middle-class parents (many of whom spoke with him in Spanish). Some favors and individual assistance led to a seat at a community college on a path to a career as a medical technician.

In contrast is Elena, who arrived from Ecuador to live with relatives in New York City. She came alone, with minimal funds and only a piece of paper with a relative's telephone number, which she lost in the course of her journey. Miraculously, she made her way from Texas to New York and somehow managed to track down her relatives. Her original plan was to complete high school and then enroll in college. Things had not turned out as she imagined. Elena worked cleaning houses, where she was primarily on her own and had little interaction with her employers and peers. Despite her aspirations, she was ridiculed at home by her relatives for goals that they called 'ridiculous', and they constantly badgered her about not earning more money to contribute to the family. None of her relatives had been to college in the US, nor did they view it as a goal or remote possibility. They saw themselves as pragmatic and considered working to make a living was a more realistic long-term goal than pursuing an education. They were not opposed to education, but they did not believe it was realistic for Elena, given the economic pressures that she and the family faced.

These anecdotal accounts do not adequately address the complex nature of social capital and how peers and networks impact the lives of the young people who have been introduced in this book. Social capital is not a tangible resource in itself, but a type of capital that *facilitates* access to institutional resources by virtue of connections to certain networks and individuals beyond those of one's immediate family (Portes, 2000). The resources that individuals have by virtue of their networks, friends, families and peers have been seen to be influential in the process of educational attainment (Bourdieu & Passeron, 1977). For example, being part of the National Honor Society in high school may put me in contact with teachers and counselors who then take me on trips to colleges and invite me to presentations on special resources for scholarships and financial aid that students in remedial or 'low track' classes are not exposed to. These types of 'connections are instrumental in furthering individual mobility' (Portes, 2000: 12).

The Influence of Peers

Peer networks have been shown to have a strong influence on the educational trajectories of both US-born and immigrant youth, sometimes positive and sometimes negative (Gaytan, 2010; Nakkula, 2006; Smith, 2006). Although they had vast networks of friends and family, most of the young people who spoke to me had no friends or acquaintances who were on similar pathways toward post-secondary education. Although a few were able to name someone they had met at work who was at a university, they were unable to provide details about where the person was studying or what the course of study was. When it came to finding information to help them plan their educational trajectories, one participant articulated succinctly what many said: *'no hay nadie quien te aconseje'* ('there is nobody who advises me about education'). Ramón explained that friends and acquaintances of his age were not interested in going to school, and elaborated:

> *Para ellos la cosa es: '¿para que estudiar?' No tienen ese plan en mente. Piensan solamente en trabajar, ahorrar, y regresar.*
> For them the thing is 'Why study?' They don't have that plan in mind. They just think about working, saving and going back.

Given the economic reasons most participants in the sample gave for interrupting their schooling, the perspectives of their peers are hardly surprising. A common barrier for many young immigrants to investing in their own education is the necessity of work and the perception that the return home is imminent (Martinez, 2009; Rivera-Batiz, 2004). Data revealed that the social networks of many participants were limited to family and close friends who were also immigrants and who themselves had no experience with higher education. For some, interactions with even one positive peer role model can have a great impact. Victor told me:

> *Y como que tu ánimo comienza a cambiar con todo esto, tu forma de pensar comienza a cambiar, conociendo a la gente......este muchacho quien yo conocí, está estudiando en Columbia ahora*
> And it's like your motivation starts to change with all of this, your way of thinking changes, getting to know people ... that guy I met, he is a student at Columbia now.

'That guy' referred to was the first immigrant peer that Victor had met who, like himself, had immigrated with undocumented status and had gained entry to post-secondary schooling. The encounter was transformative, and reinforced the importance of education, but also its potential for *'personas como yo'* ('people like me'). We cannot underestimate the impact of such interactions for young adults like Victor and Elena who have little contact with mainstream institutions and have no one in their immediate family who has entered post-secondary education.

In an exploration of the influence of peers on educational choices, each focus group that I conducted discussed how co-workers viewed education. Most respondents reported that they were the only person at their workplace who was attending school. Most differentiated clearly between *familia* (family, or the people you rely on and ask for advice) and two different kinds of friends, *amigos* (close friends) and *amistades* (acquaintances). For many participants, the people they relied upon for emotional support and advice were back in their countries of origin and despite being emotional pillars were geographically distant. Most of the family members who were identified as supports had no knowledge of the US beyond what they knew from the media, television in particular. As noted earlier, their 'point people' for education had themselves low levels of formal education. As a result, their social capital for educational purposes was quite limited. One went as far as to say *'no tengo nadie quien me ayude'* ('I have no one who can help me') and painted a picture of himself as someone very much disconnected from any sort of support network that could provide tangible advice. Even those who live with relatives reported that they had no one who could help them with their educational decisions.

The study data demonstrated a clear link between participants' social networks and their concrete educational plans. Most, like the young people above, reported having no family or friends or co-workers who were enrolled in school, and had very limited understanding of the concrete steps that would have to be made to reach post-secondary schooling. The few participants who stood out from the rest as having clearly linear and articulated pathways were ones who knew people enrolled in college or who had made strong connections with organizations that had mentors who themselves had been immigrant students. They had developed wide social networks, including friends in college and some with professional degrees. Below, a participant discusses how a connection with a peer was pivotal to his enrollment in an adult education program, despite his fear and resistance. Ramón, who had competed eight years of education before migrating to the US at age 15, worked for seven years before starting back into school:

> *Me comencé a dar más ánimo. Entonces conocí un muchacho allí que se llama Nestor y me platicaba, y le dije que quería estudiar, y me dice 'Echale ganas' Pues, le dije que eso se ve bien difícil, que no se nada de matemáticas ya. Y me dice '¿Por qué no sacas el GED?' Y le digo, 'qué eso?' Y me dice, ¿tu no sabes que es eso?' '¿Qué es?' le digo. Y me explico y le digo, naaaaaaaa, está en inglés, le digo, no, me dice, está en español. Y me explicó que allí daba la clase. Y me mete al salón donde estaban dando las clases de matemáticas. Y yo ni quería entrar, y me meto, me meto allí a ver, y era algebra, era puras letras, no hombre......no entendía nada! Entonces fui a esa clase, pero después ya no regresé. Me dio miedo. Todos los números, me dió miedo. Entonces no regresé más, dije, mejor sigo con la computación, estaba con PowerPoint y Excel, que por cosas del trabajo lo dejé. Entonces me metí otra vez en el curso de computación. Y allí adentro me encontré otra vez con Nestor, este muchacho. Y me dice, 'vamos, estoy tomando el GED apenas ahora'. Y me dio animo y digo, okay, me voy a meter, apenas comenzamos, pues.*

I started getting more motivated. I met this guy at the center named Nestor and we chatted and I told him that I wanted to go to school and he said 'go for it'. I told him it seemed really hard and that I had forgotten all my math. He asks me 'Why don't you get the GED?' and I ask him, 'what is that?' 'You don't know what that is?' he asks me. 'What is it?' I ask him. He explained it to me and I said 'noooooooo, that's in English', 'no', he says, 'it's in Spanish'. And he explained that the class was right there. And I go into the classroom where they had math class. I didn't even want to go in, but I did and they were doing algebra, it was just all letters, no way! I didn't understand anything! I went to that class but never went back. I was afraid – all those numbers, I was afraid. I decided instead to take computer classes, PowerPoint and Excel, classes I stopped taking because of work. So I started the computer class again and there I met up with this guy Nestor again. He says to me, come on, I am just starting GED classes. That motivated me and I say, Okay, I am going to enroll, let's get started.

Ramón, like Fernando, through a combination of fate and personal initiative had developed valuable networks of individuals with knowledge about post-secondary and professional pathways. They talked *con todo el mundo* (to everyone), learning how to take advantage of resources on the internet, asked questions of everyone they came in contact with, located mentors and role models, and developed a support network. Stanton-Salazar (1997, 2001) and others (Gaytan, 2010; Yosso, 2005) have identified the extreme resilience of immigrant and working-class young people who develop complex and useful social networks that provide powerful supports to help them meet their goals.

Ethnic organizations were sources of support for some of the immigrants in this study, especially Mexicans. A plethora of local community-based Mexican organizations have sprung up in New York City and provide educational services, counseling and cultural events, and connect their members with networks of individuals from their country, region or town. For Ramón and others, such organizations provided them with the first-ever contact with college-educated co-nationals in the US. Information was available in Spanish, but it was not always up to date and often did not connect with mainstream public institutions in the city. The resources available seemed contingent upon the expertise and networking skills of leaders and teachers in each particular ethnic organization and the extent to which they were connected to current educational offerings. In that sense, the opportunities provided by or through each organization were dependent upon the social capital of its leaders.

Relationships with organizational leaders, teachers and other program staff may be the only links these youth have to formal institutions and can represent the only source of accurate and informed resources on educational options. Such organizations provide invaluable support for the academic success of working-class language-minority immigrant students because they open doors to networks that are otherwise not available (Stanton-Salazar, 1997, 2001). How do students make the choice to enter a program that will help them best meet their needs?

Choosing a Path: Knowledge, Networks and Choices

The young adults discussed in this volume are a self-selected group. There is an additional factor that unites these individuals: they had all made the choice to enroll in adult education programs to further their education. We know from data discussed in Chapter 5 that thousands of people of high school age enroll in federally funded adult education. Adult education is a quite different context from high school in several significant ways. First, it is voluntary. Second, as it is often provided in a non-formal setting, there is frequently emphasis on both the academic and the affective domain, and an awareness of students' potential challenges as adults leading complex lives. Third, programs lack funding to provide the kinds of services available in K-12 settings. Just how small is the shoestring of adult education budgets? Federal investment in adult education in the US was $330 per

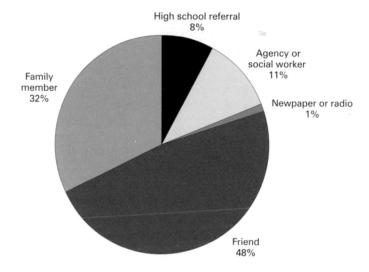

Figure 6.6 Sources of referral to the educational programs attended by study participants

student in fiscal year 2011–12, compared with $12,000 per student in high school (National Center for Education Statistics, 2013a; US Department of Education, 2013b).

Why did these young adults choose the programs in which they were enrolled? The survey that I designed and conducted for my research (see the Appendix) asked participants to identify popular and large-scale educational programs offered in New York City. Over three-quarters (77 %) knew only one option for adult education: the program in which they were enrolled. How did they come to learn about the program? Most were referred by a friend or relative (80%) (Figure 6.6). Nearly one-fifth (19%) were referred by a high school enrollment center, a high school that sent them away or by a counselor who had discharged them from school.

As discussed, individuals rely on their networks for information. When I asked the young people in my research whom they would turn to with questions about their educational choices, many indicated that they had no one or would rely on themselves. In focus groups, less than 10% of students could identify anyone they knew other than teachers or program staff who had attended college. Interview and focus group data revealed that many participants had few sources of information beyond family, friends and program staff (teachers and counselors).

When asked whom they would use as a source of information about educational decisions and educational pathways, most indicated that they

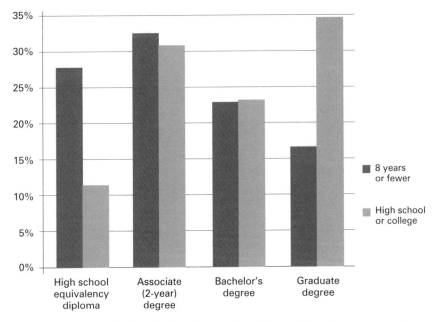

Figure 6.7 Reasons given for choice of program by study participants

would ask family members (often parents) and friends, while 11.4% (17) said that they would turn first to teachers, counselors or school administrators, and two indicated '*me da vergüenza preguntar*' ('I am too ashamed to ask'). As four-fifths of the participants relied on their friends and family members – who were equally uninformed – to refer them to educational options and to give them advice on their schooling, the knowledge and social capital of those friends and family members is vitally important.

When asked to indicate why they chose the educational program in which they were enrolled at the time of the study, 32.2% indicated because it was close to their home, 22.1% said it was the only program that they knew, 20.8% chose it because classes were offered in Spanish, 19% because it was free and 6.0% because of the schedule (Figure 6.7).

The participants in my research study came exclusively from families with low levels of formal education, a characteristic that has been linked to low educational attainment in children (Blau & Duncan, 1967; Ruiz-de-Velasco *et al.*, 2001; Togunde, 2008). My results reveal that the mother's level of education was the factor most closely correlated with children's academic levels.[2] To explore the relationship, statistical tests (Mann–Whitney) were conducted to determine the influence of the mother's prior education on the respondent's educational goals and aspirations (Figure 6.8). For the immigrant students in this study, educational goals were not uniformly low for those whose parents had low educational attainment. Being from a

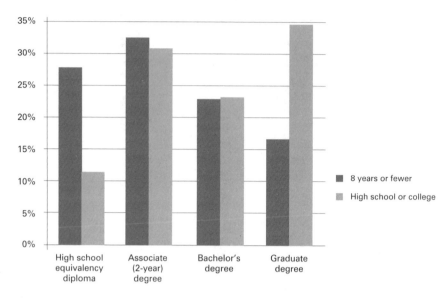

Figure 6.8 Participants' educational goals and mother's educational attainment

family with a low level of education may impact their skills, but it does not prescribe their aspirations, making high-quality instruction and resources to enhance their social capital all the more important once they have made the commitment to enroll in a second-chance educational program.

The Elephant in the Room: Immigration Status as Social Capital

Because undocumented immigrants comprise about 28% of the foreign-born population in the US (Batalova & Lee, 2012), the realities of immigrants in the US today cannot be explored thoroughly without addressing the issue of immigration status. Undocumented status is further complicated by the plight of thousands of unaccompanied minors entering the US through the border to Mexico, fleeing poverty and violence in Central America and entering a complex web of foster care and legal proceedings upon being detained at the border (Semple, 2014).

It was neither feasible nor ethical in the context of my research to ask young people to disclose their immigration status. Nonetheless, in both formal and informal conversations, many disclosed their status without prompting and discussed the resultant challenges with me. Some had specific questions about access to schooling or, as they would ask, '¿Es verdad que *tengo el derecho de ir a la universidad aquí?'* ('Do I really have a right to attend the university here?'). My experience working with public schools suggests that because of the sensitive nature of this topic, the veiled conversations about immigration status often result in misinformation or lack of information among students, teachers, counselors and administrators.

Data in this study suggest that there is a relationship between national origin and immigration status among study participants. Many, though by no means all, of the Dominican students who participated in the study reported having obtained a visa or permanent residency status through parents; many had been brought or sent for by parents or relatives who were part of the firmly established Dominican community in New York City. Dominicans number high among participants who had been shut out or pushed out of school (see Chapter 5). In contrast, a much higher proportion of Mexican and Central American participants emigrated alone and had no close relatives in New York or had joined cousins or others in the US; many were undocumented. Nonetheless, the sample is not homogeneous along these immigration status lines: some Dominican participants reported being undocumented and some Mexican and Central Americans reported having legal status. When participants were asked to rank obstacles to obtaining their educational goals, however, legal status was placed only third, behind money and knowledge of English. They appeared to consider the attainment of legal status to be rather more along the lines of a motivation to reach their goals, as this participant reports:

> *Qué pongan de su parte y no so conformen y no se pongan complacientes. No importa tu estatus legal, la educación no se te quita después de tenerla. Si trabajas 10 años no importa, sin un diploma empiezas desde 0. Un papel es la prueba de lo que sabes y puedes.*
>
> They [immigrants] should do their part and push forward and not be complacent. Your legal status is not important; education is not something that can get taken away once you have it. If you work for 10 years it doesn't even matter, not having a diploma means that you always start back at zero. A piece of paper is proof of what you know and what you can do.

The July 2012 'Deferred Action' decision by the US Department of Homeland Security (US Citizenship and Immigration Services, 2014) provided something of an amnesty for undocumented immigrants, yet it was designed to target children (in this case referring to anyone who arrived in the US under the age of 16). Despite the optimism brought by this new policy, immigration status is a real structural constraint for those who are undocumented (Smith, 2013) and an unresolved pathway to citizenship remains an insurmountable barrier to upward mobility for countless immigrant young adults. Lack of legal immigration status translates directly into lower wages and thus more hours needed away from school to earn money to pay rent and support family. For students in regions of the US that have passed laws to shut undocumented students out of higher education, it translates into a short-circuited educational pathway. Undocumented students are numerous among the growing subgroup of immigrant youth aged 16–24 and they face the greatest challenges (Gonzalez, 2007; Rumbaut & Komaie, 2010). Undocumented students face the burdens of family obligations that compel them to stay in the US to earn money for remittances, yet they lack access to jobs with anything like a good wage and may be stuck in low-wage jobs despite educational attainment. Their need for a supportive network cannot be fulfilled in ways possible for their peers with legal status. Disconnected from supportive networks, it is not possible for them to make a trip home to visit family, as it means to risk never returning, and terminating the possibility of educating themselves and improving their situation. Some reported feeling 'trapped' in this sense.

Summary and Discussion

This chapter has explored a range of educational and contextual factors that impact educational access and success for immigrant young adults with incomplete high school who seek to restart their education in the US. English language proficiency, prior education, literacy skills and content knowledge may all be tangible in a classroom setting, while young adults' contextual knowledge of education is influenced by their social capital and peers. Together, these influence where they enroll in school – and sometimes whether they locate and can access an educational program at all. Attention paid to these skills could provide invaluable information on students' academic needs, provide the programs they attend with needed background information on students' skills and knowledge gaps, and as a result prepare them for success.

For many young adult immigrants with emergent literacy and gaps in their content knowledge, the road toward developing the academic skills deemed necessary for success in college is likely a long one. The generally low levels of prior education, academic background and English proficiency suggest that they will enter post-secondary institutions in need of academic support and development. Yet the path through post-secondary education is not promising for those who enter via remediation (Adelman, 1998; Conley, 2007; City University of New York, 2008a), in that they have a much higher likelihood of abandoning their studies. The need to enroll in remedial courses has been referred to as the 'kiss of death' (Adelman, 1998) as it adds cost and time to a post-secondary trajectory that is already challenging for many students (Conley, 2007). A small proportion of students in need of remediation end up completing their degree (Conley, 2007). Additional supports and programs designed to address their specific challenges are needed for high-aspiring yet low-skilled immigrant young adults, lest their prior education be prescriptive of failure (Noguera, 2003; Portes & Zhou, 1993).

Although most are active participants in the labor market, navigate adult-like challenges and have overcome myriad obstacles to arrive in the US, the young people who are the focus of this book still face looming academic challenges and lack important contextual knowledge that will help them navigate educational pathways. They wish to complete education and enter professional careers, but many have only a vague idea about what it would entail, including locations of post-secondary institutions, requirements, format and structure and expectations in college, how to apply, financial aid, enrollment and duration. Research has demonstrated huge gaps among immigrant English language learners and low-income students in high school in what information is necessary for post-secondary access and what information they have, and that counselors and teachers were the most useful sources of information (Conley, 2007; Tornatzky et al., 2002).

This chapter has explored the ways in which gaps in knowledge may be exacerbated by lack of social capital and reliance on individuals who themselves have limited social capital and lack contextual knowledge of US educational pathways. The high level of optimism demonstrated by the young people in this volume suggests that they might not have a clear picture of the time and effort needed to reach their desired goals.

Adult education and other targeted and well-designed 'second chance' programs can play a significant role in preparing students to transition toward success. Yet many new immigrant students enter adult education programs with only a vague sense of the path that can lead to their goals and lack a nuanced understanding of the education and training options that may be available. Limited skills and lack of contextual knowledge can stifle effective participation and inhibit potentially successful learners from charting a clear, realistic path to meeting their education goals. As shown in the data presented, many immigrant students in adult education seek a pathway to post-secondary education, improved employability and higher incomes. With few friends and acquaintances with insider knowledge of post-secondary education in the US, they are sorely in need of supportive services and counseling to make informed choices. Participants seek access to college for the role they perceive it can play in their upward mobility; they present career- and workplace-oriented views of the purposes for their schooling. Yet few adult education programs are designed and funded to provide the very services that have been shown to be vital in helping low-skilled immigrant students transition successfully into post-secondary trajectories, including: career preparation, counseling supports, tracking, and monitored pipelines into and beyond post-secondary access.

The US adult education system is designed in such a way that few states incorporate career planning and advisement within funded programs.

Demands on staff are high, and teachers rightly focus on content and skills. Many do not have the intimate knowledge of post-secondary paths that could benefit their students. Nonetheless, immigrant students with limited social capital know few individuals other than their teachers or program staff with the knowledge to advise them on educational pathways and career choices.

Recent research in adult education suggests the need for seamless college transitions that provide basic skills, counseling and supports for college coursework and occupational training (US Department of Education, 2012). Promising practices focus on the range of skills and content that English language learners in post-secondary settings will need, such as challenging, college-level content, counseling, support and collaboration with outside agencies, as well as a focus on the development of reading, writing, speaking and oral English skills (Alamprese, 2004). Yet existing programs are often designed to focus on immigrant students who have already achieved high levels of English proficiency and literacy. Students who enter post-secondary programs through the pathway of adult and continuing education 'are among the most under-represented students in college' (World Education, 2010). This is a gap in the system that must be filled, otherwise there is a risk that large subgroups of students will be left behind, those who are in the process of developing the basic skills, English proficiency and social capital needed for success.

As Elena expressed when discussing the challenges she faced in tackling both basic skills and English: *'Deben de inventar algo para nosotros, ya que regresamos ahora cuando estamos grandes'* ('They should design programs for people just like us, since we come back to school when we are grown'). The next chapter takes a close look at the educational policies in the US that impact the continuing education of immigrant young adults who seek to re-enter an educational pipeline after interrupted schooling. It also explores the programs and the ways in which they address or ignore students' specific needs, and discusses opportunities for policy and programming in the future.

Additional resources

National College Transition Network, http://www.collegetransition.org/home.html
New York City Coalition for Adult Literacy, http://www.nyccaliteracy.org/
Office of Adult Education and Literacy, http://www2.ed.gov/about/offices/list/ovae/pi/
    AdultEd/index.html

Notes

(1) Participants identified college with the City University of New York (CUNY), the multi-campus public university system that enrolls more than 200,000 students

in junior and senior colleges and upwards of 200,000 in adult, continuing and professional education.
(2) Although survey respondents were asked to report the level of education attained by parents, grandparents and siblings, most were able to report only that of their mothers. Focus group and interview data revealed that many participants had lived with the mother and not the father prior to emigrating, which may explain some of this discrepancy.

7 The Road Ahead for Young Adult Migrants: Institutional Dilemmas, Nagging Questions and Open Doors

Introduction

What next? What lies ahead for young adults migrants such as Victor, Ramón, Elena, Altagracia, Rosa, Nelson, Fernando and others? In the previous six chapters, we have met and learned a bit about their histories, contexts and educational trajectories. Most young adults like them work to make ends meet and send money home. Some find their way into high schools or alternative educational settings that may or may not get them where they want to be. It would seem that the array of alternative programs are addressing only one small part of the myriad of policy issues that are central in meeting the needs of this overlooked population – young adult immigrants from Latin America who entered the US prior to completing their high school education. As 'dropouts', they fit neatly into a demographic that has to date been unexamined.

The young adults we have met and others like them are not an insignificant group: their numbers are growing. Their educational outcomes continue to be alarming. The staggering high school non-completion rates in the US among foreign-born Latinos, as discussed in Chapters 1 and 2, make it clear that for young people like the ones we have met in this volume, traditional high school settings are not working.

Is it not simply a matter of aspirations? The anecdotes, data and stories in the preceding six chapters reveal the high educational aspirations of these young people. Their experiences challenge the persistent deficit view that immigrant dropouts are low achieving and low aspiring and that they value work and money more than education. As has been discussed throughout this book, there are multiple institutional and societal barriers that may prevent young adult immigrants from ever enrolling in school in the US and myriad social, cultural and economic barriers that prevent them from inching toward their stated goals.

The previous pages have given us ample opportunity to examine an array of important factors that have impacted their school interruption prior to leaving their countries of origin. This chapter presents both dilemmas and opportunities to meet the needs of this overlooked population. The present chapter examines persistent policy and program design issues and explores institutional and societal dilemmas and how they might be addressed through broad-reaching educational, social and economic policies. It reviews a few existing models and discusses how they show promise or miss the mark in effectively serving this specific population. It also explores how human development plays a role in the lives and choices of young migrants who leave their homes often bearing the burden of adult responsibilities but with the needs of adolescents and emerging adults. Finally, the chapter presents some initial theories on how we might harness existing opportunities for policy, practice and research and seeks to pose some pertinent questions that can guide our work to better serve the needs of immigrant young adults in the years ahead, not only in New York, but across the US and internationally.

Persistent Issues for Policy and Program Design

Ramón, Elena, Altagracia, Victor, Nelson and Carmen are real people whose experiences shed light on key issues in educational policy and program design. Their stories also raise questions that reach far beyond the school and classroom. What is the role of education in enabling access to 'the American Dream?' How does the current economic structure present barriers to upward mobility? How do the history and the interdependence between the US and Latin America lead to a continued migration of young adults northward from Mexico, Central and South America and the Caribbean?

In the previous chapters, we followed the paths of these young adults out of school, into the US and back into school again in alterative settings. Is their dogged belief that education is an effective road to upward mobility in the US justified? How does the design of the programs they attend meet their needs or stand in their way? In what ways does the zeal to measure and quantify their learning and progress end up improving services or undermining access and program effectiveness? What insights have we gained that can inform educational policy and programming? What factors must we keep in mind to ensure that viable educational options exist, that schools are not penalized for enrolling students who enter as older adolescents, and that the investment of their time in education in fact reaps a reward at graduation? The sections that follow discuss lingering issues and persistent dilemmas.

The Red Herring: 'Stemming the Surge'

Much current discourse in mainstream media whips up hysteria around migration flows into the US (the same holds true in Europe for nations that receive what seems like a disproportionate number of refugees from African and the Middle East). The focus is consequently on 'stemming the surge' and building higher walls, more border protection, more restrictive entry policies. In the case of Latino immigrants to the US, what Chapter 3 made clear is that this is something of a red herring, distracting us from the issues at hand and diverting our attention away from central issues: migration has flowed northward from Latin America for nearly 200 years and is unlikely to stop now, especially as the economic fate of the US is so inextricably linked with that of Latin America. Because there is a permanent link between the US and Latin American economies, the immigration tide will not be stemmed. Building higher walls will not change that. Immigrant young adults from Latin America are here to stay. At the same time, no educational policy response can be effective in a vacuum unless immigration policies are addressed and reformed.

Dilemmas of Working and 'Making a Living'

As discussed in Chapter 3, immigrant young adults often abandon school due to family economic pressures, and the pull northward is propelled by economic necessity and the structure of the US economy, in its reliance on low-wage immigrant labor.

In the minds of the young people in this book, education is an opportunity to rise out of poverty and harness the opportunities that they perceive the US offers. The value that Altagracia, Ramón, Elena and others put on education reflects the dominant belief in the US – what some have called the 'achievement ideology' (Mickelson, 1990) and others 'the education gospel' (Grubb, 1999; Grubb & Lazerson, 2004) – that education leads unequivocally to upward mobility, stability and improved life outcomes. We know by now – and no one knows better than the millions of adults in the US and around the world who possess credentials but no viable employment – that economic upward mobility is harder and harder to come by in the 21st century. Although economic research reveals the link between post-secondary education and increased earnings (Murnane *et al.*, 2000; Tyler *et al.*, 1998), for young adults striving to improve their economic position, decades of an economy that has reduced real wages and increased the numbers of US residents who live below the poverty line (Anyon, 2005; Ehrenreich, 2001; National Employment Law Project, 2014) raise serious questions about the return on investment in current conditions. The reality of employment in the aftermath of a global recession is that recovery has meant the addition of more low-wage and poverty-level jobs and fewer jobs that pay middle- and high-end salaries (National Employment Law Project, 2014). Macroeconomic policies that have reduced real wages (Anyon, 2006) and led to global unemployment may in fact lead immigrants to strive for college education to procure entry-level jobs that may not even pay enough to live above the poverty line. While a college degree promises increased opportunity for upward mobility, it is no longer a guarantee of a living wage in the US (National Employment Law Project, 2014; Stiglitz, 2013) nor really of any job at all. Changes in the US economic structure have led to stagnant wages and increasing numbers of jobs in the low-paying retail and service industries, characterized by limited stability and meager benefits. The structure of work and the economy has made it virtually impossible to live on a minimum-wage job.

With unemployment levels high in the US and internationally, among both potential workers with limited credentials and those with post-secondary degrees, a central concern is whether there is a still direct link between education and earning. Workplaces are designed with logistical constraints that limit the ability of low-wage workers to maintain long-term, stable employment (Anyon, 2005; Ehrenreich, 2001). Work is structured not to invest in workers as human capital, but to view them as expendable, especially if they require training or flexibility with regard to scheduling, family and health concerns.

Legal status looms large as a factor that limits viable employment and upward mobility for immigrants. Undocumented youth, young adults and adults face a perpetual dilemma in the labor market as well as in education and training. Many students with unresolved immigration status remain persistently on the lowest rungs of the economy. Growing numbers of undocumented students leave college and graduate school and find themselves still waiting for a path to citizenship that will enable them to contribute to the economy (Gonzalez, 2007; Smith, 2013).

With the extreme managerial and business focus of workplaces, measuring and quantifying and making everything super-efficient, we end up not adapting to the real human needs of workers. Poverty wages in reward for a post-secondary degree mean that the time spent in college – and away from the workplace – may not be a good investment. We should be reminded of the shift away from the workplace and into high school for adolescents (Dorn, 1996). High school ended up being a popular place to spend one's adolescent years – away from the workplace – because it offered a tangible reward for time spent away from earning. For immigrant young adults with precarious legal status, the possibility of surviving with time away from earning is increasingly unrealistic. What are the implications for young adults who are forced to make a choice between hours spent away from work and earning and investing this same time in education? Will there be a payoff? How should we gauge effectiveness?

The Zeal to Measure: Accountability

While school is arguably a place to educate youth for the future, in the case of the young adults in this overlooked cohort, a central issue is ways in which the focus on ensuring accountability for public investment in education ends up undermining access and effectiveness. Current educational policies designed to make programs more accountable to certain subgroups result in disincentives, at both the K-12 and adult education level, to serve recently arrived immigrant adolescents and young adults with only emergent English and relatively poor academic skills. The current accountability system reduces program effectiveness to a very limiting set of metrics. A focus on quantifying and capturing English and math skills tends to penalize prospective students for their very real needs while overlooking the tangible skills that they bring to the educational setting. A narrow focus on quantifiable skills and gains based on test scores serves unwittingly to squander the resource of young people who come to the US bearing great risks and bring with them great potential and extensive life experience and enormous optimism about the future. Once they have embraced the American Dream that education will in fact get them somewhere, how do we make good on that promise?

Every day of the school year, faculty and staff in high schools make crucial – and potentially life-altering – decisions as to whether or not to roll the dice and grant seats to young adults who are older than average for high school, who have emergent English skills and who have spent a few years out of school. The lives of students seeking to enroll are unquestionably impacted by the decision to allow them to enroll or to send them away. Yet schools themselves are engaged in a high-stakes gamble by admitting students who risk lowering their much-watched graduation rates, leading to classification as 'low-performing' and subsequently to closure.

US high schools are strictly monitored under federal accountability guidelines to graduate a minimum percentage of all enrolled ninth-grade students within four years. As a result, staff who make registration decisions are painfully aware that a recently arrived 17-year-old immigrant who is for the first time being exposed to English and who has interrupted schooling may reach the age of 21 before completing enough credits – and in the state of New York passing enough Regents exams – to graduate. It is also likely that the young person standing at the counter hoping to enroll will lose interest before 'aging out' of high school at the age of 21 or may become frustrated at being older than average for the high school peer group and as a result drop out.

In the realm of adult education, programs that receive state or federal dollars must test students in English to demonstrate progress, or else demonstrate attainment of high school equivalency skills, or improvement in workforce status, regardless of the entering students' prior literacy or educational background or legal status. Not unlike trends in K-12 education, where schools are penalized for not demonstrating academic progress of those students who are hardest to serve, adult-education providers receiving public monies are judged on the demonstrated progress of their students in English, a reflection of monolingual ideology that fails to harness the value and potential of multilingualism among the rapidly growing immigrant populations in the US. There are few fiscal or policy incentives for adult and second-chance educational programs to serve immigrant adults with emergent literacy who may benefit from native language services (Lukes, 2009). Existing accountability structures may create disincentives. Not unlike high school administrators, program directors in adult education may be put in the position of excluding the hardest-to-serve adult learners who risk not demonstrating progress in English based on existing accountability measures. Well-designed programs that serve adults with only emergent literacy skills do exist, but funding restrictions may undermine their sustainability. How does educational language policy impact programs overall?

Language and Educational Language Policy

Despite the lack of an 'official' language for the US, English language monolingualism has been stubbornly persistent among its citizens. Some scholars have sought to examine the xenophobia they claim to be at the root of efforts to limit immigrants' use of their non-English languages, which has resulted in language loss among linguistic minorities both in the US and in other immigrant receiver nations (Menken, 2008; Phillipson, 1988; Skutnabb-Kangas, 2000: 296–374; Tollefson, 1991; Wiley, 1991; Wiley & Lukes, 1996; Wiley & Wright, 2004). Immigrant young adults who arrived as teens to the US often live in communities where multilingualism is a bonus, and literacy and proficiency in the native language are a commodity and a necessity. At the corporate level, there is a recognition that linguistic resources in the form of proficiency in a non-English language can lead to economic returns, but emergent bilinguals who are still in the process of learning English are persistently viewed as deficient in educational contexts (Callahan & Gándara, 2014).

The lack of a concrete *valuing* of bilingualism may stem in part from lack of research that shows its benefits in terms of what speaks: money. It is only recently that new approaches are being used to demonstrate the tangible value of bilingualism in the labor market, an area that was previously unexamined (Callahan & Gándara, 2014). With a growing population of immigrant youth and children of immigrants completing school and entering the workforce, empirical evidence from longitudinal research reveals a significant economic benefit for those who enter the workforce with bilingualism and biliteracy. Similarly, the costs to individuals who have lost their first language can be estimated in real economic terms (Agirdag, 2014). Scholars have recently begun to examine not only the social but also the economic costs to society that stem from language loss resulting from monolingual and subtractive schooling approaches (Agirdag, 2014).

Despite concrete evidence of the wide-reaching economic benefits to the US economy of nurturing multilingualism among newcomer students (Callahan & Gándara, 2014), monolingual and subtractive schooling approaches for immigrant English learners persist. Educational programs for immigrant students commonly position English proficiency as their only goal and view native language literacy as a problem. This subtractive approach ignores scholarship that reveals the success of translanguaging and bilingual approaches to strengthen the academic achievement of emergent bilinguals (Creese & Blackledge, 2010; García, 2011, 2012; García et al., 2008; Hornberger & Link, 2012; García & Sylvan, 2011). An understanding of students' pre-migration educational preparation should be coupled with an examination of their literacy and content knowledge in the home language as well as in English in order to help them set and reach attainable goals. We may set long-term goals for students with only emergent literacy in their home language, let alone English, and who have little understanding of the skills and competencies needed to reach those goals. Yet a multilingual approach is not the only issue. Addressing students' home languages and designing approaches that treat non-English languages as assets is but one factor in a multidimensional approach and will do little if social, economic and institutional barriers persist. An effective response must include more effective language policies, but cannot stop at addressing language.

The deficit view has created a pervasive ideology of monolingualism, often framing the maintenance of non-English literacy among immigrants as subversive and suspect. Despite a persistent belief that immigrants languish in linguistic isolation in insular enclaves where they have no access no English, the US allocates very few public resources to language learning for immigrants, relative to the numbers of English language learners over the age of 16 (Colton, 2006) and this is among the 'most neglected domestic policy issues' in the US (McHugh et al., 2009). Many immigrants work in manual jobs with peers who speak the same language and who have very limited opportunities to interact with English-speaking peers, making the need for English language instruction even more acute.

Years of research on language learning has taught us that it is possible to use students' first language as a tool and support to facilitate learning another language (Creese & Blackledge, 2010; García et al., 2008). Well-designed educational programs that harness students' home languages have been shown to promote effective learning in both English and in content areas (August & Hakuta, 1997; Cummins, 2009; García, 1999; Goldenberg, 2008; Thomas & Collier, 2003). There is a significant body of research that reveals a compelling link between strengthening students' first language and enhancing their acquisition of English (Burt & Peyton, 2003; Condelli *et al.*, 2003; Lukes, 2009). The US programs that provide education and training for immigrant adults who want to learn English and gain skills for employment rarely incorporate bilingual approaches, nor do they provide services specifically designed for adults with emergent native language literacy, resulting from limited formal schooling. Few teachers have received adequate preparation to integrate such students into a conventional, heterogeneous classroom, where much time is spent reading, writing and copying words directly from the blackboard. Students who struggle to read and write in their first language are hampered by this approach, but often teachers do not realize which students these are until it is too late.

Missing in much of program design for English language learners is the incorporation of assessments in the native language that would gather detailed information on students' skills both in their home language and in English. Existing federal adult education policy emphasizes English literacy, and programs are given few incentives – and no funding at all – to assess and harness students' native language literacy skills. Nor are there any incentives to 'leverage' or maximize the first language to maintain it or learn English. As a result, traditional, English-only, text-based approaches are perpetuated, to the detriment of a growing population of students with only emergent literacy in their first language. Much of the adult education for immigrants focuses on 'survival English', which emphasizes the kinds of language that adults need to navigate their daily lives (work, school, health care, legal system). Though practical, such approaches overlook the fact that many immigrant adults survive and thrive in their daily lives, even without access to the limited adult education services that exist.

This leads to a central question for program design: are these young people or adults? Where do they lie on the continuum of human development? Are they adolescents to be socialized in high school classrooms? Or are they adults with adult constraints, responsibilities and needs? Programs designed to serve out-of-school youth and adults struggle with ways to address students' linguistic and educational needs without boring or infantilizing them. Faced with a room full of students who may seem unfocused or who struggle to do math or write an essay, it is easy to forget that, outside of the classroom – in the *real world* as it were—these immigrant students manage jobs, households and adult responsibilities to provide for their families. The teenager who may be asleep in the back of the high school history class leaves the doors of school and enters the world as an adult. Why does it make a difference?

Youth in Adult Roles: Persistent Dilemmas for Migrant Young Adults

Ramón, Altagracia, Elena and their peers have been thrust into the world of adulthood, taking on responsibilities for families in their home countries and in the US. Research on immigrant adolescents at school does not adequately explore the dynamics of older youth in educational environments designed to socialize adolescents, assuming perhaps that educational concerns take precedence over developmental ones (Nakkula, 2006; Sadowski, 2006). Their developmental stage is central to their decision-making and the types of services they require, as they continually seek out guidance and support from adults, parents, family members and mentors, but at the same time they are faced with unequivocally adult responsibilities, such as financial support for those same individuals to whom they go for advice. They are also faced with long work hours, family obligations and concerns about their future that position them with both feet firmly in an adult world. But in some ways they *are* youth, and their developmental needs must be attended to. Yet in many areas of their lives they live as adults.

Paradoxical for the young adults in this study is that although they would be well-served by programs designed for disconnected youth, they are disconnected from neither work nor school. In contrast, regardless of their goals for entering the US or the circumstances of their migration, all have made a choice to enter school – and all appear to be seeking the correct door to find their way back into education. Nonetheless, their quest for guidance (Aron & Zweig, 2003; Zarrett & Eccles, 2006) and support reflects developmental needs as older adolescents, not as adults. Well-designed interventions, to ensure their success, have both to take into account their needs and to consider the divergent roles they play in the world.

Literature on disconnected youth (O'Connor, 2008; Ouellette, 2006) cites widespread disengagement by over-age and under-credited youth, who are thought to lack motivation and direction. Stereotypes often depict urban youth of color as inherently 'at risk' and focus on their ostensible pathologies (Way, 1998) rather than taking a more positive and proactive approach to youth development (Golstein & Noguera, 2006). Models shown to be successful have included those that incorporate an array of supportive practices, including high expectations, work-based learning, teacher collaboration and continuous improvement (Frome, 2001). Youth who are defined as 'disconnected' – out of school and disconnected from the workforce – constitute a population that differs greatly from the participants in this study, yet promising practices in youth development can inform policy for immigrants enrolled in alternative pathways to graduation. Programs for credit recovery and alternative pathways to graduation often intersect with the programs in which the participants in this study found themselves. Pathways to high school equivalency, as discussed below, are one example.

Many immigrant teens and young adults are financial anchors for families in their countries of origin and shifted into these adult roles at a young age (Martinez, 2009), supporting families with remittances (Somerville *et al.*, 2008), serving as liaisons between parents and US institutions, and making major life decisions in the absence of adults. For many, the reality is that school and work must coexist.

Adult Education for Youth

As early as the progressive era and later in the development of the adult education movement in the US, scholars criticized traditional education for not being appropriate for the learning needs of adults. Traditionalists who claimed that most adults were not self-directed nor interested in learning were attacked using the argument that the main problem was the design of the learning systems (Lindeman, 1926). The argument was that because adults are not motivated by traditional instruction designed with the in-strumentalist goal of socializing young people, such programs were bound to fail (Knowles, 1973; Lindeman, 1926). Failure in adult education is often predicated on lack of attendance, as students who lose interest simply leave. For students like Altagracia and others, who have found their way into programs designed for adults, attendance is a choice made every single day of class, not an educational mandate (Comings *et al.*, 2000).

Once students are beyond compulsory school age, they are in school only if they perceive a practical need or benefit (Knowles, 1973; Comings *et al.*, 2000; Vella, 2002). 'Persistence' in adult education is defined as adults' ongoing participation in educational programs, their engagement in self-directed study when circumstances allow, interruptions in voluntary participation when they don't and a return to participation when life demands allow (Comings *et al.*, 2000). Key to understanding their participation are their perspectives on why they want an education and where they believe this education can lead. According to adult learning theorists, children are dependent learners, relying on the teacher to determine what needs to be learned, whereas adults are independent, with life experience and personal goals playing a central role in learning (Knowles, 1973; Lindeman, 1926).

Because we understand that young adults who are placed in the position of shouldering financial responsibilities, caring for families and making major life decisions are in adult-like roles, then we have much to learn from adult learning theory about what works best for them. In his theories of adult learning, Knowles (1973) cites four characteristics of educational contexts that promote learning in adults: (1) respect for individuals, (2) shared decision-making, (3) freedom of expression, and (4) shared goal setting, planning and evaluation. A broad study of adults who were success-ful in adult education programs revealed four very similar factors that lead to success and the persistence of adults and older youth who have made the decision to continue their schooling: (1) awareness and management of the forces that can help and hinder persistence; (2) self-efficacy and the ability to make responsible choices and manage obstacles; (3) student-articulated goals; and (4) tangible progress toward articulated goals (Comings *et al.*, 2000).

The literature on adult learning stresses its potentially transformative nature, especially when the adults concerned are in marginal positions in society (Auerbach, 1993; Knowles, 1973; Vella, 2002). In many community-based adult learning contexts, critical pedagogy is used as a means to help students articulate the challenges they face structurally and institutionally and to explore alternatives to oppressive social conditions (Auerbach, 1993; Freire, 1993; Shor & Freire, 1987; Wallerstein, 1983). Such learning environments are designed with the goal of developing 'self-efficacy' and enabling often marginalized, minority and low-income students to take charge of their lives. This is a very different goal from many high school settings or even from settings on which 'survival' is the operating framework. It is perhaps no wonder that so many youth find their way into settings designed for adults.

Who is Disconnected and Why?

The term 'disconnected youth' refers to a range of types of 'non-participation' in school among high school dropouts aged 16–24 and must be understood across multiple dimensions of school and labor market participation: youth who are neither working nor enrolled in school, as well as youth with incomplete high school who are working but are disconnected from school. The Urban Institute underscores the diversity among this population and identifies them broadly as 'youth who are currently struggling to be successful in their roles as adolescents and who are socially, educationally, and economically disadvantaged relative to their peers' (Aron & Zweig, 2003: 3). Policy literature explores how the current emphasis on standards and assessment exacerbates barriers to participation among many at-risk youth and examines the need for alternative programs for youth. Yet even with extensive research and investment in this subsection of the youth population, challenges persist. Two of the most glaring difficulties are how to locate the young adults who are in need of services and how to find adequate programming for them (Fine & Jaffe-Walter, 2007; Wald & Martinez, 2003).

Obstacles to participation in adult education and the reasons why some young people may be disengaged from education and the workforce have been researched in depth. There are ample reasons why some do not make the shift into second-chance education. Below, Victor shares his views on his peers and their priorities:

Creo que son las circunstancias. A veces se ve que hay responsabilidades. A veces hay muchachos de 18 años, 18, 19 años, ya tienen 2 o 3 niños. He pensado que los estudios entonces, pasan a segundo o a tercer lugar, porque la prioridad es mantener su familia, sus hijos, la esposa, todo eso.

I think it is the circumstances. Sometimes you can see that there are responsibilities. Sometimes there are kids who are 18 years old, 18, 19 years old, they already have two or three kids. I think that maybe education sort of moves to second or third place, because the priority is to support his family, his kids, his wife, all that.

Nearly half of the participants in this study were parents (44%), with a total of 165 children, some of them born in the US and some foreign-born. Although finding childcare and balancing work, study and family may be challenging, they had made education their priority, despite what their peers might believe. For some, being a parent may even be a key motivating factor for prioritizing education, as Hector discusses:

Yo tengo una niña. Yo no puedo pensar en mi, tengo que pensar en ella, porque si pienso solo en mi, no está bien … entonces en este país le dan a uno la oportunidad de estudiar y se tiene que hacerlo.

I have a daughter. I can't just think of myself; I have to think of her, because if I only think of myself, it's not right … anyway, this country gives you the opportunity to study and you have to take it.

The step into an educational pathway as an adult after an interruption in schooling is a conscious one and can be sustained only through persistence (Knowles, 1973; Vella, 2002). No truant officer will arrive for adult education students and haul them back to school. For Ramón, Elena, Altagracia and their peers, their investment in their education is the hook upon which they hang all their hopes for upward mobility. Through their words, we see that they perceive a lasting value in education. We also see that their decisions to leave home were often motivated by a sense of obligation to help their families economically, as Victor tells us:

Pues mi propósito en llegar aquí era hacer mi negocio … arreglar la casa de mi mama, entiendes, pagar los estudios a mis hermanos, para que no les vaya a pasar que me pasó a mí, me entiendes.

So, my reason for coming here was to make money… fix my mother's house, you know, pay for my younger siblings to study, so they don't have to have the same experience as I did, you know.

Across the range of ages, the young people in this book discussed roles that stood often in direct opposition: (1) the adult role of supporting the family chafes against (2) an adolescent's developmental need for emotional support from parents and caring adults. The constant balancing of responsible adult and emerging adult and adolescent roles suggests a need for a developmental approach educational programs, in which participants have the flexibility to work but also receive emotional nurturing and guidance. As discussed in Chapter 6, the young people presented here are largely on their own regarding educational decisions, revealing the importance of programmatic supports to ensure they reach their goals.

In her exploration of life stages among Mexican immigrant youth in New York City, Martinez (2009) examines how those who emigrate in their teens and do not enroll in high school understand their life stages. Among immigrant groups in New York City, Mexicans top the list for school-age youth not enrolled in high school. Martinez (2009) posits that in order to understand their reasons for staying out of school, we must examine their experiences of childhood and adolescence, especially as they take on adult responsibilities so early in life, as demonstrated here as well. This concept of choice and agency is woven through scholarly work on young adult transitions (Arnett, 2004; Evans, 2002). Data presented here reveal that it cannot be assumed that these young adults will never return to school, nor can we understand their failure to enroll in high school as a 'choice' based upon weighing options and having complete information.

Current literature on alternative programs for disconnected youth suggests multiple components that must be in place to ensure success. In addition to well-trained staff, ongoing professional development and visionary leadership, programs must be designed to include: (1) a thorough intake and admissions process, (2) skills assessment, (3) orientation, (4) instruction, (5) support and, finally, (6) planning for the next life phase ('transition planning') (Joselowsky, 2009). Yet a survey of the programs in which most of the participants in this study were enrolled reveals that very few of them included more than one of these six components. Let us examine existing programs and explore how they might meet the needs of Altagracia, Ramón, Elena, Victor and others like them.

Existing Models: Strengths and Weaknesses

What is a typical high school program for immigrant English language learners? The most common model involves two components: (1) instruction in English as a second language (or English language development); and (2) content instruction, in credit-bearing classes such as math, history or science. These two elements, English learning and content learning, are treated as separate entities. In the first element of this model, students classified as English language learners receive a prescribed amount of instruction in English by teachers trained to teach grammar, reading and writing in English to students whose first language in not English. Students in these classes are generally grouped by English proficiency as gauged by a test in

English. Typically, students are discouraged from using their first language in the classroom, as was discussed earlier in this chapter. In the second element, teachers who are experts in their disciplines teach algebra, calculus, biology, chemistry and US and global history. In general, these teachers have little or no connection to the teachers assigned to teach language, and they generally work in separate departments and do not meet to collaborate or discuss students. English language learners with very different levels of English are grouped in content classes, often with native English speakers. The teachers in these classes generally have received little or no training in how they might adapt their lectures – as these classes are often lectures or whole-group discussions – to accommodate students who are just developing academic vocabulary and proficiency in English.

The approach described has resulted in less than exemplary high school graduation rates for immigrant youth who enter the US at high school age. With four years to become both proficient in academic English and to master the academic content, more than half do not make it. Yet programs have emerged designed to meet the needs of students of high school age and young adults who have not experienced academic success. In the pages that follow, I will address some existing programs in New York City and ways in which they address or overlook the needs and realities of recently arrived Latino immigrant young adults.

Young Adult Borough Centers[1]

In New York City, Young Adult Borough Centers (YABCs) are an innovative 'alternative pathway to graduation' for young people who are on a trajectory that does not lead to graduation. They target those who are at risk of dropping out, who are 'over-age and under-credited', and who must work during school hours to support themselves or their families. This description fits many immigrant newcomer students, yet YABCs do not generally admit or target this population. In their design, they preclude participation of newcomers until they are too far behind in their progress toward graduation to be able to benefit because, to enroll in such a program, a student of high school age must be have completed the school year in which they turn 17, have 17 credits toward graduation, be in their fifth year of high school and be enrolled in a high school. For students like Ramón and Victor, who never managed to procure a seat in a high school, a YABC is not an option, and the same holds true for a wide range of transfer school options. Altagracia would in theory have been eligible, as she had the credits and had turned 17, but she was never referred to such a program because she was encouraged to leave school before she had completed her fourth year of high school. Although these programs have demonstrated effectiveness, their criteria shut out newcomer immigrants who may be gone, discharged from the system, long before they meet the criteria.

GED and high school equivalency options[2]

The year 2014 was when the world of high school equivalency, formerly known as the GED test, began to shift dramatically. The GED and its equivalents allow students to complete a credential that enables them to enter college without having completed high school in the US. Because there is a test available in Spanish, students who arrive from Spanish-speaking countries, even with only emergent basic language skills, are able to circumvent traditional high school pathways and have the opportunity to enter post-secondary pathways.

The GED is the ticket to college for many immigrant students without a high school diploma but, paradoxically, the process of preparing for, taking and passing the GED may not ensure college readiness. A report by the City University of New York's Office of Institutional Research and Assessment indicates that although GED recipients are less prepared than high school graduates to be successful in academic instruction, only 20% ever take advantage of existing remediation programs at the University's community colleges (City University of New York, 2008a). However, those who do persist achieve higher grades than their peers holding high school diplomas, although they tend to accumulate credits at a slower rate due to multiple demands of family and work. Data presented here highlight the challenge shown in the data from the City University of New York, as fewer GED graduates than eligible enroll in programs designed to support disadvantaged students. Currently in the US, a college education is a prerequisite for many types of gainful employment and upward mobility for all subgroups in the population. Starting in the late 1980s, individuals with less than post-secondary education began to fare far worse economically than those with college and beyond, making the returns to college preparation rise dramatically (National Center for the Study of Adult Learning and Literacy, 2004).

Without the option to obtain a high school credential, the GED is a necessity at this point for immigrants seeking post-secondary schooling (Fry, 2010). In the past, education that focused solely on test preparation was short-sighted and often failed to provide students with the skills and knowledge to navigate the next steps along a post-secondary pathway. Without transition planning, immigrant students with a GED diploma may in fact have little more than a piece of paper.

The new initiative spearheaded by the GED Testing Service (GEDTS) in the US is meant to align the test with emerging standards for college and career readiness that are being implemented in schools across the US under the umbrella of the Common Core State Standards. The new standards-aligned GED is meant to be a test that not only confirms the skills to graduate high school but also demonstrates and certifies career and college readiness. The focus of the GEDTS '21st century initiative' is 'transitions', in recognition of the fact that students who try to move on to college with credentials but limited skills face often insurmountable obstacles. The changes appear promising, but questions remain for this new generation of tests. The Common Core State Standards being implemented across the US have paid scant attention to the needs of English language learners and provide few specifics as to how to leverage home language knowledge, develop academic English and build on the strengths of students like Victor, years away from having left school but wanting now to enter a post-secondary pathway.

Recent research on the retention and completion rates of post-secondary institutions reveals a disturbing trend: 30% of college students leave after their first year, without gaining their qualifications but nonetheless costing more than $6.2 billion in state appropriations and $1.5 billion in student grants. States with the highest costs included New York at $403 million (Schneider, 2010). Although dropout rates and college completion rates have not increased, the cost of college has gone up. This underscores the importance of providing non-traditional, first-generation and new-immigrant college-goers with the support not only to access post-secondary education but also to be prepared and to continue through to be successful. How will the new GED account for Victor's challenges and address his needs while also providing him with the knowledge and social capital to make a transition into a post-secondary system that is completely foreign to him? Would a student like him be better off in a vocation track, preparing directly for the workforce in a vocational training program?

Workforce Development[3]

Workforce development and career pathways programs exist in many contexts all over the US, some funded by the US Department of Labor. Existing career pathway programs typically require levels of English proficiency beyond that of recently arrived immigrant youth or those with limited formal education. The majority of programs – for example, those that target the health care field with its growing labor needs – are designed for students with a fairly high level (high intermediate or advanced) of English proficiency (CAELA Network 2009), making them unattainable for many students who are recent recipients of a GED in Spanish. With their linear approach, such programs can run the risk of replicating the same institutional barriers that led some of our immigrant young adults to adult education and second-chance options in the first place. Rather than excluding students who do not meet skill and English proficiency benchmarks, programs should extend the pathway to lower levels of proficiency, and incorporate native language instruction, English language development, career counseling and skills.

Yet such models are designed to provide precisely what the types of students who participated in this study need: contextualized or integrated instruction (Perin, 2011); support for career planning; and post-secondary success strategies (e.g. study skills, and assistance with the college application and financial aid processes) that helps students enter and succeed in college-level academic and occupational courses. In addition, many programs require proof of legal work authorization, something that would shut out students like Ramón and Victor.

Immigration status is a central factor when considering which individuals might be served by programs intended to train workers and provide labor market skills. Much of the funding restricts participation to individuals with legal immigration status. There are an estimated 11 million unauthorized immigrants currently in the US, with the majority (72%) of working age but nowhere near retirement (Capps et al., 2013). Limited to low-skilled jobs with little options for career advancement, they could benefit greatly from Workforce Development but are essentially shut out of many of the training services, despite their numbers in low-skilled jobs in many sectors of the US economy.

Models That Offer Promise

The previous pages have discussed the limitations of existing high school programs, workforce development, GED preparation and programs designed for struggling high school students. This is not to suggest that we throw up our hands and give up on this population of students. Are there promising models currently enrolling immigrant students like Ramón, Victor, Altagracia and Elena and showing some success? In the following pages I explore programs that appear to be working.

CUNY College Transition Programs[4]

When students apply for admission to the City University of New York (CUNY), immigrant status and a lack of English proficiency can make them eligible for low-cost intensive classes to develop academic proficiency in English to promote their college success. At present, community colleges within CUNY offer an intensive academic program for English language learners – both GED recipients and high school graduates. This program, the CUNY Language Immersion Program (CLIP),[5] is designed to prepare students for the demands of a college classroom and also provides counseling and orientation to a college pathway, including how to select courses, plan for study, and register. CUNY has two other initiatives at present – CUNY Start and the High School Equivalency program – that also are designed to help students spend less time in development education (i.e. remedial classes) and to speed their successful entry to college-level courses. These programs have specially designed instruction, incorporate high expectations, mentors and peer role models – precisely what was lacking for many of the participants in this research study. Some programs include opportunities for leadership development, such as a partnership that CLIP has begun with the Mayor's Office of the City of New York to train and place students as volunteer community discussion leaders for adults learning English.

Native language literacy services in community-based settings

Some services that appear to offer promise for immigrants seeking a door back into an educational pipeline are offered outside of publicly funded institutions, at community-based programs, some run exclusively by volunteers. Some community-based and volunteer programs offer education, counseling, high school equivalence preparation, workforce development in culturally responsive settings. Some programs provide services, including basic education for adults, in the native language.

In several neighborhoods in New York City with large populations of Mexicans, both foreign-born and US-born (e.g. East Harlem in Manhattan, Sunset Park in Brooklyn, Crotona, Elmhurst and Jackson Heights in Queens), community programs, often unfunded or volunteer-run, have sprung up to targeted a large population of Mexican and Central American immigrant women. Many have children in public schools in the area and some of these adults and young adults have three years or fewer of formal schooling. The students in these free programs enter basic literacy classes in Spanish, learn computer skills and can enroll in classes in English as a second language, parenting, entrepreneurship and high school equivalency classes. Students who have not yet learned the alphabet, of whom there are a significant and growing number, work collaboratively to develop the skills to read and write simple texts, including memoirs, personal narratives and poetry. Students, many of them women with small children, also learn the basic math to make a family budget and the skills to navigate the public school system and the health care system.

Sadly, such programs are often the victim of precarious funding and high staff turnover, as several in the East Harlem neighborhood of Manhattan have been. Among programs that existed to provide native language literacy and basic education services, some have student retention rates well above the averages typical of adult education programs. Notable is that such community-based programs are often recommended by word of mouth and accessible to residents of immigrant neighborhoods who may be reluctant to attend programs in large institutions – or unaware that such programs exist. There is also a level of trust and support when community members provide services for others from their own community and ethnic group. However, due to public funding constraints, such programs are often not able to muster the resources needed to sustain long years of service.

I-BEST[6]

An example of the type of program that can be adapted is Washington State's Integrating Basic Education and Skills Training (I-BEST), where instruction is contextualized around career goals. Similarly, the City University of New York's LaGuardia Community College has designed contextualized GED programs for three career pathways – business, health and professions – where students work with texts and materials from the given profession. Due to funding that sets restrictions on their participation, undocumented students who seek to improve their skills and career opportunities are often precluded from participating in such programs, especially those funded by the US Department of Labor. Nonetheless, in response to existing need, several programs have made professional training certification available to very specific populations through partnership agreements. For instance, New York City College of Technology, through its Division of Continuing Education, provides certification on occupational competence in the hospitality industry, one that employs large numbers of undocumented immigrants. Students build on existing English and workforce skills and are eligible to apply without regard to their immigration status.

Internationals Network for Public Schools[7]

The focus here on workforce training and community-based programs is not meant to suggest that high school is a lost cause for immigrant young adults. On the contrary, a school model to serve the very immigrant young adults whom typical high schools are reluctant to serve has emerged out of the small public high schools movement in the US and has demonstrated far-reaching success. Schools that are part of the Internationals Network for Public Schools seek to understand the realities of immigrant students, build a support system for them, leverage their existing strengths, and graduate them within six years, ready for college and career.

The Internationals Network Public Schools (currently 18 small public, non-charter high schools in New York City, California and Virginia) have developed a model that addresses the weaknesses of traditionally unsuccessful approaches to teaching English language learner adolescents. All teachers are trained to teach both English language and content, and teams of teachers share students and work across interdisciplinary lines. Rather than being graded into ability groups or by language proficiency levels, students at Internationals schools are mixed in heterogeneous classes, which include recently arrived labor migrants like Victor and students who have attended high school like Altagracia, as well as undocumented students and unaccompanied minors. To leverage their learning, students are encouraged to work collaboratively on structured projects that allow for different levels of participation, depth of learning and output, and students leverage their home languages for understanding and critical thinking, with complex assignments and presentations completed in English. It is common in an Internationals school classroom to see students grappling with complex content in their first language, helping each other in groups, while completing assignments in English.[8]

Teachers at Internationals schools are well aware that one of the greatest challenges for many immigrant young adults are the shifting circumstances of leaving familiar territory like the homeland and adapting to a new context that is not only foreign but may also be hostile. The negative social mirror of a hostile receiving environment can have dire consequences for identity, even for adolescents who come with a solid sense of self (Suárez-Orozco, 2004). This is precisely why Internationals schools take an asset-based approach to educating students whom some schools consider 'off limits'. Relationship-building is key, and teams of teachers travel with a fixed cohort of students, providing advice and sharing resources.

Outcomes at Internationals high schools have far exceed those at traditional high schools serving English language learners, with graduation rates nearly double those of schools that using traditional models, in which classes in English as a second language are completely separate from content area classes. The majority of their students, who enter at the lowest levels of English proficiency and some with significant schooling gaps, go on to college. At the same time, administrators must grapple constantly with accountability pressures to demonstrate progress in four years, which is often unrealistic for students who first enter school at age 17. While successful, these schools also struggle with the economic reality of many students and the pressure not only from the accountability system but from the economy, as students face demands of the workforce on top of those of school.

Opportunities, Lingering Questions and Possibilities for the Road Ahead

As a society, it would be a mistake to continue to propagate the questionable logic that conflates tangible institutional, political, economic and programmatic barriers to school completion by immigrant young adults with their ostensible lack of interest in education. We stand before an opportunity to address specific policy and program design issues in order to create opportunities that specifically target the very students whom we have long considered to be uninterested in education. Our hope should be that policies result in increased educational access and equity for immigrant young adults with interrupted schooling and lead to a better-educated workforce, broad-reaching economic gains and positive societal impact.

This chapter has presented an array of issues that are central to policy and program design, shared snapshots of some promising practices, and raised far more questions than can be answered in this brief volume. We have had a chance to glimpse the realities faced by students who have long been overlooked. Rather than ignoring these students or writing them off as failures, we have an opportunity to invest in them. By examining what works via a targeted research agenda, we have an opportunity also to improve the lives of Generation 1.5 youth and other young adults whom our institutions have failed to serve effectively. Addressing the needs of young adults who have not found their way back into education after abandoning their schooling is a systemic and societal challenge, not one for classroom teachers or school administrators to address alone. How can we address their needs? What are possible alternatives and solutions?

One final question must be asked, as it relates to immigrant young adults. What policy shifts can lead to a tangible return on investment for staying in school, especially when working full time undermines progress toward graduation, but being out of the labor force may not be viable? Especially for youth with unresolved immigration status, what educational options really provide a benefit, in the absence of a viable pathway to permanent residency or citizenship? What is the return on investment to schooling in the current economy? Is there an opportunity that lies ahead to create vocational pathways that lead to well-paying jobs with some modicum of security?

A policy response for young adult migrants with interrupted schooling must harness the flexibility and potential of adult education and address its under-funding and restrictive policies that limit creative solutions in program design. We have an opportunity to address as well the artificial disconnect between adult programs and secondary schools. In addition, a human development response will address viable job training pathways, healthy communities, personal and community investment and initiative, and pathways to citizenship.

Potential policy responses to the persistent problems discussed in this book are multifaceted. Some key dimensions are explored in the pages that follow. Again, it cannot be emphasized enough that educational solutions are bound closely with issues of the political economy, and that we must move our attention away from the constant distracting discourse that would have us invent ways to 'disappear' millions of immigrants who are currently in the US and those who are destined to arrive. The solutions proposed below presume that our goal is a healthy society that values all of its members and harnesses their potential. Central to these solutions are the ways in which they are closely linked to immigration policies – this holds true in the US and in other industrialized nations that receive large numbers of migrants.

Effective policies must together address factors that include: (1) young adults' need for employment that leads to self-sufficiency; (2) viable pathways to legal residency and citizenship; (3) flexible educational programming that adapts to students' very real life circumstances. Incentives are needed for programs that bring these youth out of the shadows, and organizations must not be penalized for opening their doors to them. Organizations and institutions attempting to develop flexible solutions must be given real incentives to adapt their services to meet students' pressing needs, and not leave students to adapt to services.

Potential solutions must move beyond simple test scores and English and math skills to provide a lifelong learning approach that enables students to improve their lives. Many immigrant students bear adult responsibilities at a very young age and without some of the supports typical of US-born youth. Effective programs must be designed to create opportunities for students to demonstrate and validate their life and work skills, as many have life and labor market experiences beyond their years.

For the young adults in this book and many others like them, the need for employment is persistent. Educational policies must incentivize, document and track the outcomes of creative programs designed with the flexibility to address the needs of a population with significant, and often shifting, work demands. Viable programmatic solutions would take into account students' developmental needs and provide counseling and academic training in bilingual formats while offering modular, short-term training schemes that result in job mobility. Students' status in adult roles could be addressed by short-term, project-based, interdisciplinary courses that align to and leverage work experience, addressing adults' desire for their learning to be applicable to the real world.

Programmatic solutions would integrate the learning of English with the learning of academic content and workplace skills and leverage students' home languages. We cannot continue to promote approaches that limit access by forcing students to wait until they are sufficiently English proficient before they get into the 'meat' of learning or training. Rather than constraining approaches to English-only, we must leverage and strengthen the non-English home languages that students bring, as we know that there is a payoff in the workforce. At the same time, to imply that the solution is simply an issue of learning English or fostering their home languages would be a gross oversimplification that ignores the broader social and political realities of these young adults and the ways in which race and class impact both access and equity.

We must focus on viable labor market options. Despite low skills and limited knowledge of pathways, the educational aspirations of the young people whom we have met in these pages are directed toward the workplace and a profession. New models of education for students otherwise classified as remedial – including new immigrants, GED recipients and disconnected youth – have a strong focus on workforce development and career and technical education (Brown & Thakur, 2006; Fischer & Bowles, 2008). Of utmost importance for the young people in this book is integration – into schools that lead to improvements, into the mainstream workforce, into jobs with opportunities for growth, into communities where they can make a contribution, into a pathway for legal residency and citizenship where they can become full members of their host society.

Immigration trends indicate that the population of young adult immigrants is permanent, not temporary, and that the greatest growth in the next decade will be among immigrants with limited literacy and interrupted formal schooling. Regardless of immigration status, and despite unprecedented numbers being deported, their numbers are growing. The Supreme Court's decision in the 1982 *Plyler v. Doe* case (see Chapter 5, page 92) ensures legal access to free public schooling for all immigrant students, regardless of their legal immigration status. Policies are needed to stem the tide of students forced out of schools. In New York City, the Department of Education has begun to look at its own school data to explore college transitions and to identify schools that 'beat the odds' with hard-to-serve populations like English language learners. Yet this examination could go farther, by gathering data on students who have been discharged and providing schools with incentives to better serve these young adults. The implications of discharging – or never allowing entry to – ill-prepared youth with few skills and limited supports into a workforce where they cannot succeed are dire. An investment in the future of this population that has already made a commitment to higher education will have long-term impacts on both their lives and the lives of their children (Kasinitz *et al.*, 2008), as well as on their host communities and the nation as a whole.

Future research should examine alternative approaches in ways that do not limit outcomes to test scores and graduation rates. Economic self-sufficiency, participation in the community and adult pathways must all be central factors to a research agenda that incentivizes creative approaches and flexibility.

Gauging Success

What about 'accountability?' A system that documents outcomes and the impact of schools at all levels of the educational continuum would make it possible to know how effective they are and whether public investment gets a worthwhile return. How do we gauge programmatic success? Can impact be measured? How should we chart the impact of investments in education over the lifespan? How much does it cost to implement a system that measures and documents what we think really matters about student progress? What would a good and useful accountability system look like? How much should it cost? Should it include test scores, empirical data, mixed methods, self-assessments or something else entirely? How do we gather results that are consistent and comparable across classrooms, schools, cities, states and nations?

Measures based solely on test scores have obvious limitations. How can we create a system to actually follow students from the time they enter to the time they leave, return, transition to other programs, stop out and then re-enter? It is clearly difficult to know what is really happening on the ground in schools and how students are faring; current accountability systems often make schools look better (or worse) than they really are and overlook large elements. How much time and money should we spend collecting data and how much should we invest in actual instruction and supportive services for students themselves? What would a system look like that actually provides incentives for schools to serve students who are currently shut out or pushed out of school? States across the US have begun to develop alternative approaches to demonstrate mastery of high school content. As one example, New York State is piloting a combination of tests and performance-based assessments that address issues of equity and provide alternative pathways for students from diverse backgrounds, including English language learners, to demonstrate mastery and achieve high school credentials (Advocates for Children of New York, 2013; New York Immigration Coalition, 2014). What can be learned from such approaches? How can research provide alternative models to gauge success and impact?

Conclusions: The Road Ahead

What lies ahead for Altagracia, Victor, Ramón and Elena? What is next for Fernando, Nelson and Rosa? What must we keep in mind as we seek to serve them effectively and others like them? First and foremost, although they may fit the profile of 'immigrant dropouts', they did not actively *choose* to abandon school. It is not acceptable or realistic to design programs and policies that impact their lives and the lives of young people like them simply by looking at statistics on educational attainment, as the number may be misleading. We have an imperative to listen to the voices of the young adults we claim to want to serve well, to understand their experiences.

Moreover, overlaying a conventional dropout paradigm on Latin American immigrants with incomplete schooling masks the contexts in which they interrupted school and their reasons for attempting to restart. Knowing a bit about their experiences, as we now do, should lead us to challenge the conventional wisdom on dropouts and reframe our thinking.

We have also learned how many factors go into being 'successful' in education of any type. To design policies that truly facilitate upward mobility, we must attend to those factors, including economic opportunity, minimum wage, labor market factors, constraints and opportunities for a path to citizenship, literacy, skills, language proficiency and multilingualism; we must also attend to program design and adolescent and adult development. Access to college is needed for both documented immigrants and those shut out of a path to citizenship. Although research reveals that the second generation is doing well in comparison with their parents, incentives to serve new arrivals are few and far between, even as their numbers rise. There is concern about how the economy, especially in the aftermath of the recession, can provide enough employment opportunities for young people coming of age. Research conducted in the 1990s (Kasinitz *et al.*, 2008; Portes & Rumbaut, 2001) demonstrated that the second generation of immigrants were doing better than their parents, but the future is unclear in the aftermath of the recession and given the fact that the impact of racism can be felt in daily life (Kasinitz *et al.*, 2013).

To address the realities of young adults like Ramón, Altagracia and their peers, funding and educational policy must meet the needs of hard-to-serve populations, increase capacity and address workforce development, not only for those who can easily transition but also for those with emergent English and literacy (Capps *et al.*, 2010). As birth rates shift, immigration increases and US demographics change, it has become clear that the coming generations of workers will comprise primarily immigrants. A strong economy and labor force in the future requires that the US invest in their education (Wrigley *et al.*, 2003).

What will happen if there is continued inattention to this growing group of young adults? This is difficult to say with any certainty, but we may continue to see young people with high aspirations stuck at the bottom rungs of the labor market and increasingly aware of the institutional and societal barriers that constrain them. The long-term detrimental impact of ignoring the need to develop effective policies for education and workforce training that fosters upward mobility will result in a negative generational impact on the children of US immigrants, on the communities in which they live, and ultimately on the US economy.

Central to the US national education agenda is a push for higher standards in K-12 education, increased graduation rates and higher numbers of of college entrants. Graduation rates for Latinos have been made a national priority (Kelly *et al.*, 2010). 'One key to the nation's future will be how it incorporates young adults of immigrant origin in its economy, polity, and society, and especially how it enables these young adults to have access to, and to attain, post-secondary education and its manifold payoffs' (Rumbaut & Komaie, 2010: 43).

Bright, and with high hopes for themselves, the young people in this study are often referred to in research as 'non-college-bound' students because of emergent skills and status as dropouts (Immerwahr, 2003). They face multiple challenges of misinformation, lack of information, competing options, unrealistic expectations and a low sense of efficacy (Immerwahr, 2003).

Research on youth development and adult learning underscores factors that promote academic engagement and help students build positive support networks. Successful programs are both culturally and developmentally responsive, keeping in mind students' levels of prior education, their socio-emotional needs, their language background and their knowledge of educational pathways. To design programs for this population, practitioners must move beyond pathologizing them (Fine, 1991; Golstein & Noguera, 2006; Way, 1998) and recognize that those who have overcome multiple obstacles have 'beaten the odds' – by arriving, succeeding and entering school. Successful programs are safety zones (Camino & Zeldon, 2002), where students find ample social and academic support. Integrated into the program and staff competencies are developmentally and culturally responsive strategies to address students' fears of failure and fear of being underprepared, which might otherwise lead them to become discouraged and abandon their studies (Cervone, 2010; Comings et al., 2000). Effective programs must be not punitive, but provide appropriate supports when students slip up, recognizing that they are still adolescents in some ways. At the same time, they must recognize the adult demands placed upon immigrant youth who are economic cornerstones for their family and put in place opportunities for them to develop competencies that will lead to academic success and to a profession.

Finally, for all the emphasis in the US about improving educational outcomes, it would be shortsighted to leave a generation of high-aspiring, over-age and low-skilled young adults out of the educational pipeline just as the need for post-secondary schooling for upward mobility becomes most acute. Policy and programmatic solutions that address individual needs must also be understood in a larger perspective. Ill-conceived policies that create institutional constraints for immigrant young adults often perpetuate educational failure, rather than upward mobility. As a result, they impair the economy and the workforce, negatively impacting society as a whole.

We cannot talk about immigrant youth and their aspirations without talking about immigration status and the perpetually stalled attempts to create a pathway to citizenship for millions of US residents, many of them high school and college graduates, in whom the US has invested time and resources. Any analysis of their situation and of programs designed to serve them is solidly positioned in the context of national immigration policies, including current policies about post-secondary access for undocumented students, access to secondary programs for immigrant students, and immigration reform.

As a society, it would be counterproductive to discourage education, but without pushing for significant economic and labor reform, do we risk perpetuating the belief that education is still a guarantee? Without changes in the political economy and without reforms in the immigration system, education reforms that provide well-designed programs for immigrant young adults seeking to complete their education will be efforts that fall short of having a significant impact in the long term. We must challenge perspectives that focus blame on individual immigrants for their failures, otherwise we may risk ignoring significant, persistent weaknesses in larger institutional structures and as a result lose the opportunity to remedy them.

Young adults like Victor, Ramón, Elena, Altagracia, Nelson, Fernando and Rosa have bought into the dream. The US and other immigrant host nations stand before an immense opportunity to invest in and make real these young people's dreams. Our collective response to the hopes of these young people will be one of the most pressing societal issues in the years ahead.

Notes

(1) http://schools.nyc.gov/ChoicesEnrollment/SpecialPrograms/AlternativesHS/YoungAdult/default.htm
(2) http://www.gedtestingservice.com/educators/2014-faqs
(3) http://www.dol.gov/opa/media/press/eta/eta20111409.htm
(4) http://www.cuny.edu/academics/programs/notable/CATA.html
(5) http://www.clip.cuny.edu/index.htm
(6) http://www.sbctc.ctc.edu/college/e_integratedbasiceducationandskillstraining.aspx
(7) http://internationalsnps.org/
(8) https://www.teachingchannel.org/internationals-network-video-library-inps

Appendix

Site Selection: Listening for Voices

Starting in 1996, I began my work in New York City's vibrant and multifaceted adult education community. New York City is unique in that it has a network of diverse institutional providers that offer free, publicly funded classes for adults in English as a second language, basic literacy in English, basic education in the native language (for non-English-speaking immigrants) and preparation for the high school equivalency (GED) exam. The field of provider institutions is wide and includes: three library systems (Queensborough, Brooklyn and New York Public Libraries) spanning all five boroughs; the vast City University of New York, which serves 200,000 degree-seeking students and an additional 200,000 individuals in adult and continuing education programs; community-based programs in churches and social service agencies; union-based programs that serve union members and their families; and the New York City Department of Education, with its own Office of Adult and Continuing Education.

With its diverse offerings of second-chance and alternative educational options, New York City provides an ideal setting to examine the pathways and aspirations of immigrant young adults with incomplete high school education. The City's coordinated system of adult education providers receives funding from federal, state and city sources (Literacy Assistance Center, 2008). This network of programs and classes is one of the largest providers in the US of adult and youth education; in 2006–07 it provided basic education, GED and English as a second language to 62,000 out-of-school youths and adults in New York City, 44% of whom were Latino. More than 70% of students attending adult programs in New York City are immigrant English language learners (Colton, 2006).

After more than a decade dedicated to providing professional development and program support in every corner of this vast network, I had been in innumerable classrooms and built professional relationships with teachers and program managers. Knowing the limitations of available public data to identify immigrant students in adult education programs by level of education and country of origin, I set out to counter the need to estimate and to get beyond solely numerical representations of individuals' experience, to uncover their stories.

Using the US Census as a tool, I determined that Latino immigrant young adults with incomplete high school education in New York City number highest among Mexicans, Dominicans, Central Americans and some South Americans. To address the need to estimate that resulted from the lack of detail in both Census and program enrollment data, I constructed a purposeful sample. Data from the 2000 US Census were a valuable tool to identify neighborhoods with high concentrations of Latino immigrants. New York State adult education program data were used along with listings of community-based programs to identify organizations that serve them. From among the institutional diversity of New York City program providers that serve immigrant young adults, I selected seven very different sites that provided English as a second language and Spanish GED classes at no cost and that had high Latino enrollments.

The seven sites that I selected from which to recruit participants for my study were chosen because, together, they provided a broad geographic distribution and represented a diverse institutional and fiscal base (publicly funded, privately funded and run by volunteers). The selected sites were: three community-based programs, one public library, two school district-run programs (one for students aged 17–21 and one for those aged 21 and over) and one community college program in English as a second language.

Table A1 Study sites

Site	Institution	Program
Youth GED (for 17–21-year-olds)	Public school district	English as a second language and GED in Spanish
Adult Learn	Public school district	English as a second language and GED in Spanish
ESOL Intensive	Public community college	English as a second language
Community Learn	Public library	English as a second language
Neighborhood Learn	Community-based organization	English as a second language and GED in Spanish
Neighbors Unite	Community-based organization	English as a second language and GED in Spanish
Paisanos Unidos	Community-based organization	GED in Spanish

The community-based programs served primarily Mexican and Dominican students, two of the largest immigrant subgroups in New York City and those demonstrating the lowest levels of formal education. Table A1 lists the sites (with pseudonyms), all of which are located in New York City.

Participant Selection and Recruitment

All of the young adults who participated in this research did so as volunteers. Within each program, enrollment data were used to select a subset of youths who fitted the criteria – Latino immigrants who entered the US between the ages of 15 and 24, native Spanish-speakers, born in Mexico, Central America, South America or the Spanish-speaking Caribbean. Two overlapping methods were used to select participants. The first was enrollment data, as two participating sites (ESOL Intensive and Community Learn) had available sufficient student data to identify enrolled youths who fitted the study criteria. In the remaining programs, student data did not include year or age at entry or prior schooling, making data-based selection impossible and, as a result, students self-selected to attend an orientation. At each of the seven sites, orientations in Spanish were conducted to explain the research and conditions of participation. Far from demonstrating reluctance to participate, many more students than anticipated were interested in participating and nearly all expressed a desire to be interviewed about their educational experiences.

Purposeful, criterion-based sampling (Merriam, 2009) was used to select participants and to ensure diversity in country of origin, gender, prior education and geographic region. Because it is a purposeful rather than a random sample, results from this sample of 149 participants cannot be broadly generalized across the US, but they are nonetheless relevant for locales both in the US and abroad that are receiver communities for migrant youths. Without question, large statistical datasets provide powerful evidence across a representative sample of the population in ways that case studies from a purposeful sample cannot. My research explores a corner of the immigrant population and, though significant, is not meant to be generalized in the same way that large statistically powerful samples are.

Limitations

Another possible limitation is the potential inaccuracy of self-reported years of schooling. Actual educational attainment of some participants may be lower than their self-reports indicate. Teachers and staff in the programs with which I worked reported that students often exaggerate their years of schooling, for a variety of reasons. Analysis of writing, vocabulary and word choice in open-ended survey responses suggest that skill levels did not always match the years of education reported. This is merely anecdotal and suggests a need for further research.

An obvious limitation results from the use of a survey tool. Only participants with the literacy skills able to complete a written survey could be included in this sample. Due to resource limitations of this study, students with very limited literacy were not included, even if they otherwise fitted the study criteria, as they were unable to complete the written survey. As such, this subset of the population remains invisible and should be the subject of future research on this topic.

Trustworthiness and credibility are concerns central to a mixed methods study. To ensure validity, methodological triangulations were used to compare data from different sources to check for inconsistencies or irregularities (Bogdan & Biklen, 1998; Willis, 2007). Analytical validity was addressed using member checks (both with study participants and with staff at each center) in the process of coding and analyzing the data. Participatory research methods like the focus group have built-in validity, as participants 'actively participate in the formulation of conclusions' (Willis, 2007: 220).

Instruments for Data Collection

The Spanish version of the survey, which is presented after the English translation below, was used with the study participants.

Survey

Today's date:
Center where you study:

To learn about educational goals of Latinos in New York, please answer the following questions. All of your answers will remain anonymous.

Personal information
1.
    a. Age:
    b. Year you were born:
2. Sex: Male/Female
3.
    a. Are you employed? Yes/No
    b. How many hours/week do you work?
    c. What kind of work do you do?

4.
　　a. Do you have children? Yes/No
　　b. Do your children live with you? Yes/No
　　c. Ages of your children:

Your country
5. Birthplace:
6.
　　a. In your country do you come from: A village/Small town/City, metropolitan area
　　b. Do you speak an indigenous language? Yes/No, What language?

Coming to the US
7. What year did you come to the US?
8. How old were you when you arrived?
9. Who did you migrate to the US with? Parents/Other relatives/Alone, with relatives in the US/Alone, with no one here
10. Who do you live with now? Parents/Other relatives/Domestic partner/ Husband/wife/Friends/Alone

Your education in your country
11. How old were you when you stopped attending school in your country?
12. Were you still in school when you left to come to the US? Yes/No
13. Indicate the level of education (elementary, secondary, high school, baccalaureate, university) achieved by the following people in your family:
　　mother
　　father
　　brother
　　sister
　　grandmother
　　grandfather
14. Did you complete **primary** school? Yes/No
15. Did you complete **secondary** school? Yes/No
16.
　　a. Did you begin baccalaureate studies in your country? Yes/No
　　b. Did you complete baccalaureate studies in your country? Yes/No
17. If you did not finish school in your country, why did you leave school?
　　There was no school to go to/I had no access to school
　　I had to work
　　My parents did not let me continue school
　　My family did not have the money to send me to school
　　I left my country to come to the US
　　Other (please explain)

High school in the US

18. Have you attended high school in the US? Yes/No
    (If your answer is NO, continue to question 24)
19. How long did you go to high school in the US?
    Less than 1 year
    1–2 years
    2–3 years
    4 years
    more than 4 years
20. At what age did you start high school in the US?
21. In what grade did you start US high school?
22. Why did you leave high school? (Check all that apply)
    I did not like it
    I felt like I was too old to be in high school
    I had to work
    My school sent me to another educational program
    I was not a good student/I did not pay attention in school
    I did not like my teachers
    It was too difficult
    Other:
23. Please mark all of the below that are true about your high school in the US:
    In my classes there were very few students who did not speak English
    Most of the classes I had were in *English*
    Most of the classes I had were in *Spanish*
    I had special education classes
    Most of my classmates were immigrants

Your education Now

24. Which of the following programs do you know about? (Check all that apply)
    Newcomer high school
    Free English classes
    International high school
    English classes for fee
    GED Plus Program
    Community College Transition
    GED en Español
    Plaza Comunitaria
25. Are you taking classes in any other program? Yes/No
26. If you answered 'yes' to #25, what is the name of the program?

27. Who told you about or how did you find out about the program you are now attending?

Friend
Relative/family member
Radio ad
Newspaper ad
The consulate
My church
My high school sent me
Referred by another educational program
Other

28. Who do you ask when you want to know something about continuing your education?

My parents
My friends
A family member/relative
Officials from the consulate
Someone in my church
Other members of an ethnic club
Other

29. When did you start studying in this program? (month and year)

30. Why did you choose this program or school? (Check all that apply)

Close to home/work
My friends go here
Classes here are in Spanish
The schedule works for me
Because it is free
It is the only program I knew about
I looked at many programs and it was best
Other:

Your goals

31. Mark the level of education you *want* to achieve:

Take the GED exam
Go to college/university (2 years)
Go to college/university (4 years)
Master's degree
Doctorate (PhD)

32. Mark the level of education that you think you will be *able* to achieve:

Take the GED exam
Go to college/university (2 years)
Go to college/university (4 years)
Master's degree
Doctorate (PhD)

33. What obstacles that might prevent you from getting the education you want? (Check all that apply)

Money

Being undocumented/no having legal immigration status

Racism

Work

Not speaking English

Not knowing how the system works

Being an immigrant

Other

34. How much you agree or disagree with each of the following statements about education (strongly disagree; disagree; agree; strongly agree):

Education is the key to success in the future

If everyone in America gets a good education, we can end poverty

Achievement and effort in school lead to job success later on

The way for poor people to become middle class is for them to get a good education

School success is not necessarily a clear path to a better life

Getting a good education is a practical road to success for a person like me

Young people like me have a chance of making it if we do well in school

Education really pays off in the future for a young person like me

35. How has attending school helped you in your work or your life?

36. What questions do you have about continuing your education?

37. What advice would you give to an immigrant like yourself about education?

Many thanks for your participation

Spanish version of survey

Fecha de hoy:

Escuela donde estudias ahora:

Para investigar sobre la educación y experiencias de Latinos en Nueva York, favor de contestar las siguientes preguntas. No es necesario que escribas tu nombre.

Sobre ti

1.

a. Edad:

b. Año en que naciste

2. Sexo: M/F

3.
  a. Tienes empleo? Sí/No
  b. ¿Cuántas horas trabajas durante la semana?
  c. ¿A qué te dedicas?
4.
  a. ¿Tienes hijos? Sí/No
  b. ¿Viven tus hijos contigo? Sí/No
  c. Edades de tus hijos:

Tu país de origen
5. País de origen:
6.
  a. En tu país vivías en: Un pueblo/Una ciudad mediana/Una aérea metropolitana
  b. ¿Hablas un idioma indígena? Sí/No ¿Cual?

Llegando al EU
7. ¿En qué año llegaste a Estados Unidos?
8. ¿Qué edad tenías al llegar?
9. ¿Con quién viniste a Estados Unidos? Con mis padres/Con otros familiares/Solo, pero tenía familiares aquí/Solo sin conocer a nadie
10. ¿Con quién vives ahora? Mis padres/Otros parientes/Pareja/esposo/a Amigos/Vivo sólo

Tu educación en tu país
11. ¿Cuántos años asististe a la escuela en tu país?
12. ¿Estabas asistiendo a la escuela todavía cuando saliste para Estados Unidos? Sí/No
13. Indica el nivel de educación (primaria, secundaria, bachillerato, universidad) logrado por las siguientes personas en tu familia
  madre
  padre
  hermano
  hermana
  abuela
  abuelo
14. ¿Terminaste la **escuela primaria** en tu país? Sí/No
15. ¿Terminaste la **escuela secundaria** en tu país? Sí/No
16.
  a. ¿Empezaste el bachillerato/preparatoria en tu país? Sí/No
  b. ¿Terminaste el bachillerato/preparatoria en tu país? Sí/No

17. Si no terminaste la escuela en tu país ¿cuáles fueron las razones por las que dejaste la escuela?

No había escuela

Tenía que trabajar

Mis padres no me dejaron asistir a la escuela

Mi familia no tenía dinero para mandarme a la escuela

Salí para Estados Unidos

Otro razón (favor de explicar) :

El high school en USA

18. ¿Has asistido a *High School* en USA? Sí/No

(Si contestaste NO, siga a la pregunta 24)

19. ¿Por cuánto tiempo asististe al *High School*?

1–3 meses

4 meses –1 año

más de 1 año

2 años

3 años

20. ¿A qué edad empezaste el *High School* en USA?

21. ¿En qué grado (*grade*) empezaste?

22. ¿Por qué saliste del High School en E. U? (indica todos que son verdad)

no me gustaba

me sentía muy grande para estar en la escuela

tenía que trabajar

la escuela me mandó para otro programa

no era buen estudiante/no ponía atención

no me gustaban los maestros

era muy difícil

Otro

23. ¿Cuáles de las siguientes materias has tomado en el *High School* en USA?

ESL (Inglés como segunda lengua)

Materias académicas en español (p. ej., Ciencias, Matemáticas, etc.)

Materias académicas en inglés (p. ej., World History, Math, Algebra)

Música, Arte, etc.

Preparación vocacional

Otro

Tu educación ahora

24. ¿Cuáles de los siguientes programas conoces?

Newcomer high school

Clases de inglés gratis

Internacional high school

Clases de inglés pagadas

Programa de GED Plus

Programa de transición de colegio
Comunitario
GED en Español
Plaza Comunitaria
25. ¿Estás tomando clases en otro centro además de este? Sí/No
26. Si contestaste sí a la pregunta anterior, ¿cómo se llama el otro programa?
27. ¿Cómo supiste o quién te dijo de esta escuela?
Un amigo
Un familiar/pariente
Radio
Periódico
El Consulado
Mi iglesia
El High School me mandó
Me mandaron de otro programa
Otro:
28. ¿A quién preguntas si quieres información sobre tu educación?
Mis padres
Mis amigos
Un familiar/pariente
Los oficiales del Consulado
Alguien en mi iglesia
Otros miembros de un club de oriundos
Otro:
29. ¿Cuándo empezaste a estudiar aquí? Indica la fecha
30. ¿Por qué escogiste esta escuela en particular?
Está cerca a mi casa o mi trabajo
Mis amigos vienen a esta escuela
Aquí dan clases en español
El horario me sirve
Es gratis
Es el único programa que conozco
Fue el mejor de los programas que ví
Otro:

Tus metas
31. Indica el nivel de educación que *quieres* lograr.
Tomar el GED
Ir a *College*/Universidad (2 años)
Certificación vocacional / profesional
Ir a *College*/Universidad (4 años)
Terminar la Maestría
Terminar un doctorado (PhD)

32. Indica el nivel de educación que crees que vas a *poder* lograr.
    Tomar el GED
    Ir a *College*/Universidad (2 años)
    Certificación vocacional / profesional
    Ir a *College*/Universidad (4 años)
    Terminar la Maestría
    Terminar un doctorado (PhD)

33. Indica cuales de los siguientes son obstáculos en lograr tus metas educacionales.
    El dinero
    No tener papeles, no tener estatus legal
    El racismo
    El trabajo
    No poder hablar inglés
    No conocer el sistema
    Ser inmigrante
    Otro:

34. Indica quetanto esta o *no* esta de acuerdo con lo siguienre (muyo de acuerdo; un poco de acuerdo; no de acuerdo; completemente no de acuerdo):
    L education es las clave para el exito en un futuro
    Si todos en Eastdo Unidos se educan bien, podemos terminar con la pobreza
    Los es fuersoz y lo gros en las escuela reltan en el exitor future en el trabajo
    Las personas sin muchos recursos economicos pueden llegara a la calse media por medio de una Buena educacion
    El exito escolar no es necesariamente el camino pra una vida major
    Una persona como yo puede obtener el exitor por medio de una Buena educacion
    Jovenes como yo tienela oportunidad deternexitor en la vida si so bresalenen en las escuela
    La educacion result definitive mentee n lo gros en el furuo para personas como yo
    Sus comentarios:

35. ¿Cómo te ha ayudado asistir a la escuela aquí?

36. ¿Qué preguntas tienes acerca de tu educación?

37. ¿Qué consejor darias a un inmigrante como tu acerca de su educación?
    Otros comentarios:

Muchas gracias por tu valiosa colaboración

Focus Group Protocol

1. Review of goals of research

You have been invited to take part in a research study to understand the goals of immigrant newcomers aged 18–24 in New York City and their educational choices. This study will be conducted by Marguerite Lukes of the Steinhardt School of Education at New York University.

Some of the interviews will be audio-taped or video-taped. You may review these tapes and request that all or any part of the tapes that includes your participation be destroyed.

2. Review of risks of research – Ensure that each participant has signed a consent form

There is no risk connected with your participation in this research beyond the regular risks you face in your daily life. Even though you will not gain anything personally from participating, being part of this research will help the investigator understand better how to design good educational programs for people like yourself.

3. Rules of anonymity of research – No names – What is said in the room stays in the room

Your responses will be kept strictly confidential by not including your name or any specific personal information in any of the records. The only persons with direct access to this information collected from you will be the investigator and the faculty sponsor. If you choose to participate in the small focus group interview, your responses will be kept confidential by the researcher, but the researcher cannot guarantee that others in the group will do the same.

4. Discussion topics

- Introductions – Names and country.
- Vision for the future.
- Goals prior to emigrating? Current goals? How have they changed?
- How do you plan to reach your goals?
- What are the milestones along your path to reach your goals?
- What are your educational options?
- Social networks – How do you obtain information about educational opportunities?
- How do you make your choices? How do you know they are good choices?

- Who do you go to for advice? Who advises you?
- What are the obstacles along your path to your goals?
- What resources do you have that help you reach your goals?
- What advice would you give to other young people like yourself who emigrate to the US?

Interview Protocol

- Name, age.
- Year and age at migration.
- Reasons for coming to the US.
- Circumstances of migration.
- Background of family – tell me about your family.
- Expectations and goals upon migrating.
- When and how did you come to enroll in the present educational program?
- What are your goals in this program?
- What are next steps after you finish the program? Draw a picture for me of how you will get from here to your goal.
- Who do you know who has reached this same goal that you aspire to?
- Who advises you on your goals and who do you get information from?
- What is helping you reach your goal?
- What obstacles have you encountered?
- Are there people like you among your friends who are trying to reach this same goal?
- Are there people like you among your family who are trying to reach this same goal?

Empirical Data and Statistical Significance

A Mann–Whitney test and an independent-samples t-test were conducted to determine whether there were significant differences in goals between the younger subset of participants (age < 24) and the older subset (age > 25). Educational goals were quantified from 1 (GED) to 4 (graduate degree) and a score assigned. The tests revealed no significant difference in scores for educational goals between younger participants (mean $= 2.5$, SD $= 1.1$) and older (mean $= 2.3$, SD $= 1.00$). Table A2 illustrates these results.

The Mann–Whitney test for the hypothesis that the goals of the two age groups are drawn from same distribution: $Z = -1.023$, $p = 0.31$.

A Mann–Whitney test was also conducted to determine whether being a parent had a significant effect on goals, but there was no significant difference ($p = 0.62$) in goals between parents (mean $= 2.45$, SD $= 1.08$) and non-parents (mean $= 2.38$, SD $= 1.06$).

Table A2 Differences in educational goals by age

Goals	Age 25 or older (%)	Age 18-24 (%)
GED	25.0	22.8
Associate	32.8	29.1
Bachelor's	28.1	22.8
Graduate	14.1	25.3
Total	100.0	100.0

Table A3 Differences in educational goals by region of origin

Goals	Not urban (%)	Urban (%)
GED	26.5	21.3
Associate	26.5	34.7
Bachelor's	29.4	21.3
Graduate	17.7	22.7
Total	100.0	100.0

The literature on economic development and education indicates that the area of a country in which a person lives in Latin America can be a strong predictor of educational access and attainment (Arnett, 2007; UNICEF, 2010). To explore the possible effect of geographic region on educational goals, I collapsed the variable for the area in which the participant had grown up in the country of origin into a dichotomous variable with only two categories: urban or rural. The goal was to differentiate between participants from primarily agricultural areas and those from town and urban areas, to see whether this factor correlated with having more access to education. As illustrated in Table A3, the Mann–Whitney test revealed no significant difference ($p = 0.72$) between the educational goals of participants from rural areas (mean = 2.38, SD = 1.06) and towns/urban areas (mean = 2.45, SD = 1.07).

Mann–Whitney test for hypothesis goals of groups are drawn from same distribution: $Z = -0.360$, $p = 0.72$ ($n = 143$).

Prior education and goals

Educational level attained prior to emigrating was revealed to be significant according to the Mann–Whitney test ($p = 0.05$) (Table A4). Participants who completed eight years of schooling and began their pre-college baccalaureate studies (mean = 2.6, SD = 1.03) had goals that were significantly

Table A4 Differences in educational goals by prior education in home country

Goals	Less than eight years of schooling (%)	Completed eight or more years of schooling (%)
GED	28.1	18.0
Associate	32.9	27.9
Bachelor's	23.2	27.9
Graduate	15.9	26.2
Total	100.0	100.0

higher than the goals of those who had completed less than eight years of schooling (mean = 2.17, SD = 1.06). In this sample, 65 participants (43.6%) began their *bachillerato*, or pre-college high school education. An eta-squared value of 0.04 indicated a small to moderate effect, with 4% of the variance in goals related to education attained prior to emigrating. Mann–Whitney test for hypothesis goals of groups are drawn from same distribution: $Z = -1.967$, $p = 0.05$, $n = 143$.

Table A5 provides a summary of the differences in educational goals by participant subgroup. Using both parametric independent-samples t-tests and non-parametric Mann–Whitney tests, no significant differences between subgroup means were found based on sex, age, parental status or region of origin.

Table A5 Subgroup differences in educational goals

| | Mean | SD | Test of null hypothesis that groups have same goals | | | Effect size (eta) |
| | | | t-test | Mann–Whitney test | | |
			p-value	p-value	Z	
Men	2.45	1.06				
Women	2.38	1.07				
Difference	0.07	–	0.69	0.67	–0.431	
Age<24	2.50	1.1				
Age>25	2.31	1.0				
Difference	0.19	–	0.28	0.31	–1.023	
Parent	2.47	1.08				
Not parent	2.38	1.06				
Difference	0.09	–	0.64	0.63	–0.491	
Urban	2.45	1.07				
Non-urban	2.38	1.06				
Difference	0.07	–	0.69	0.72	–0.360	
Working	2.70	0.96				
Not working	2.25	1.10				
Difference	0.46	–	0.01	0.01	–2.513	0.040
Prior schooling > 8 years	2.62	1.07				
Prior schooling <8 years	2.27	1.04				
Difference	0.35	–	0.05	0.05	–1.967	0.026
Mother's education > 8 years	2.29	1.05				
Mother's education < 8 years	2.81	1.06				
Difference	0.52	–	0.03	0.03	–2.125	0.031

Note: Educational goals is a variable ranging from 1 (GED) to 4 (graduate degree). The test in column 3 is an independent samples t-test; the test in columns 4 and 5 is the Mann–Whitney non-parametric test

Bibliography

Adelman, C. (1998) The kiss of death? An alternative view of college remediation. *National Crosstalk*. At http://www.highereducation.org/crosstalk/ct0798/voices0798-adelman. shtml (accessed November 2014).

Adelman, C. (2006) *The Toolbox Revisited: Paths to Degree Completion from High School Through College*. Washington, DC: US Department of Education.

Advocates for Children (2010) *Students with Interrupted Formal Education: A Challenge for New York City Public Schools*. New York: Advocates for Children of New York. At http://www.advocatesforchildren.org/sites/default/files/library/sife_2010.pdf?pt=1 (accessed November 2014).

Advocates for Children of New York (2013) *Rethinking Pathways to High School Graduation in New York State. New York: Coalition for Multiple Pathways to a Diploma*. At http:// www.advocatesforchildren.org/sites/default/files/library/rethinking_pathways_to_ graduation.pdf?pt=1 (accessed November 2014).

Advocates for Children of New York (n.d.) Litigation. The trilogy of push-out cases. At http://www.advocatesforchildren.org/litigation/class_actions/trilogy (accessed November 2014).

Agirdag, O. (2014) The long-term effects of bilingualism on children of immigration: Student bilingualism and future earnings. *International Journal of Bilingual Education and Bilingualism*, 17 (4), 449–464.

Aguilar, J. (2012) Twenty years later, Nafta remains a source of tension. *New York Times*, December 7.

Alamprese, J. (2004) *GED Transitions: Focus on Basics, 6(D)*. Cambridge, MA: Harvard, University, National Center for the Study of Adult Learning and Literacy (NCSALL).

Alba, R. and Nee, V. (2003) *Remaking the American Mainstream: Assimilation and Contemporary Immigration*. Cambridge, MA: Harvard University Press.

Alexander, M. (2010) *The New Jim Crow: Mass Incarceration in an Age of Colorblindness*. New York: New Press.

Alvarez, L. (2009) In uncertain times, valedictorians look ahead. *New York Times*, June 26.

Alvarez, R.M. and Butterfield, T.L. (1997) The resurgence of nativism in California? The case of Proposition 187 and illegal immigration. Pasadena, CA: California Institute of Technology, September 25.

American Civil Liberties Union (2010) One in five New York State districts puts up illegal barriers for immigrant children. At https://www.aclu.org/immigrants-rights/ nyclu-analysis-1-5-new-york-state-school-districts-puts-illegal-barriers-immigrant (accessed November 2014).

American Council on Education (2008) *GED Testing Program Statistical Report*. Washington, DC: GED Testing Service, American Council on Education.

Anderson, E. (1994) The code of the streets. *Atlantic Monthly* 273 (5), 80–94.

Anderson, J. (2013) Is this the best education money can buy? *New York Times*, May 2.

Anyon, J. (2005) *Radical Possibilities: Public Policy, Urban Education, and a New Social Movement*. New York: Routledge.

Apple, M. (2006) *Educating the Right Way: Markets, Standards, God and Inequality* (2nd edn). New York: Routledge.

Arnett, J. (2004) *Emerging Adulthood: The Winding Road from the Late Teens Through the Twenties*. New York: Oxford University Press.

Arnett, J. (2007) Mexico. In *International Encyclopedia of Adolescence* (pp. 632–644). New York: Routledge, Taylor and Francis.

Arnez, N.L. (1978) Implementation of desegregation as a discriminatory process. *Journal of Negro Education* 47 (1), 28–45.

Aron, L. and Zweig, J. (2003) *Educational Alternatives for Vulnerable Youth: Student Needs, Program Types, and Research Directions*. Washington, DC: Urban Institute.

Aud, S., Hussar, W., Kena, G., Bianco, K., Frohlich, L., Kemp, J. and Tahan, K. (2011) *The Condition of Education 2011* (NCES 2011–033). US Department of Education, National Center for Education Statistics. Washington, DC: US Government Printing Office.

Auerbach, E.R. (1993) Reexamining English-only in the ESL classroom. *TESOL Quarterly* 27 (1), 9–32.

August, D. and Hakuta, K. (1997) *Improving Schooling for Language-Minority Children*. Washington, DC: National Academy Press.

August, D. and Shanahan, T. (eds) (2008) *Developing Reading and Writing in Second-Language Learners: Lessons from the Report of the National Literacy Panel on Language-Minority Children and Youth*. New York: Routledge for the American Association of Colleges for Teacher Education.

Bacon, D. (2004) *Children of NAFTA: Labor Wars on the US/Mexico Border*. Riverside, CA: University of California Press.

Baer, J., Mark, K. and Sabatini, J.P. (2009) *Basic Reading Skills and the Literacy of America's Least Literate Adults: Results from the 2003 National Assessment of Adult Literacy (NAAL) Supplemental Studies* (NCES 2009–481). Washington, DC: National Center for Educational Statistics, Institute for Educational Statistics.

Barro, R.J. and Lee, J.W. (1996) International measures of schooling years and school quality. *Economic Reform and Growth* 82 (2), 218–223.

Barro, R.J. and Lee, J.W. (2010) *A New Data Set of Educational Attainment in the World, 1950–2010*. Washington, DC: National Bureau of Economic Research.

Barron, L. (2013) State cuts $1M from adult-education program in Washington Heights, forcing immediate cuts. *New York Daily News*, June 10. At http://www.nydaily news.com/new-york/uptown/big-state-cuts-upper-manhattan-adult-programs-article-1.1368664 (accessed October 2014).

Batalova, J. and Fix, M. (2011) *Up for Grabs: The Gains and Prospects of First- and Second-Generation Young Adults*. Washington, DC: Migration Policy Institute. At http://www.migrationpolicy.org/pubs/youngadults-upforgrabs.pdf (accessed October 2014).

Batalova, J. and Lee, A. (2012) Frequently requested statistics on immigrants and immigration in the United States. *Spotlight*. Washington, DC: Migration Policy Institute, March 21, 2012. Accessed at http://www.migrationpolicy.org/article/frequently-requested-statistics-immigrants-and-immigration-united-states-0.

Batalova, J. and Terrazas, A. (2007) *The Recently Arrived Foreign-Born in the United States*. Migration Information Source. Washington, DC: Migration Policy Institute. At http://www.migrationinformation.org/feature/display.cfm?ID=603#3 (accessed October 2014).

Belfield, C.R. and Levin, H.M. (2007) *The Economic Losses from High School Dropouts in California*. Santa Barbara, CA: California Dropout Research Project.

Belzer, A. (1998) Stopping out, not dropping out: *Focus on Basics*, 2 (A). At http://www.ncsall.net/index.php@id=417.html (accessed November 2014).

Bergad, L.W. (2011) *The Latino Population of New York City, 1990—2010. Latino Data Project – Report 44 – November 2011*. New York: City University of New York, Center for Latin American and Caribbean Studies. At http://clacls.gc.cuny.edu/files/2013/10/The-Latino-Population-of-New-York-City-1990-2010.pdf (accessed October 2014).

Bernstein, N. (2010) No visa, no school, many New York districts say. *New York Times*, July 22.

Blau, P.M. and Duncan, O.D. (1967) *The American Occupational Structure*. New York: Wiley.

Boesel, D., Alsalam, N. and Smith, T.M. (1998) *Research Synthesis: Educational and Labor Market Performance of GED Recipients*. Washington, DC: US Department of Education. At http://www.edpubs.gov/document/ed001441b.pdf (accessed October 2014).

Bogdan, R.C. and Biklen, S.K. (1998) *Qualitative Research in Education: An Introduction to Theory and Methods* (3rd edn). Needham Heights, MA: Allyn and Bacon.

Bohon, S.A., Kirkpatrick, M. and Gorman, B.K. (2006) College aspirations and expectations among Latino adolescents in the United States. *Social Problems* 53 (2), 207–225.

Bourdieu, P. (1980) Le capital social: Notes provisoires. *Actes de la Recherche en Sciences Sociales* 31, 2–3.

Bourdieu, P. (1986) The forms of capital. In J. Richardson (ed.) *Handbook of Theory and Research for the Sociology of Education* (pp. 241–258). New York: Greenwood.

Bourdieu, P. and Passeron, J.C. (1977) *Reproduction in Education, Culture and Society*. Beverly Hills, CA: Sage.

Brookfield, S. (1991) *Understanding and Facilitating Adult Learning*. San Francisco, CA: Jossey-Bass.

Brown, D.E. and Thakur, M.B. (2006) Workforce development for older youth. *New Directions for Youth Development* 111, 91–104.

Bureau of Labor Statistics (2012) Foreign-born workers: Labor force characteristics. News release, May 24. Washington, DC: US Department of Labor. At http://www.bls.gov/news.release/pdf/forbrn.pdf (accessed October 2014).

Burt, M. and Peyton, J.K. (2003) *Reading and Adult English Language Learners: The Role of the First Language*. Washington, DC: National Center for ESL Literacy Education.

Burt, M., Peyton, J.K. and Adams, R. (2003) *Reading and Adult English Language Learners: A Review of the Research*. Washington, DC: Center for Applied Linguistics.

Bush, M. (2010) *Compulsory School Age Requirements*. Denver, CO: Education Commission of the States. At http://www.ncsl.org/documents/educ/ECSCompulsoryAge.pdf (accessed October 2014).

Bynner, J. (2005) Rethinking the youth phase of the life-course: The case for emerging adulthood. *Journal of Youth Studies* 8 (4), 367–384.

Byrne, O. and Miller, E. (2012) *The Flow of Unaccompanied Children through the Immigration System: A Resource for Practitioners, Policy Makers, and Researchers*. New York: Vera Institute for Justice. At http://www.vera.org/sites/default/files/resources/downloads/the-flow-of-unaccompanied-children-through-the-immigration-system.pdf (accessed October 2014).

CAELA Network (2009) *Education for Adult English Language Learners in the United States: Trends, Research, and Promising Practices*. Washington, DC: Center for Applied Linguistics. At http://www.cal.org/caelanetwork/pdfs/education-for-adult-ells-with-new-copyright.pdf (accessed November 2014).

Callahan, R. and Gándara, P. (eds) (2014) *The Bilingual Advantage: Language, Literacy and the US Labor Market*. Bristol: Multilingual Matters.

Cameron, S.V. and Heckman, J.J. (1999) *The Dynamics of Educational Attainment for Blacks, Hispanics and Whites*. NBER Working Paper No. 7249. *Journal of Political Economy* 109 (3), 455–499.

Camino, L. and Zeldin, S. (2002) Making the transition to community youth development: Emerging roles and competencies for youth-serving organizations and youth workers. *Community Youth Development Journal* 3, 70–78.

Capps, R., Fix, M. and Lin, Y. (2013) Still an hourglass? Immigrant workers in middle-skilled jobs. At http://www.migrationpolicy.org/research/immigrant-workers-middle-skilled-jobs (accessed November 2014).

Capps, R., Bachmeier, J.D., Fix, M. and Van Hook, J. (2013) *A Demographic, Socioeconomic, and Health Coverage Profile of Unauthorized Immigrants in the United States*. Washington, DC: Migration Policy Institute. At http://www.migrationpolicy.org/research/demographic-socioeconomic-and-health-coverage-profile-unauthorized-immigrants-united-states (accessed November 2014).

Carnevale, A.P., Rose, S.J. and Cheah, B. (2011) *The College Payoff: Education, Occupations, Lifetime Earnings. Executive Summary*. Washington, DC: Georgetown University Center on Education and the Workforce. At http://cew.georgetown.edu/collegepayoff/ (accessed October 2014).

Carter, L. (1997) Intermediate scrutiny under fire: Will *Plyler* survive state legislation to exclude undocumented children from school? *University of San Francisco Law Review*, 31 (winter), 345.

Center for an Urban Future (2011) *Failing the Test*. New York: Center for an Urban Future. At http://www.nycfuture.org/images_pdfs/pdfs/FailingtheTest.pdf (accessed October 2014).

Center for the Study of Brooklyn (2012) *Educational Attainment Trends of New York City Latinos*. New York: Brooklyn College.

Cervone, B. (ed.) (2010) *Hear Us Out: High School Students in Two Cities Talk About Going to College*. Providence, RI: Center for Youth Voice in Policy and Practice.

Chapman, C., Laird, J., Ifill, N. and KewalRamani, A. (2011) *Trends in High School Dropout and Completion Rates in the United States: Compendium Report*. Washington, DC: National Center for Education Statistics. At http://nces.ed.gov/pubs2012/2012006.pdf (accessed November 2014).

Chishti, M. and Hipsman, F. (2014) Dramatic surge in the arrival of unaccompanied children has deep roots and no simple solutions. *Migration Information Source: Policy Beat*, July 13. At http://www.migrationpolicy.org/article/dramatic-surge-arrival-unaccompanied-children-has-deep-roots-and-no-simple-solutions (accessed November 2014).

City University of New York (2008a) *College Readiness of New York City's GED Recipients. A Report of the CUNY Office of Institutional Research and Assessment*. New York: City University of New York.

City University of New York (2008b) *A New Community College: Concept Paper*. New York: Office of Academic Affairs, City University of New York.

City University of New York (2014) *CUNY Start*. At http://www.cuny.edu/academics/programs/notable/CATA/cti-cunystart.html (accessed November 2014).

Clark, M.A. and Jaeger, D.A. (2006) Natives, the foreign-born and high school equivalents: New evidence on returns to the GED. *Journal of Population Economics* 19 (4), 769–793.

Coleman, J.S. (1988) Social capital in the creation of human capital. *American Journal of Sociology* 94, 95–121.

Coleman, J.S., Campbell, E., Hobson, C., McPortland, J., Mood, A., Weinfeld, F. and York, R. (1966) *Equality of Educational Opportunity*. Washington, DC: US Government Printing Office.

Colombi, M.C. (2002) Academic language development in Latino students' writing in Spanish. In M.J. Schleppengrell and M.C. Colombi (eds) *Developing Advanced Literacy in First and Second Languages: Meaning with Power* (pp. 67–86). New York: Routledge.

Colton, T. (2006) *Update: Still Lost in Translation*. New York: Center for an Urban Future.

Comings, J., Parella, A. and Soricone, L. (2000) Helping adults persist: Four supports. *Focus on Basics*, 4(A). At http://ncsall.net/index.html@id=332.html (accessed November 2014).

Community Education Pathways to Success (CEPS) (2006) *College Access and Success for Young Adult Learners: A Research Summary for Schools and Programs.* New York: Fund for the City of New York/Youth Development Institute.

Condelli, L., Wrigley, H. and Yoon, K.S. (2009) 'What works' for adult literacy students of English as a second language. In S. Reder and J. Bynner (eds) *Tracking Adult Literacy and Numeracy Skills: Findings from Longitudinal Research* (pp. 132–159). New York: Routledge.

Condelli, L., Wrigley, H., Yoon. K., Cronen, S. and Seburn, M. (2003) *What Works Study for Adult ESL Literacy Students.* Washington, DC: US Department of Education.

Conley, D.T. (2007) *Redefining College Readiness.* Washington, DC: Educational Policy Improvement Center.

Cook, J.L. (2008) *Our Chance for Change: A Four-Year Reform Initiative for GED Testing in New York City.* New York: New York City Department of Youth and Community Development.

Cornelius, W. (2001) Death at the border: Efficacy and unintended consequences of US immigration control policy. *Population Development Review* 27 (4), 661–685.

Cortina, R. and Gendreau, M. (eds) (2003) *Immigrants and Schooling: Mexicans in New York.* New York: Center for Migration Studies.

Covarrubias, A. and Lara, A. (2013) The undocumented (im)migrant educational pipeline: The influence of citizenship status on educational attainment for people of Mexican origin. *Urban Education,* http://uex.sagepub.com/content/early/2013/01/31/0042085912470468 (accessed November 2014).

Cowan, R. (2014) Waves of unaccompanied minors present crisis for Obama, Congress. *Reuters.* May 28. At http://www.reuters.com/article/2014/05/28/us-usa-immigration-children-idUSKBN0E814T20140528 (accessed November 2014).

Creese, A. and Blackledge, A. (2010) Translanguaging in the bilingual classroom: A pedagogy for learning and teaching? *Modern Language Journal* 94 (1), 103–115.

Cuban, L. (2004) *The Blackboard and the Bottom Line: Why Schools Can't Be Businesses.* Cambridge, MA: Harvard University Press.

Cummins, J. (1979) Linguistic interdependence and the educational development of bilingual children. *Review of Educational Research* 49 (2), 222–251.

Cummins, J. (1991) *Interdependence of First- and Second-Language Proficiency in Bilingual Children.* Cambridge: Cambridge University Press.

Cummins, J. (2000) BICS and CALP. In *Encyclopedia of Language Teaching and Learning.* Toronto: University of Toronto.

Cummins, J. (2009) Literacy and English language learners: A shifting landscape for students, teachers, researchers and policy-makers. *Educational Researcher* 38 (5), 382–383.

Cummins, J. and Sayers, D. (1995) *Brave New Schools: Challenging Cultural Illiteracy.* New York: St Martin's Press.

Cummins, J., Brown, K. and Sayers, D. (2007) *Literacy, Technology, and Diversity: Teaching for Success in Changing Times.* Boston, MA: Pearson.

Díaz, J. (2008) *The Brief Wondrous Life of Oscar Wao.* New York: Penguin.

Dorn, S. (1996) *Creating the Dropout: An Institutional and Social History of Failure.* Westport, CT: Praeger.

Durkheim, E. (1893) *The Division of Labor in Society.* New York: Simon and Schuster (2014).

Eccles, J. and Zarrett, N. (2006) The passage to adulthood: Challenges of late adolescence. *New Directions for Youth Development* 111, 13–28.

Ehrenreich, B. (2001) *Nickled and Dimed: On (Not) Getting By in America.* New York: Macmillan.

Empire State Coalition for Youth and Family Services (2013) Section II: School. At http://www.empirestatecoalition.org/main/legal/school.html (accessed October 2014).

Erikson, E. (1968) *Identity: Youth and Crisis.* New York: W.W. Norton.

Evans, K. (2002) Taking control of their lives? Agency in young adult transitions in England and the new Germany. *Journal of Youth Studies* 5 (3), 245–269.

Fass, P. (1991) *Outside In: Minorities and the Transformation of American Education.* Oxford: Oxford University Press.

Fass, P. (2007) *Children of a New World: Society, Culture and Globalization.* New York: New York University Press.

Fine, M. (1991) *Framing Dropouts: Notes on the Politics of an Urban Public High School.* Albany, NY: State University of New York Press.

Fine, M. and Jaffe-Walter, R. (2007) Swimming: On oxygen, resistance, and possibility for immigrant youth under siege. *Anthropology and Education Quarterly* 38 (1), 76–96.

Fingeret, H.A. (1994) *Adult Literacy Education: Current and Future Directions. An Update.* Columbus, OH: College of Education, Ohio State University, Center on Education and Training for Employment.

Finn, C. and Jackson, T. (1989) The dropout controversy: Dropouts and grownups. *Public Interest* 96 (summer), 131–136.

Fiscal Policy Institute (2010) *Across the Spectrum: The Wide Range of Jobs Immigrants Do.* Washington, DC: Fiscal Policy Institute.

Fischer, D.J. and Bowles, J. (2008) *Schools That Work.* New York: Center for an Urban Future. At https://nycfuture.org/pdf/Schools_That_Work.pdf (accessed November 2014).

Foddy, W. (1993) *Constructing Questions for Interviews and Questionnaires: Theory and Practice in Social Research.* Cambridge: Cambridge University Press.

Foner, N. (ed.) (2013) *One out of Three: Immigrant New York in the Twenty-First Century.* New York: Columbia University Press.

Forderaro, L.W. (2010) CUNY adjusts amid tide of remedial students. *New York Times*, March 3.

Fowler-Finn, T. (2004) Listening to minority students: One district's approach to closing the achievement gap. In M. Sadowski (ed.) *Adolescents at School* (pp. 42–46). Cambridge, MA: Harvard Education Press.

Freire, P. (1993) *Pedagogy of the Oppressed.* New York: Continuum.

Freire, P. and Macedo, D. (1987) *Literacy: Reading the Word and the World.* London: Routledge.

Frome, P. (2001) *High Schools That Work: Findings from the 1996 and 1998 Assessments.* Research Triangle Park, NC: Research Triangle Institute.

Fry, R. (2002) *Latinos in Higher Education: Many Enroll, Too Few Graduate.* Washington, DC: Pew Hispanic Research Center.

Fry, R. (2005) *The Higher Dropout Rate of Foreign-born Teens: The Role of Schooling Abroad.* Washington, DC: Pew Hispanic Research Center.

Fry, R. (2010) *Hispanics, High School Dropouts and the GED.* Washington, DC: Pew Hispanic Research Center.

Fry, R. and López, M.H. (2012) *Hispanic Student Enrollments Reach New Highs in 2011.* Washington, DC: Pew Hispanic Research Center.

Fuligni, A.J. (2007) Family obligation, college enrollment, and emerging adulthood in Asian and Latin American families. *Child Development Perspectives* 1 (2), 96–100.

Fuller, B., Bridges, M., Bein, E., Jang, H., Jung, S., Rabe-Hesketh, S., Halfon, N. and Kuo, A. (2009) The health and cognitive growth of Latino toddlers: At risk or immigrant paradox? *Maternal and Child Health Journal* 13 (6), 755–768.

Gambetta, D. (1987) *Were They Pushed or Did They Jump? Individual Decision Mechanisms in Education* (Studies in Rationality and Social Change). Cambridge: Cambridge University Press.

Gándara, P. and Contreras, F. (2009) *The Latino Education Crisis: The Consequences of Failed Social Policies.* Cambridge, MA: Harvard University Press.

Gándara, P., O'Hara, S. and Gutierrez, D. (2004) The changing shape of aspirations: Peer influence on achievement behavior. In M.A. Gibson, P. Gándara and J.P. Koyama (eds) *US Mexican Youth, Peers and School Achievement* (pp. 39–62). New York: Teachers College Press.

García, E.E. (2006) Early academic achievement of Hispanics in the United States: Implications for teacher preparation. *The New Educator* 2, 123–147.

García, O. (1999) Educating Latino high school students with little formal schooling. In M. Faltis (ed.) *So Much To Say* (1st edn, pp. 61–82). New York: Teachers College, Columbia University.

García, O. (2011) From language garden to sustainable languaging: Bilingual education in a global world. *Perspective. A Publication of the National Association for Bilingual Education* (September/October), 5–10.

García, O. (2012) Theorizing translanguaging for educators. In C. Celic and K. Seltzer (eds) *Translanguaging: A CUNY-NYSIEB Guide for Educators* (pp. 1–6). New York: CUNY-New York State Initiative on Emergent Bilinguals.

García, O. and Sylvan, C. (2011) Pedagogies and practices in multilingual classrooms: Singularities and pluralities. *The Modern Language Journal* 95 (3), 385–400.

García, O., Kleifgen, J. and Falachi, L. (2008) *From English Language Learners to Emergent Bilinguals* (Equity Matters: Research Review No. I. A Research Initiative of the Campaign for Fiscal Equity). New York: Teachers College, Columbia University.

Gates Foundation (2010) *United States Programs and Partnerships*. At http://www.gatesfoundation.org/united-states/Pages/program-overview.aspx (accessed October 2014).

Gaytan, F. (2010) The role of social capital and social support from adults in the academic self-efficacy, identity, and engagement of Mexican immigrant youth in New York City. PhD dissertation (Publication No. AAT 3390452). New York University.

GED Testing Service (2014) New GED test and comprehensive GED program launches today (Press release, January 2). At http://www.gedtestingservice.com/uploads/files/3abc4d490b455d0aafc7372a171927fd.pdf (accessed October 2014).

Gibson, M.A., Gándara, P. and Koyama, J.P. (2004a) The role of peers in the schooling of US Mexican youth. In M.A. Gibson, P. Gándara, J.P. Koyama, M.A. Gibson, P. Gándara and J.P. Koyama (eds) *School Connections: U.S. Mexican Youth, Peers, and School Achievement* (pp. 1–17). New York: Teachers College Press.

Gibson, M.A., Gándara, P. and Koyama, J.P. (eds) (2004b) *School Connections: US Mexican Youth, Peers, and Achievement*. New York: Teachers College Press.

Goldenberg, C. (2008) Teaching English language learners. *American Educator* 37 (3), 8–23 and 42–44.

Goldenberg, C., Reese, R., Gallimore, R. and Garnier, H. (2000) Longitudinal analysis of the antecedents of emergent Spanish literacy and middle-school English reading achievement of Spanish-speaking students. American Educational Research Journal 37 (3), 633–662.

Golstein, M.J. and Noguera, P.A. (2006) Designing for diversity: Incorporating cultural competence in prevention programs for urban youth. *New Directions for Youth Development* 111, 29–40.

Gonzalez, J. (2000) *Harvest of Empire: A History of Latinos in America*. New York: Viking Penguin.

Gonzalez, R. (2007) Wasted talent and broken dreams: The lost potential of undocumented students. *Immigration Policy in Focus* 5 (13).

Gordon, M. (1964) *Assimilation in American Life: The Role of Race, Religion, and National Origins*. New York: Oxford University.

Goss, J.D. and Leinbach, T.R. (1996) Focus groups as alternative research practice: Experience with transmigrants in Indonesia. *Area* 28 (2), 115–123.

Gotbaum, B. and Advocates for Children (2002) *Pushing Out At-Risk Students: An Analysis of High School Discharge Figures*. New York: Office of the Public Advocate and Advocates for Children. At http://www.advocatesforchildren.org/sites/default/files/library/pushing_out_2002.pdf?pt=1 (accessed October 2014).

Grieco, E.M., Acosta, Y.D., De La Cruz, G.P., Gambino, C., Gryn, T., Larsen, L.J., Trevelyan, E.N. and Walters, N.E. (2012) *The Foreign-Born Population in the United States: American Community Survey Reports*. Washington, DC: US Census Bureau. At http://www.census.gov/prod/2012pubs/acs-19.pdf (accessed October 2014).

Grubb, W.N. (1999) *Honored But Invisible: An Inside Look at Teaching in Community Colleges*. New York: Routledge.

Grubb, W.N. and Lazerson, M. (2004) *The Education Gospel: The Economic Power of Schooling*. Cambridge, MA: Harvard University Press.

Hakimzadeh, S. and Cohn, D. (2007) *English Usage Among Hispanics in the United States*. Washington, DC: Pew Hispanic Center.

Hall, K.H. (2002) *Lives in Translation: Sikh Youth as British Citizens*. Philadelphia, PA: University of Pennsylvania Press.

Hammack, F.M. (1986) Large school systems' dropout reports: An analysis of definitions, procedures, and findings. *Teachers College Record* 87 (3), 324–341. At http://www.tcrecord.org (ID No. 675) (accessed October 2014).

Hanson, S.L. (1994) Lost talent: Unrealized educational aspirations and expectations among US youths. *Sociology of Education* 67 (3), 159–183.

Harkavy, I. and Hartley, M. (2009) University–school–community partnerships for youth development and democratic renewal. *New Directions for Youth Development* 122, 7–18.

Harklau, L. (2003) *Generation 1.5 Students and College Writing* (EDO-FL-03-05). Washington, DC: Center for Applied Linguistics.

Heckman, J. and Rubinstein, Y. (2001) The importance of non-cognitive skills: Lessons from the GED testing program. *American Economic Review* 91 (2), 145–149.

Heron, J. and Reason, P. (1997) A participatory inquiry paradigm. *Qualitative Inquiry* 3 (3), 274–294.

Hilliard, T. (2012) *Bad English*. New York: Center for an Urban Future.

Hirschman, C. (2001) The educational enrollment of immigrant youth: A test of the segmented-assimilation hypothesis. *Demography* 38 (3), 317–336.

Hochschild, J.L. (1995) *Facing Up to the American Dream: Race, Class and the Soul of the Nation*. Princeton, NJ: Princeton University Press.

Hornberger, N. and Link, H. (2012) Translanguaging and transnational literacies in multilingual classrooms: A biliteracy lens. *International Journal of Bilingual Education and Bilingualism* 25 (3), 261–278.

Immerwahr, J. (2003) *With Diploma in Hand: Hispanic High School Seniors Talk About Their Future* (National Center Report #03-2). Washington, DC: Tomas Rivera Policy Institute.

Instituto Nacional de la Educacion para Adultos (INEA) (2009) *Rezago educativo*. Mexico City: Mexican Ministry of Public Education.

Jennings, J.L. and Haimson, L. (2009) *High School Discharges Revisited: Trends in New York City's Discharge Rates 2000–2007*. New York: Class Size Matter.

Johnson, J., Rochkind, J., Ott, A. and DuPont, S. (2009) *With Their Whole Lives Ahead of Them: Myths and Realities About Why So Many Students Fail to Finish College*. New York: Public Agenda for the Bill and Melinda Gates Foundation.

Johnson, R.B. and Onwuegbuzie, A.J. (2004) Mixed methods research: A research paradigm whose time has come. *Educational Researcher* 33 (7), 14–26.

Joselowsky, F. (2009) *Tailor Made: Attracting, Engaging, and Retaining Hard-to-Reach Youth*. New York: Youth Development Institute.

Kalmar, T. (2001) *Illegal Alphabets and Adult Biliteracy: Latino Migrants Crossing the Linguistic Border*. New York: Routledge.

Kao, G. and Tienda, M. (1998) Educational aspirations of minority youth. *American Journal of Education* 106 (3), 349–384.

Karp, M.M., O'Gara, L. and Hughes, K.L. (2008) *Do Support Services at Community Colleges Encourage Success or Reproduce Disadvantage? An Exploratory Study of Students in Two*

Community Colleges (CCRC Working Paper No. 10). New York: Teachers College, Columbia University. At http://ccrc.tc.columbia.edu (accessed October 2014).

Karp, S. (2013) The problem with the common core. *Rethinking Schools* 28 (2). At http://www.rethinkingschools.org/archive/28_02/28_02_karp.shtml (accessed November 2014).

Kasinitz, P., Mollenkopf, J.H., Waters, M.C. and Holdaway, J. (2008) *Inheriting the City: Children of Immigrants Come of Age*. New York: Russell Sage Foundation.

Kasinitz, P., Mollenkopf, J.H. and Waters, M.C. (2013) The next generation emerges. In N. Foner (ed.) *One Out of Three: Immigrant New York in the Twenty-First Century* (pp. 267–281). New York: Columbia University Press.

Kelly, A., Schneider, M. and Carey, K. (2010) *Rising to the Challenge: Hispanic College Graduation Rates as a National Priority*. Washington, DC: American Enterprise Institute.

Kerckhoff, A.C. (1976) The status attainment process: Socialization or allocation? *Social Forces* 55, 368–381.

Kett, J.F. (1994) *The Pursuit of Knowledge Under Difficulties: From Self-improvement to Adult Education in America, 1750–1990*. Stanford, CA: Stanford University Press.

Kimura-Walsh, E., Yamamura, E.K., Griffin, K.A. and Allen, W.R. (2009) Achieving the college dream? Examining disparities in access to college information among high achieving and non-high achieving Latino students. *Journal of Hispanic Higher Education* 8 (3), 298–315.

Kirst, M. and Venezia, A. (2001) Bridging the great divide between secondary schools and postsecondary education. *Phi Delta Kappa* 83 (1), 92–97.

Kirst, M. and Venezia, A. (2006) *Improving College Readiness and Success For All Students: A Joint Responsibility Between K–12 and Postsecondary Education* (Issue Brief for the Secretary of Education's Commission on the Future of Higher Education). Washington, DC: US Department of Education, Secretary's Commission on the Future of Higher Education.

Klapper, M.R. (2007) *Small Strangers: The Experiences of Immigrant Children in America, 1890–1925*. Chicago: Ivan R. Dee.

Knowles, M. (1984) *The Adult Learner: A Neglected Species* (3rd edn). Houston, TX: Gulf.

Kremer, M. (2003) Randomized evaluations of educational programs in developing countries: Some lessons. *American Economic Review* 93 (2 – Papers and Proceedings of the One Hundred Fifteenth Annual Meeting of the American Economic Association, Washington, DC, January 3–5, 2003), 102–106.

Kronick, R.F. and Hargis, C.H. (1998) *Dropouts: Who Drops Out and Why – And the Recommended Action*. Springfield, IL: Charles C. Thomas.

Legal Information Institute, Cornell University (n.d.) *Plyler v. Doe*, 457 US 202. At http://www.law.cornell.edu/supct/html/historics/USSC_CR_0457_0202_ZO.html (accessed October 2014).

Levinson, A. (2011) Unaccompanied immigrant children: A growing phenomenon with few easy solutions. At http://www.migrationinformation.org/Feature/display.cfm?ID=823 (accessed October 2014).

Limonic, L. (2007) *The Latino Population of New York City, 2007*. New York: City University of New York, Graduate Center, Center for Latin American, Caribbean and Latino Studies.

Lindeman, E. (1926) *The Meaning of Adult Education*. New York: New Republic.

Literacy Assistance Center (2008) *Final Report*. New York: New York City Office of the Mayor.

Lobo, P. and Salvo, J.J. (2013) A portrait of New York's immigrant mélange. In N. Foner (ed.) *One Out of Three: Immigrant New York in the Twenty-First Century* (pp. 35–63). New York: Columbia University Press.

Loewen, J. (1995) *Lies My Teacher Told Me: Everything Your American History Book Got Wrong*. New York: Touchstone.

Lopez, M.H. (2009) Latinos and education: Explaining the attainment gap. Washington, DC: Pew Hispanic Research Center. At http://www.pewhispanic.org/2009/10/07/latinos-and-education-explaining-the-attainment-gap (accessed October 2014).

Louie, V. (2007) Who makes the transition to college? Why we should care, what we know, and what we need to do. *Teachers College Record*, 109 (10).

Lukes, M. (2009) We thought they had forgotten us: Research, policy and practice in the education of Latino immigrant adults. *Journal of Latinos and Education* 8 (2), 161–172.

MacLeod, J. (1995) Ain't no makin' it: Aspirations and attainment in the low-income neighborhood. In D. Conley (ed.) *Wealth and Poverty in America: A Reader* (pp. 115–125). New York: Wiley.

Mansilla, V.B. and Jackson, A. (2011) *Educating for Global Competence: Preparing Our Youth to Engage the World*. New York: Asia Society. At http://asiasociety.org/files/book-globalcompetence.pdf (accessed October 2014).

Maralani, V. (2003) *From GED to College: The Role of Age and Timing in Educational Stratification* (On-line Working Paper Series). Los Angeles, CA: University of California Center for Population Research. At http://papers.ccpr.ucla.edu/papers/PWP-CCPR-2003-005/PWP-CCPR-2003-005.pdf (accessed October 2014).

Martinez, I. (2009) What's age gotta do with it? Understanding the age-identities and school-going practices of Mexican immigrant youth in New York City. *High School Journal* 92 (4), 34–48.

Massey, D., Durand, J. and Malone, N. (2002) *Beyond Smoke and Mirrors: Mexican Immigration in an Era of Economic Integration*. New York: Russell Sage Foundation.

Mather, M. (2009) *Children in Immigrant Families Chart New Path*. Washington, DC: Population Reference Bureau.

McClelland, K.E. (1990) The social management of ambition. *Sociological Quarterly* 31 (2), 225–251.

McHugh, M., Gelatt, J. and Fix, M. (2009) *Adult English Language Instruction in the United States: Determining Need and Investing Wisely*. Washington, DC: Migration Policy Institute.

Meade, B., Gaytan, F.X., Fergus, E. and Noguera, P. (2009) *A Close Look at the Dropout Crisis: Examining Black and Latino Males in New York City*. New York: New York University. At http://steinhardt.nyu.edu/scmsAdmin/uploads/004/453/Dropout_Crisis.pdf (accessed October 2014).

Mellard, D.F. and Anderson, G. (2007) *Challenges in Assessing for Postsecondary Readiness*. New York: Council for Advancement of Adult Literacy.

Menken, K. (2008) *English Learners Left Behind: Standardized Testing as Language Policy*. Clevedon: Multilingual Matters.

Menken, K., Kleyn, T. and Chae, N. (2012) Spotlight on 'long-term English language learners': Characteristics and prior schooling experiences of an invisible population. *International Multilingual Research Journal* 6, 121–142.

Merriam, S.B. (2009) *Qualitative Research: A Guide to Design and Implementation* (2nd edn). San Francisco, CA: Jossey-Bass.

Mezirow, J. (1990) *Fostering Critical Reflection in Adulthood: A Guide to Transformative and Emancipatory Learning*. San Francisco: Jossey-Bass.

Mickelson, R.A. (1990) The attitude–achievement paradox among black adolescents. *Sociology of Education* 63 (1), 44–61.

Migration Policy Institute (MPI) (n.d.) State immigration data profiles. At http://www.migrationinformation.org/datahub/acscensus.cfm# (accessed October 2014).

Migration Policy Institute (MPI) (2008) MPI data hub immigration statistics by state: New York. At http://www.migrationinformation.org/datahub/state.cfm?ID=NY (accessed October 2014).

Morgan, S.L. (2005) *On the Edge of Commitment: Educational Attainment and Race in the United States*. Stanford, CA: Stanford University Press.

Murnane, R., Willett, J. and Tyler, J. (2000) Who benefits from a GED? Evidence from high school and beyond. *Review of Economics and Statistics* 82 (1), 23–37.

Nakkula, M. (2006) Identity and possibility: Adolescent development and the potential of schools. In M. Sadowski (ed.) *Adolescents at School: Perspectives on Youth, Identity, and Education* (3rd ed) (pp. 7–18). Cambridge, MA: Harvard Education Press.

Napoli, T.P. and Bleiwas, K.B. (2010) *The Role of Immigrants in the New York City Economy* (Report 17-2010). New York: Office of the New York State Comptroller. At http://www.osc.state.ny.us/osdc/rpt17-2010.pdf (accessed October 2014).

National Center for Education Statistics (NCES) (2008) *High School Dropout and Completion Rates in the United States: 2007 Compendium Report.* Washington, DC: United States Department of Education. At http://nces.ed.gov/pubs2009/2009064.pdf (accessed October 2014).

National Center for Education Statistics (NCES) (2010) *Trends in High School Dropout and Completion Rates in the United States: 1972–2008 Compendium Report.* Washington, DC: United States Department of Education. At http://nces.ed.gov/pubs2011/2011012.pdf (accessed October 2014).

National Center for Education Statistics (NCES) (2013a) Summary of expenditures for public elementary and secondary education, by purpose: Selected years, 1919–20 through 2009–10. At http://nces.ed.gov/programs/digest/d12/tables/dt12_205.asp (accessed October 2014).

National Center for Education Statistics (NCES) (2013b) *National Education Data Model.* Washington, DC: United States Department of Education, Institute of Education Sciences. At http://nces.ed.gov/forum/datamodel/eiebrowser/datasets.aspx?instance=eden_043 (accessed October 2014).

National Center for the Study of Adult Learning and Literacy (NCSALL) (2004) A conversation with FOB: Why go beyond the GED? *Focus on Basics* 6 (D). At http://www.ncsall.net/index.php@id=171.html (accessed November 2014).

National Conference of State Legislatures (2005) Unaccompanied immigrant and refugee minors. At http://www.ncsl.org/default.aspx?tabid=13128 (accessed October 2014).

National Conference of State Legislatures (2014). *Child migrants to the United States.* At http://www.ncsl.org/research/immigration/child-migrants-to-the-united-states.aspx#trends (accessed November 2014).

National Employment Law Project (2014) *An Unbalanced Recovery: Real Wage and Job Growth Trends.* Data brief. At http://www.nelp.org/page/-/Reports/Unbalanced-Recovery-Real-Wage-Job-Growth-Trends-August-2014.pdf?nocdn=1 (accessed November 2014).

Nee, V. and Sanders, J. (2001) Understanding the diversity of immigrant incorporation: A forms of capital model. *Journal of Ethnic and Racial Studies* 24 (3), 386–411.

New York Immigration Coalition (2014) NYIC and Internationals Network for Public Schools release joint comments on the New York State Education Department's request for waiver. At http://www.thenyic.org/node/2763 (accessed November 2014).

New York City College of Technology (2010) New program prepares Mexican immigrants for hospitality industry careers. At http://www.citytech.cuny.edu/aboutus/newsevents/2010sp/hosp_mex/index.shtml (accessed October 2014).

New York City Department of Education (NYCDOE) (2009) *Diverse Learners on the Road to Success: The Performance of New York City's English Language Learners.* New York: New York City Department of Education.

New York City Department of Education (NYCDOE) (2013a) Other ways to graduate. At http://schools.nyc.gov/ChoicesEnrollment/AlternativesHS/default.htm (accessed October 2014).

New York City Department of Education (NYCDOE) (2013b) *Office of English Language Learners 2013 Demographic Report.* New York: New York City Department of Education. At http://schools.nyc.gov/NR/rdonlyres/FD5EB945-5C27-44F8-BE4B-E4

C65D7176F8/0/2013DemographicReport_june2013_revised.pdf (accessed October 2014).

New York City Department of City Planning (2004) *The Newest New Yorkers: Immigrant New York in the New Millennium*. New York: New York City Office of the Mayor, Department of City Planning.

New York State Education Department (2013a) *Recommendations for Engaging the Field to Review, Enhance, and Strengthen Commissioner's Regulations Part 154*. Albany, NY: Office of Bilingual Education and Foreign Language Services.

New York State Education Department (2013b) *Public School District Total Cohort Graduation Rate and Enrollment Outcome Summary, 2011–12 School Year*. Albany, NY: NYSED. At http://www.p12.nysed.gov/irs/pressRelease/20130617/District-enroll-outcomes-and-diplomas-June172013.pdf (accessed October 2014).

New York State Regents (2012) Memo on graduation rates of 2006 cohort. Albany, NY: New York State Education Department. At http://www.p12.nysed.gov/irs/pressRelease/20120611/GradRates2012.pdf (accessed October 2014).

Nieto, S. and Raible, J. (2006) Beyond categories: The complex identities of adolescents. In M. Sadowski (ed.) *Adolescents at School* (3rd edn) (pp. 145–161). Cambridge, MA: Harvard Education Press.

Noguera, P.A. (2003) *City Schools and the American Dream*. New York: Teachers College and Columbia University Press.

Noguera, P.A. (2004) 'Joacquín's dilemma': Understanding the link between racial identity and school-related behaviors. In M. Sadowski (ed.) *Adolescents at School* (3rd edn) (pp. 19–30). Cambridge, MA: Harvard Education Press.

Nwosu, C., Batalova, J. and Auclair, G. (2014) *Frequently Requested Statistics on Immigrants and Immigration in the United States*. Washington, DC: Migration Policy Institute.

O'Connor, J. (2007) *Disconnected Youth: An Answer to Preventing Disengagement* (White Paper). Albany, NY: Schuyler Center for Analysis and Advocacy.

O'Connor, J. (2008) *Disconnected Youth: An Answer to Preventing Disengagement (Volume 2)* (White Paper No. 2). Albany, NY: Schuyler Center for Analysis and Advocacy.

Ogbu, J. (1990) Minority education in comparative perspective. *Journal of Negro Education* 59 (1), 45–57.

Ogbu, J. and Simons, H. (1998) Voluntary and involuntary minorities: A cultural–ecological theory of school performance with some implications for education. *Anthropology and Education Quarterly* 29 (2), 155–188.

Olsen, L. (1997) *Made in America: Immigrant Students in Our Public Schools* (1st edn). New York: New Press.

Orfield, G. and Eaton, S. (1997) *Dismantling Desegregation: The Quiet Reversal of Brown v. Board of Education*. New York: New Press.

Orfield, G., Losen, D. and Wald, J. (2004) *Losing Our Future: How Minority Youth Are Being Left Behind*. Cambridge, MA: Harvard University, Harvard Civil Rights Project.

Oropesa, R.S. and Landale, N.S. (2009) Why do immigrant youths who never enroll in US schools matter? An examination of school enrollment among Mexicans and non-Hispanic Whites. *Sociology of Education* 82 (3) 240–266.

Orr, M.T. (2009) Transitions to college: An in-depth look at the selected influences of demographics, development, and policy. *Teachers College Record* 111 (10), 2311–2319.

Oudenhoven, E.D. (2006) Caught in the middle: Generation 1.5 Latino students and English language learning at a community college. Doctoral dissertation, Loyola University Chicago. *Digital Dissertations,* AAT 3212980.

Ouellette, M. (2006) Going the distance: Serving the needs of older youth at scale. *New Directions for Youth Development* 111, 105–115.

Pallas, A.M., Natriello, G. and Mcdill, E.L. (1987) The high costs of high standards: School reform and dropouts. *Urban Education* 22 (1), 103–114.

Pandya, C., McHugh, M. and Batalova, J. (2011) *Limited English Proficient Individuals in the United States: Number, Share, Growth, and Linguistic Diversity*. Washington, DC: Migration Policy Institute.

Park, R.E. and Burgess, E.W. (1924) *Introduction to the Science of Sociology*. Chicago, IL: University of Chicago Press.

Patterson, M.B., Zhang, J., Song, W. and Guison-Dowdy, A. (2010) *Crossing the Bridge: GED Credentials and Postsecondary Educational Outcomes*. Washington, DC: American Council on Education.

Pavlish, C. (2005) Refugee women's health: Collaborative inquiry with refugee women in Rwanda. *Health Care for Women International* 26 (10), 880–896.

Perin, D. (2011) *Facilitating Adult Learning Through Contextualization*. CCRC Working Paper No. 29. Teachers College of Columbia University, Community College Research Center. At http://knowledgecenter.completionbydesign.org/sites/default/files/232%20Perin%20February%202011-1_0.pdf (accessed November 2014).

Perreira, K., Mullan Harris, K. and Lee, D. (2006) Making it in America: High school completion by immigrant and native youth. *Demography* 43 (3), 511–536.

Pew Hispanic Center (2013) *Statistical Portraits of the Foreign-Born Population in the United States*. Washington, DC: Pew Hispanic Center.

Phillipson, R. (1988) Linguicism: Structures and ideologies in linguistic imperialism. In T. Skutnabb-Kangas and J. Cummins (eds) *Minority Education: From Shame to Struggle* (pp. 339–358). Clevedon: Multilingual Matters.

Poros, M. (2011) *Migrant Social Networks: Vehicles for Migration, Integration and Development*. Washington, DC: Migration Policy Institute.

Portes, A. (1998) Social capital: Its origins and applications in modern sociology. *Annual Review of Sociology* 24, 1–24.

Portes, A. (2000) The two meanings of social capital. *Sociological Forum* 15 (1), 1–12.

Portes, A. and Rumbaut, R.G. (1996) *Immigrant America: A Portrait*. Berkeley, CA: University of California Press.

Portes, A. and Rumbaut, R.G. (2001) *Legacies: The Story of the Immigrant Second Generation*. Oakland, CA: University of California Press.

Portes, A. and Rumbaut, R.G. (2006) *Immigrant America: A Portrait*. Berkeley, CA: University of California Press.

Portes, A. and Zhou, M. (1993) The new second generation: Segmented assimilation and its variants. *Annals of the American Academy of Political and Social Science* 530, 74–96.

Quigley, B. and Uhland, R.L. (2000) Retaining adult learners in the first three critical weeks: A quasi-experimental model for use in ABE programs. *Adult Basic Education* 10 (2), 55–68.

Ramirez, J.D., Yuen, S.D. and Ramey, D.R. (1991) *Longitudinal Study of Structured English Immersion Strategy, Early-Exit, and Late-Exit Transitional Bilingual Education Programs for Language-Minority Children* (Contract No. 300-87-0156). Washington, DC: US Department of Education.

Rampell, C. (2013) It takes a B.A. to find a job as a file clerk. *New York Times*, February 19.

Reyes, M. (2011) *Words Were All We Had: Becoming Biliterate Against the Odds*. New York: Teachers College Press.

Reynolds, J.R. and Pemberton, J. (1997) Rising college expectations among youth in the United States: A comparison of the 1979 and 1997 NLSY. *Journal of Human Resources* 36 (4), 703–726.

Riessman, C.K. (2008) *Narrative Methods for the Human Sciences*. Thousand Oaks, CA: Sage.

Rivera-Batiz, F.L. (2004) Newyorktitlán: A socioeconomic profile of Mexican New Yorkers. *Regional Labor Review* 6 (2), 32–43.

Rosen, R., Wieler, S. and Pereira, J. (2005) New York City immigrants: The 1990s wave. *Current Issues* 11 (6). At http://www.newyorkfed.org/research/current_issues/ci11-6.pdf (accessed November 2014).

Ross, S. and Gray, J. (2005) Transitions and re-engagement through second chance education. *Australian Educational Researcher* 32 (3), 103–140.

Rouse, C.E. (2007) Quantifying the costs of inadequate education: Consequences of the labor market. In C.R. Belfield and H.M. Levin (eds) *The Price We Pay: Economic and Social Consequences of Inadequate Education* (pp. 99–124). Washington, DC: Brookings Institution Press. At http://mea.org/tef/pdf/social_costs_of_inadequate.pdf (accessed October 2014).

Ruiz-de-Velasco, J., Fix, M.E. and Clewell, B.C. (2001) *Overlooked and Underserved: Immigrant Students in US Secondary Schools*. Washington, DC: Urban Institute.

Rumbaut, R.G. (1997) Assimilation and its discontents: Between rhetoric and reality. *International Migration Review* 31 (4), 923–960.

Rumbaut, R.G. and Komaie, G. (2010) Immigration and adult transitions. *Future of Children* 10 (1), 43–66.

Rumberger, R.W. (1987) High school dropouts: A review of issues and evidence. *Review of Educational Research* 57, 101–121.

Sadowski, M. (ed.) (2006) *Adolescents at School: Perspectives on Youth, Identity, and Education* (3rd edn). Cambridge, MA: Harvard Education Press.

Sander, L. (2012) In a secret classroom in Georgia, immigrants learn to hope. *Education Week* December 10.

Schneider, M. (2010) *Finishing the First Lap: The Cost of First-Year Student Attrition in America's Four Year Colleges and Universities*. Washington, DC: American Institutes for Research.

Scott, R.E. (2011) *Heading South: US–Mexico Trade and Job Displacement after NAFTA* (Economic Policy Institute Briefing Paper No. 308). Washington, DC: Economic Policy Institute. At http://epi.3cdn.net/fdade52b876e04793b_7fm6ivz2y.pdf (accessed October 2014).

Semple, K. (2014) Surge in child migrants reaches New York, overwhelming advocates. *New York Times,* June 17. At http://www.nytimes.com/2014/06/18/nyregion/immigration-child-migrant-surge-in-New-York-City.html?_r=0 (accessed October 2014).

Sewell, W.H., Haller, R.M. and Portes, R. (1969) The educational and early occupational attainment process. *American Sociological Review* 34 (1), 82–92.

Shor, I. and Freire, P. (1987) *A Pedagogy for Liberation: Dialogues on Transforming Education*. South Hadley, MA: Bergin and Garvey.

Skutnabb-Kangas, T. (2000) *Linguistic Genocide in Education, or Worldwide Diversity and Human Rights?* Mahwah, NJ: Lawrence Erlbaum Associates.

Slavin, R.E. and Cheung, A. (2005) A synthesis of research on language of reading instruction for English language learners. *Review of Educational Research* 75 (2), 247–284.

Smith, R.C. (2006) *Mexican New York: Transnational Lives of New Immigrants*. Berkeley, CA: University of California Press.

Smith, R.C. (2013) Mexicans: Civic engagement, education and progress achieved and inhibited. In N. Foner (ed.) *One Out of Three: Immigrant New York in the Twenty-First Century* (pp. 246–266). New York: Columbia University Press.

Smith, T. (2003) Who values the GED? An examination of the paradox underlying the demand for the general educational development credential. *Teachers College Record* 105 (3), 375–415.

Somerville, W., Durana, J. and Terrazas, A.M. (2008) *Hometown Associations: An Untapped Resource for Immigrant Integration?* Washington, DC: Migration Policy Institute.

Soper, D. (2007) Statistical calculations. At http://www.danielsoper.com/statcalc (accessed October 2014).

Soto-Hinman, I. and Hetzel (2009) *The Literacy Gaps: Bridge-Building Strategies for English Language Learners and Standard English Learners.* New York: Corwin.

Spencer, M.B. and Dornbush, S.M. (1990) Challenges in studying minority youth. In S.

Feldman and G. Elliott (eds) *At the Threshold: The Developing Adolescent* (pp. 123–145). Cambridge, MA: Harvard University Press.

Staff, J. and Mortimer, J.T. (2007) Educational and work strategies from adolescence to early adulthood: Consequences for educational attainment. *Social Forces* 85 (3), 1169–1196.

Stanton-Salazar, R.D. (1997) A social capital framework for understanding the socialization of racial minority children and youths. *Harvard Educational Review* 6 (7), 1–40.

Stanton-Salazar, R.D. (2001) *Manufacturing Hope and Despair: The School and Kind Support Networks of US–Mexican Youth.* New York: Teachers College Press.

State of California (1998) Proposition 227: English for the Children. English Language in Public Schools Initiative Statute. At http://primary98.sos.ca.gov/VoterGuide/Propositions/227text.htm (accessed October 2014).

St Bernard, G. (2003) *Major Trends Affecting Families in Central America and the Caribbean.* United Nations Division of Social Policy and Development, Department of Economic and Social Affairs Program on the Family. At http://www.un.org/esa/socdev/family/Publications/mtstbernard.pdf (accessed October 2014).

Steele, C.M. (1997) A threat in the air: How stereotypes shape intellectual identity and performance. *American Psychologist* 52 (6), 613–629 (doi: 10.1037/0003-066X.52.6.613).

Stiglitz, J. (2013) Equal opportunity, our national myth. *New York Times*, February 16.

Stone, V. (n.d.) *Latino Educational Enrollment and Attainment Levels in New York City.* New York: City University of New York, Latino Data Project.

Suárez-Orozco, C. (2004) Formulating identity in a globalizing world. In M. Suárez-Orozco and D. Qin-Hilliard (eds) *Globalization: Culture and Education in the New Millennium* (pp. 173–199). Berkeley, CA: University of California Press.

Suárez-Orozco, C. and Suárez-Orozco, M. (1995) *Transformations: Immigration, Family Life, and Achievement Motivation Among Latino Adolescents.* Stanford, CA: Stanford University Press.

Suárez-Orozco, C. and Suárez-Orozco, M. (2001) *Children of Immigration* (1st edn). Cambridge, MA: Harvard University Press.

Suárez-Orozco, C., Suárez-Orozco, M. and Torodova, I. (2008) *Learning a New Land.* Cambridge, MA: Belknap Press of Harvard University Press.

Suárez-Orozco, M. (2000) Everything you ever wanted to know about assimilation but were afraid to ask. *Daedalus* 129 (4), 1–30.

Takaki, R. (1993) *A Different Mirror: A History of Multicultural America.* New York: Little, Brown.

Tanners, L. (1997) Immigrant students in New York City Schools. *Urban Education* 32 (2), 233–255.

Thomas, W. and Collier, V. (2003) *A National Study of School Effectiveness for Language Minority Students' Long-Term Academic Achievement.* Santa Cruz, CA: Center for Research on Education, Diversity and Excellence, University of California.

Thonus, T. (2003) Serving Generation 1.5 students in the university writing center. *TESOL Journal* 12 (1) 17–24.

Toby, J. and Armor, D.D. (1992) Carrots or sticks for high school dropouts? *Public Interest* 106, 76–90.

Togunde, D. (2008) Children's educational and occupational aspirations in urban Nigeria: Implications for policy development. *Research Journal of International Studies* 7, 19–31.

Tollefson, J.W. (1991) *Planning Language, Planning Inequality: Language Policy in the Community.* New York: Longman.

Tornatzky, L.G., Cutler, R. and Lee, J. (2002) *College Knowledge: What Latino Parents Need to Know and Why They Don't Know It.* Los Angeles, CA: Tomás Rivera Policy Institute.

Tornatzky, L.G., Pachon, H.P. and Torres, C. (2004) *Closing Achievement Gaps: Improving Educational Outcomes for Hispanic Children.* Washington, DC: Tomás Rivera Policy Institute, Center for Latino Educational Excellence.

Treschan, L. (2010) *Latino Youth in New York City: School, Work, and Income Trends for New York's Largest Group of Young People* (Policy Brief). New York: Community Service Society. At http://www.cssny.org/publications/entry/latino-youth-in-new-york-cityoct2010 (accessed October 2014).

Treshan, L. and Mehrotra, A. (2013) *Young Mexican-Americans in New York City: Working More, Learning and Earning Less*. New York: Community Service Society.

Tyler, J. (2004) Does the GED improve earnings? Estimates from a sample of both successful and unsuccessful candidates. *Industrial and Labor Relations Review* 57 (4), 579–598.

Tyler, J. and Lofstrom, M. (2005) *Is the GED an Effective Route to Postsecondary Education*. Working Paper 13816. Cambridge, MA: National Bureau of Economic Research.

Tyler, J. and Lofstrom, M. (2009) Finishing high school: Alternative pathways and dropout recovery. *Future of Children* 19 (1), 7.

Tyler, J., Murnane, R. and Willett, J. (1998) *Estimating the Impact of the GED on the Earnings of Young Dropouts Using a Series of Natural Experiments*. Cambridge, MA: National Bureau of Economic Research.

Tyler, J., Murnane, R. and Willett, J. (2000) Estimating the labor market signaling value of the GED. *Quarterly Journal of Economics* 115 (2), 431–468.

UNESCO (2011) *Global Education Digest 2011: Comparing Education Statistics Across the World*. Montreal: UNESCO Institute for Statistics.

UNICEF (2010) Basic education and gender equality: Equal access to education. At http://www.unicef.org/education/index_access.html (accessed October 2014).

United Nations (2000) The Millennium Development Goals. At http://www.un.org/millenniumgoals/bkgd.shtml (accessed October 2014).

United Nations (2011) *Challenges for Education with Equity in Latin America and the Caribbean*. Buenos Aires: Regional Preparatory Meeting 2011 United Nations Economic and Social Council Annual Ministerial Review ECOSOC – AMR.

United Nations High Commissioner for Refugees (UNHCR) (2014) *Children on the Run: Unaccompanied Minor Children Leaving Central America and Mexico and the Need for International Protection*. Washington, DC: UNHCR. At http://www.unhcrwashington.org/children (accessed October 2014).

US Census Bureau (2010) American community survey: 2009 data release new and notable 2005–2009 ACS 5-year estimates. At http://www.census.gov/acs/www/data_documentation/2009_release (accessed October 2014).

US Citizenship and Immigration Services (2014) Consideration of deferred action for childhood arrivals process. At http://www.uscis.gov/humanitarian/consideration-deferred-action-childhood-arrivals-daca (accessed November 2014).

US Committee for Refugees and Immigrants (2013) Leaders gather to address the plight of unaccompanied immigrant youth. At http://www.refugees.org/about-us/in-the-news/press-releases/children-migrating-all-alone.html (accessed October 2014).

US Department of Education (2002) *Public Law 107–110, 107th Congress: No Child Left Behind Act of 2001*. Washington, DC: US Department of Education. At http://www2.ed.gov/policy/elsec/leg/esea02/107-110.pdf (accessed October 2014).

US Department of Education (2009) *High School Dropout and Completion Rates in the United States: 2007. Compendium Report*. Washington, DC: National Center for Education Statistics.

US Department of Education (2010a) *National Reporting System, Version 9.1, Public Use Data*. Washington, DC: Office of Vocational and Adult Education. At https://wdcrobcolp01.ed.gov/CFAPPS/OVAE/NRS/main.cfm (accessed November 2014).

US Department of Education (2010b) *A Blueprint for Reform: Reauthorization of the Elementary and Secondary Education Act*. At http://www2.ed.gov/policy/elsec/leg/blueprint/blueprint.pdf (accessed October 2014).

US Department of Education (2010c) *The Condition of Education 2010* (NCES 2010-028,

Indicator 19). Washington, DC: National Center for Education Statistics. At http://nces.ed.gov/programs/coe/2010/pdf/19_2010.pdf (accessed October 2014).

US Department of Education (2012) *Promoting College and Career Readiness: Bridge Programs for Low-Skill Adults* (Community College Virtual Symposium). Washington, DC: Office of Vocation and Adult Education, USDOE.

US Department of Education (2013a) *Carl D. Perkins Career and Technical Education Act of 2006. Report to Congress on State Performance, Program Year 2009–10.* Washington, DC: US Department of Education, Office of Vocational and Adult Education. At http://www2.ed.gov/about/offices/list/ovae/resource/aefla-report-to-congress-2010-accessible.pdf (accessed October 2014).

US Department of Education (2013b) *Adult Education – Basic Grants to States.* Washington, DC: US Department of Education, Office of Vocational and Adult Education. At http://www2.ed.gov/programs/adultedbasic/funding.html (accessed October 2014).

US Department of Education (2013c) *Adult Education and Family Literacy Act of 1998 Annual Report to Congress, Program Year 2010–11.* Washington, DC: US Department of Education, Office of Vocational and Adult Education. At http://www2.ed.gov/about/offices/list/ovae/resource/aefla-report-to-congress-2010-accessible.pdf (accessed October 2014).

Valdés, G., Kibler, A. and Walqui, A. (2014) *Changes in the Expertise of ESL Professionals: Knowledge and Action in an Era of New Standards.* Alexandria, VA: TESOL International Association.

Vella, J. (2002) *Learning to Listen, Learning to Teach: The Power of Dialogue in Adult Education* (2nd edn). New York: Jossey-Bass.

Wald, M. and Martinez, T. (2003) *Connected by 25: Improving the Life Chances of the Country's Most Vulnerable 14–24 Year Olds.* William and Flora Hewlett Foundation Working Paper. At http://www.ytfg.org/documents/connectedby25_OOS.pdf (accessed November 2014).

Wallerstein, N. (1983) *Language and Culture in Conflict: Problem-Posing in the ESL Classroom.* Reading, MA: Addison Wesley.

Warner, W.L. and Srole, L. (1945) *The Social Systems of American Ethnic Groups.* New Haven, CT: Yale University Press.

Way, N. (1998) *Everyday Courage: The Lives and Stories of Urban Teenagers.* New York: New York University Press.

Weaver, C. (1998) *Reading Process and Practice: From Sociolinguistics to Whole Language.* Portsmouth, NH: Heinemann.

Webster, B.H. and Bishaw, A. (2007) *Income, Earnings, and Poverty Data from the 2006 American Community Survey* (American Community Survey Reports). Washington, DC: US Census Bureau.

Wiley, T.G. (1996) Language planning and policy. In S. McKay (ed.) *Sociolinguistics and Language Teaching* (pp. 103–132). Cambridge: Cambridge University Press.

Wiley, T.G. and Lukes, M. (1996) English-only and standard English ideologies in the US. *TESOL Quarterly* 30 (3), 511–535.

Wiley, T.G. and Wright, W. (2004) Against the undertow: Language minority education policy and politics in the age of accountability. *Educational Policy* 18 (1), 142–168 (doi: 10.1177/0895904803260030).

Willis, J. (2007) *Foundations of Qualitative Research: Interpretive and Critical Approaches.* Thousand Oaks, CA: Sage.

Wilson, B.J. (2006) Why America's disadvantaged communities need twenty-first century learning. *New Directions for Youth Development* 110, 47–52.

Wilson, W.J. (1996) *When Work Disappears: The World of the New Urban Poor.* New York: Knopf.

Wirth, L. (1928) *The Ghetto.* Chicago, IL: University of Chicago Press.

World Education (2010) Post secondary success of young adults: System impact opportunities in adult education. Executive summary. Boston, MA: National College

Transition Network at World Education. At http://www.collegetransition.org/docs/Gates-Executive-Summary.pdf (accessed December 2014).

Wrigley, H.S. (2008) *Adult ESL and Literacy: Issues and Options.* Montreal: Centre for Literacy. At http://www.centreforliteracy.qc.ca/sites/default/files/Adult%20ESL_Literacy_Issues_Opti.pdf (accessed October 2014).

Wrigley, H.S., Richer, E., Martinson, K., Kubo, H. and Strawn, J. (2003) *The Language of Opportunity: Expanding Employment Prospects for Adults with Limited English Skills.* Washington, DC: Center for Law and Social Policy. At http://www.sbctc.ctc.edu/college/education/career_pathways_wrigley_language_opportunity_brief_june07.pdf (accessed October 2014).

Yosso, T.J. (2005) Whose culture has capital? A critical race theory discussion of community cultural wealth. *Race Ethnicity and Education* 8 (1), 69–91.

Zarrett, N. and Eccles, J. (2006) The passage to adulthood: Challenges of late adolescence. *New Directions for Youth Development* 111, 13–28.

Ziolek-Skrzypczak, M. (2013) *Integrating Immigrant Youth: Transatlantic Perspectives.* Washington, DC: Migration Policy Institute.

Index